RHETORIC
A Synthesis

RHETORIC
A Synthesis

W. Ross Winterowd
UNIVERSITY OF SOUTHERN CALIFORNIA

HOLT, RINEHART AND WINSTON, INC.

New York · Chicago · San Francisco · Atlanta
Dallas · Montreal · Toronto · London

For

Henrietta and Howard Locke

PN 175
.W54

Copyright © 1968 by Holt, Rinehart and Winston, Inc.

Library of Congress Catalog Card Number: 68–16377

2686202

Printed in the United States of America

1 2 3 4 5 6 7 8 9

Jacket photograph (on right)
© Lincoln Center for the Performing
Arts, Inc., 1967—Photograph by
Morris Warman.

preface

With only a few notable exceptions, the art of rhetoric has been static for two hundred years. In the latter half of the eighteenth century, Blair and Campbell in their "new" rhetoric said virtually the last word. Rhetoricians have been at work (I. A. Richards, Francis Christensen, and most notably Kenneth Burke), but a modern rhetoric has not emerged. The rhetoric of composition and speech classes turns out to be the most arid of all academic disciplines, and recent work in the subject remains generally unknown and universally unapplied in pedagogy. But there are stirrings. Kenneth Burke is coming to be understood and accepted as one of the seminal minds of our age; Professor Christensen's work is being published.

One initial problem in the development of a new rhetoric is semantic. To the great majority, rhetoric means (a) handbook rubrics on "how to" write or "how to" speak; (b) mendacious bombast. Even avowed rhetoricians limit themselves to narrow ranges of their subject, as, for instance, the methods of writing good sentences and paragraphs, the art of public speaking, or the study of figures. But rhetoric is much more than this, much more than the handbooks or the textual critics imply. It is a broad art encompassing all aspects of discourse,

v

and a new rhetoric must reflect the breadth of the subject. Even more, a new rhetoric must look to the future.

The present volume makes no claim to definitiveness. But it does establish a basis for a new kind of rhetoric.

The rationale of *Rhetoric: A Synthesis* is this: only the genuinely new has been included. Whatever is adequately available in other sources has been excluded. For instance, I could hardly hope to add to Ong's, Howell's, Tuve's, and Baldwin's work on rhetoric in the Renaissance, so I have said very little of that period. On the other hand, I do have something to add concerning the Age of Reason. There currently exists no complete history of rhetoric in the eighteenth century; so I have included a chapter on that period. (Furthermore—and perhaps most important for purposes of the book—the neoclassical age represents a paradigm par excellence of the forces that create a rhetorical milieu.) To be sure, commentaries on Aristotle abound; however, none of them, it seems to me, makes precisely the points that give the Greek master relevance for our age. Rhetoric has been too much given to rehashing. In this book, hopefully, the reader will find no warmed-overs.

Rhetoric: A Synthesis is planned to accomplish several ends. First— and most obviously—the attempt is to bring together in coherence the various fragments of a new rhetoric, most notably in the chapters on style and form. Second, the book usually takes the difficult course of putting theory into practice; hence the extended analyses of style and form and the lengthy discussion of a novel. The chapter on pedagogy may well dangle precariously on a limb waiting for the sawers—but better such a situation than a noncommittal, general statement about the necessity for teaching rhetoric. Finally, I have attempted to synthesize the theory and practice of rhetoric in a way that will make the book a real introduction to the subject.

The yawning lacuna in the book is its lack of a chapter on invention. I can plead that this omission represents the failure of modern rhetoric and rhetoricians to make use of new psychological discoveries in learning theory, verbal ability, and creativity. Aristotle admonished all rhetoricians of the need for psychology, but we have not paid attention to the advice. Modern studies, particularly in creativity, ought to shed new light on the problem of invention. Thus, in ways direct and indirect the whole of *Rhetoric: A Synthesis* concerns invention.

Gentle reader, beware of the modern reflexive distaste for rhetoric and all things rhetorical. Aristotle is much more exciting than generations of commentators have led us to believe. The odious freshman rhetoric course was not rhetoric at all. And rhetoric is not purely or even primarily mendacity.

In fact, it seems clear to me that rhetoric offers a logical way out of a great many modern dilemmas—for instance, the dilemma of a vigorous literary tradition preserved by fossilized studies in English departments. A rhetorical view of esthetics will always judge the effect of the work for good or ill upon someone, including the artist himself. Rhetoric simply refuses to judge the work in a moral and social vacuum (this statement does not mean, however, that the esthetics of rhetoric are democratic). Focusing as it does on the wherewith and wherefor of all kinds of discourse among human beings, rhetoric proffers the hope of meaningful and humane courses in high school and college—courses to replace the unsuccessful hybrids that discourage so many students from interest in the central studies of any true education. Furthermore, rhetoric does synthesize; it is the ecumenical umbrella under which grammar, poetry, logic, composition, and public speaking can find shelter. One might say that rhetoric is a metasubject that can serve to unify the diverse aspects of the study of discourse of all kinds.

There is just a slim chance that, in this unpredictable world, rhetoric will be the subject that is meaningful to the educable man.

Rhetoric: A Synthesis is, I think, a beginning. There is more, much more, to come.

Kenneth Burke and Francis Christensen put their stamp on this book. I consulted with neither, but I borrowed liberally from both. I hope they approve of the results, and I thank them for the important work they have done.

In the chapter on esthetics, I point out that Amelia was Fielding's creation in the human sublime. I think the reason for my love for Fielding's novel is that Amelia reminds me of my wife, Norma. It was she who encouraged me to work on through a period of persistent illness that left me apathetic about any undertaking. A preface is not the place for a recital of personal matters, but the work that my wife did over a period of three months was at great personal sacrifice. I thank her for her help.

W.R.W.

HUNTINGTON BEACH, CALIF.
FEBRUARY 1968

contents

chapter I

Introduction

Some Basic Assumptions

The Myth of Neutral Language

There is no such thing as neutral language. This proposition demands a bit of analysis, for currently we are laboring under the myth that some language is loaded, whereas some is objective, fair, and neutral. We continually hear about the objectivity of wire-service reports; scientists assure us that their reports are only reports, not inferences; and the mass-circulation news magazines piously disclaim their own implied judgments. One of the common misconceptions about language is that the mathematical "language" of science is not loaded—that it is purely objective and that it carries no emotional overtones. The intimidated college freshman looking at a page in the text for his required course in math would certainly not agree that the precise language of mathematics is "unloaded," and that the simple equation $E = MC^2$ is not perhaps one of the most portentous utterances of our era.

The notion that some language can be neutral while other language is freighted with all sorts of connotative suggestions has a long and complex history, starting in the latter part of the seventeenth century. But currently, the general semanticists suggest that we not only be aware of, but also indicate, the differences in meaning among several uses of the same word, thus: mother$_1$ mother$_2$ mother$_3$, and so on. Their insistence that we be aware of differences in meaning of the same word variously used is all to the good; any suggestion that we try to use language neutrally is futile.

In short, no language—not even the language of mathematics $(E = MC^2)$—is neutral. Nor is it desirable that language be neutral.

The Persuasiveness of Language

Another basic assumption in this discussion is that all language is persuasive. Aristotle defined rhetoric as discovering the best possible means of persuasion on any subject whatever. This definition of rhetoric is standard and influential; therefore, we tend to think of language as persuasion in terms of forceful arguments or powerfully effective advertising campaigns or sermons that move the congregation to reform. But suppose that we strip language of all its argumentation, all its overt appeal to do something or to accept some idea. Is it then nonpersuasive? Sometimes language is used in a way that semanticists call presymbolic; that is, frequently what we say does not convey ideas (or impressions or whatever) through the symbolic medium of words. In some instances, language has approximately the "semantic" value of a smile or of a pat on the head—or of a frown. Though the words convey an impression, they do not symbolize something in the way that the code marks c o w symbolize a ruminatory quadruped commonly domesticated. . . . Examples of the presymbolic use of language are the following common series of remarks:

"Hello. How are you?"
"I'm fine. And how are you?"

If the first question in this series evokes a real answer, the whole purpose of the "communication" has broken down, thus:

"Hello. How are you?"
"Oh, I don't feel so well. You see, last year I was bending over to pick up a large rock in my garden, and I hurt my back. Now, every time the weather is cloudy, I . . . ."

The first question—"How are you?"—was not intended to elicit information. Or at least that particular question seldom is intended to bring any

answer but the formulary "Fine." That is, the common "How are you?—
I'm fine. How are you?" series does not try to say so many things in almost
an equal number of words. It is a communication of quite a different class
from the verbal series that this question will bring about: "How do I get
to the corner of Higgins Avenue and Pine Street?" One way in which we
can characterize the "How are you?" formula is to say that it is an un-
meditated (or subconscious or even preconscious) attempt at persuasion.
It is one way in which human beings establish rapport with one another.
In this sense, it is not talk merely for the sake of talk.[1] It is talk for the sake
of *courtship*. In rhetorical theory—particularly that of Kenneth Burke—
courtship is the overcoming of social estrangement. It is opening the lines of
communication among human beings. Here is how a kind of presymbolic
language makes it work:

> Twenty-five people (male and female) in a room; each holds a glass; they
> talk together (rather boisterously) in groups of two or three. Person num-
> ber twenty-six comes into the room. A maid hands him a glass. He looks
> about uncomfortably, finds a pretty redhead who has just walked away
> from two men in an animated discussion, and says to her:
> "Hasn't it been a beautiful spring?"
> This exchange follows:
> "It certainly has—much better than last year. We had rain almost
> every day until June last year."
> "But once summer really did arrive, we had some beautiful weather."

And so on. As the progress of courtship through presymbolic language
continues, Number Twenty-Six and the redhead may gradually or suddenly
deviate into a topic about which the words will carry a true semantic
meaning as opposed to the suasive "meaning" of the process of courtship.
Of course, in the foregoing exchange the words do in fact mean something;
they are not nonsense syllables (like the Falalala in songs). But their
intention is not to mean; their intention is to overcome social estrangement, and this intention is rhetorical in that it is persuasive, though not
necessarily on a conscious level.

Other common language situations may seem devoid of a suasive
element, for instance, a dictionary definition:

> dermatology: the study of the skin, its structure, its function, and its
> diseases

---

[1] Much talk is for its own sake. Man might be *homo sapiens*. He is certainly the talking
animal. If we can classify singing as a kind of talking, we can say that there is a great
deal of talking for the sake of talk in bathtubs and showers; we "talk" ourselves through
to solutions of problems. And *Imaginary Conversations* is a literary figuration of one of
the characteristics of our species.

or a set of instructions:

> Lift receiver. Listen for dial tone. Deposit coins. Dial number.

The neutrality of these utterances is, however, only apparent, not actual. We can say that the definition of "dermatology" is framed in such a way that it will be informative and acceptable to users of the dictionary; in this sense each entry is a carefully planned use of language to a suasive end, though the primary end of these entries is informative. And in the illustration of the set of instructions: the very form of the utterances is imperative, the "mood" of the sentence that is commonly defined in English as a command or urgent request.

Language is persuasive almost willy-nilly, simply because it is language. Try as we may, we cannot frame an utterance in such a way that it will be totally informative or totally affective. Whenever we use language, we are using persuasion. Even nonsense syllables, as long as we interpret them as language of some kind, work their persuasive magic. (Remark overheard during a performance of *Tosca* with Renata Tebaldi in the starring role: "I love opera in Italian. It's so much better than when I can understand the words.") Of course, if language is always persuasive, it is axiomatic that there are degrees of persuasion, ranging from the almost imperceptible suasiveness of a lyric poem through the overt and heavy-handed suasiveness of an automobile ad.

The Ambiguity of Language

The next basic assumption is that language is always ambiguous and that this ambiguity is a virtue, not a liability. John Donne eloquently argued that no man is an island, and in the frame of reference and context of his argument, no man is an island:

> No man is an *Iland*, intire of it selfe: every man is a peece of the *Continent*, a part of the *maine*; if a clod be washed away by the Sea, Europe is the less, as well as if a promontorie were, as well as if a Mannor of thy Friend or of thine own were; any mans death diminishes me because I am involved in Mankind; and therefore never send to know for whom the bell tolls; it tolls for thee.   —*Devotion* xvii

But in another frame of reference, and another context, every man is an island. In fact, the metaphor "every man is an island" might well be an apt metaphor for summing up the philosophy of Kant. Or consider the metaphorical—if not actual—implications of such works as *The Loneliness of the Long Distance Runner*, "Uncle Wiggily in Connecticut," even *The*

Man in the Gray Flannel Suit. Thus, depending on how one looks at it, man either is or is not an island. Because I am imprisoned within the walls of my own sense and sensibility, I am an *isolato* on the Island of Me. At least, that is one way—a very common way—of viewing the human situation. What kind of lines of communication can I set up between this Island of Me and the rest of humanity? At best, imperfect means of sending my messages. A mirrored flash code? A teletype line? A telephone cable? These allow me to communicate indeed, but imperfectly. Perhaps the metaphor has already been extended beyond its breaking point, but it is curiously apt, this concept of the individual as an *isolato* trying to "get through" to other islands or to the mainland. For no man can achieve total communication. That is, we never "say" everything we have to say. The highest degree of approximation possible is all that one can intend in language.

The following sentence is ambiguous because of a structural fault:

He saw her in the house.

It might mean something like this:

As he looked through the window from the porch, he saw her in the house.

Or something like this:

As soon as he walked in the door of the house, he saw her sitting in an easy chair in the front room.

It is not this type of ambiguity that we are concerned with. We are concerned with inherent ambiguity rather than that which comes about through the inept use of language. Some ambiguity can be eliminated. Some cannot. It is the latter with which we are concerned.

The very nature of language demands ambiguity, and this ambiguity results from the process of generalization. Conversely, all language must be generalized. For instance, there is little, but nonetheless some, ambiguity in the term "Franklin Delano Roosevelt." We can determine a great deal about the meaning of those eight syllables: date of birth, date of death, family affiliations, tastes in music and food, opinions on government, and the like. Not only that, there will be a great consistency—though not total consistency—in the ideas that the name Franklin Delano Roosevelt evokes —even though one person might squirm uneasily at the mention of the socialist who started America on the road to collectivistic ruin while another might smile contentedly to be reminded of the great leader who rescued America from depression. In any event, there will be almost no disagreement about the person to whom the words "Franklin Delano Roosevelt" refer. In this sense, the utterance will be as free from ambiguity as language can ever hope to be. (In fact, the ambiguity will be minimal in the so-called denotative meaning of the term, but great in the connotative meaning. That is, roughly, everyone will agree about *who* FDR was, but not about how they feel toward him.) When we take one step toward generalization and speak about *a* Roosevelt, ambiguity increases sharply. Which Roosevelt? Franklin? Teddy? F.D.R., Jr.? When we speak of *a* president of the United States, the ambiguity decreases in one respect, but increases in another, and so on. Again, we can generalize further and speak of *man* in the generic sense. Obviously, this ability of language to generalize and hence to bring about ambiguity is one of its most useful aspects. Linguists tell us that in some American Indian languages there is no word for "wash," but rather separate words for "wash the hands," "wash the face," and so on. Any such limitation of generalized terms is a definite linguistic loss.

Generally speaking, language has two kinds of features: the obligatory and the optional. For instance, the following lists of words are optional choices:

> house man the the enter saw I
> man the dog the bit

The order in which they must appear in the language called English is not optional, but obligatory, thus:

> A B   C   D   B   C   D
> I saw the man enter the house
> The dog bit the man

>   *or*

> The man bit the dog

For the class of utterances to which *I saw the man enter the house* belongs, we can set up an equation thus:

$$A \; B \; C \; D \; B \; C \; D = S$$

For this type of utterance, the form of the equation will not change; it is obligatory. The specific values that we assign may change if

$$A = \text{pronoun}$$
$$B = \text{verb}$$

$$C = article$$
$$D = noun$$
$$S = sentence$$

but the form of the "equation" may not change.

$$A \ + \ B \ + \ C \ + \ D \ + \ B \ + \ C \ + \ D = S$$
We   heard   the   wind   rustle   the   leaves

These paradigms are not meant to be linguistically accurate, but rather to serve as illustrations of the difference between obligatory and optional aspects of language.

The reader is by now undoubtedly aware that the discussion is bordering on theories of transformational grammar. Because our purpose is not to discuss the structure and linguistic functioning of language, we have no need, I think, to get into the deep water of Noam Chomsky's discoveries. Rather, a few examples in layman's terms will serve to illustrate the point that transformational grammar works out in detail. If we make certain choices about language, other choices must necessarily follow, thus:

Jim is but not *Jim are*

or

The man bit the dog

from which we can derive

Did the man bite the dog?
The dog was bitten by the man
The man was biting the dog

and so on. So long as we make choices that are within the possibilities of English structure, we shall have eliminated one source of ambiguity—and, of course, virtually every native speaker makes the "right" choices, even if he says "He aint got no money," for that locution is "right" so far as one level of usage is concerned. We have cited one instance of structural ambiguity that resulted, not from the speaker's having made the wrong structural choice, but from the way in which the "right" structural choice worked out in a given locution: *He saw her in the house.* We have also said that by structural rearrangement or by rephrasing, this kind of ambiguity can be eliminated.

But what about the ambiguity inherent in a word such as "man"—

that ambiguity so necessary if language is to function at all? Suppose, for instance, we move "man" down the scale of generalization and speak of a Danish Prince and then go a step further and speak of a Danish Prince called Hamlet who avenged the murder of his father. Suppose, in fact, we write a play called *Hamlet* in which we use a great many well-chosen words to define this man. Surely the ambiguity will be eliminated. Or suppose I want desperately to tell you about my dog, not about *a* dog or about dogs in general. The result could well be *The Call of the Wild*, and yet you and I would never reach total agreement about the meaning of "my dog." The mathematical language of science is in a happier situation, for there is little ambiguity in the proposition that $2 \times 2 = 4$, even though, paradoxically, the proposition may not be true at all. The whole problem of eliminating ambiguity stops short of establishing the truth of propositions and concentrates on bringing about understanding. The reason language can never eliminate all ambiguity is simply—to return to the proposition of man's isolate condition—that no two men have exactly the same tools for perception, and if they did have, they would not have the same conditioning. Simply, each would have had different experiences with dogs during lives that, no matter how similar in some respects, were different in important and fundamental ways. If language were not to a high degree ambiguous, we could not communicate, for D O G would mean to you only a given animal in a given place.

At the same time that the inherent ambiguity of language allows us to communicate, it also allows us to delude ourselves inadvertently and others intentionally.

The Morality of Language

Another basic assumption is that any use of language is a human action and that every human action has moral consequences. Thus, the act of communicating through language entails moral responsibility.

We have said that all language is to some extent suasive and hence rhetorical. No utterance can be completely devoid of suasiveness, not even a presymbolic utterance such as a small boy's emphatic "Guck!" when he sees what his mother has prepared for dinner. In fact, the language of children and particularly their prelanguage is predominantly and highly suasive, whether or not they intend it to be. Matter-of-fact statements ("The Mets beat the Cards today") have a great many perceptible suasive qualities. In short, to reiterate, language is suasive. Thus, in discussing the morality of language or of linguistic acts, the problem is not one of abstract ethics but of practical morality. The moral questions of language belong to exactly the same class as questions concerning the decision to drop the first atom bomb or to conduct raids on targets north of the 17th parallel in

Viet Nam. The difference is in degree, not in kind. And at crucial moments in history, the moral decisions concerning language have probably been as momentous as those concerning the use of arms. For instance, the decision to declare war results in a simple verbal act: "yes" or "no" or some equivalent of these. The decision to convince a nation that it should go to war results in a complex verbal act, or a concatenation of complex verbal acts, or, more probably, a concatenation of verbal acts stemming from an earlier concatenation of verbal acts. That is, the president (or king or whoever) decides to declare war or to ask for a declaration of war. His speech will be an attempt to convince the nation that it should go to war, but it will not be the first utterance tending to arouse a nation to the martial spirit, for there will have been a long series of other utterances that preceded it: bellicose editorials in newspapers, statements by various members of the government, perhaps warnings from the leader himself. Once the leader has made the final decision and has formally urged the nation to go to war, he and his government must sustain the aura of bellicosity—more properly, of righteous bellicosity—through a series of carefully planned utterances that appear regularly until the war is over.

None of this is astounding. It is, however, astounding that the moral ramifications of human utterance receive so little consideration. The general semanticists, of course, begin from a moral premise, namely, that if man is to prevail he must learn to prevail through the cooperation brought about by (a more exact) use of language. The linguists, however, that proliferation of modern scholars who have contributed so much to our understanding of the function of language, have largely (like the good scientists whom they emulate and after whose condition they aspire) ignored the question of ethics or morality. In fact, for two millennia and longer, the question of the ethics of the use of language has been almost the peculiar province of the rhetorician. And finally perhaps, the most beautiful statement about the morality and moral responsibility of language appears in Plato's *Phaedrus*. This remarkable work is worth some discussion. One suspects that it is neglected, and certainly it has been misunderstood. In fact, it was only in 1953 that a modern scholar and critic gave us what appears to be a correct interpretation of the *Phaedrus*. I refer to Richard M. Weaver's essay, "The Phaedrus and the Nature of Rhetoric," and it is to this remarkable work that I am indebted for most of the ideas in the following discussion of the *Phaedrus*.

In discussing the *Phaedrus*, one immediately encounters a terminological difficulty. The work uses love as an allegorical basis on which to build a discussion of discourse, and this love, or these kinds of love, that form the rationale for the work are not in any sense the popularly construed Platonic variety. That is, Plato speaks of love that involves physical relations; hence, one would like to avoid coyness, and include in the present discussion the term "sexual intercourse." Unfortunately, but not surprisingly, the love of which Plato speaks is pederastic. We shall, therefore, resort to the euphemistic term "relations" in speaking of the love acts involved in the love that Plato describes.

The *Phaedrus* is a dialogue between Plato and Phaedrus, but our present discussion will ignore this nature of the work and treat it as an expository essay. The sacrifices of such an approach are considerable, for we must necessarily lose sight of the *modus operandi* of the work; the gain is brevity.

The first kind of relation that Plato describes is that in which the nonlover seeks satisfaction. His partner is an object, perhaps enjoying the relations, perhaps not, but nonetheless bestowing satisfaction or release. Note that Plato speaks of a love that involves acts, not merely passive adoration. The relations of the nonlover bestow approximately the kind of release that the linguistic ejaculation gives to the man who vents his annoyance by shouting, "God damn it!" The double meaning of the word "ejaculation" is in this sense completely fitting, and the nonlover to whom relations give release is momentarily free of the drives which had propelled him into the love-act situation. Furthermore, what he has done has not been *merely* cold and calculating; as Weaver says,

> . . . the non-lover follows a policy of enlightened self-interest. First of all, the non-lover does not neglect his affairs or commit extreme acts under the influence of passion. Since he acts from calculation, he never has occasion for remorse. No one ever says of him that he is not in his right mind, because all of his acts are within prudential bounds. The first point is, in sum, that the non-lover never sacrifices himself and therefore never feels the vexation which overtakes lovers when they recover from their passion and try to balance their pains with their profit.[2]

The second kind of person who enters into love relations is the evil lover. Although the nonlover is never vicious, the evil lover commits the cardinal sin of debasing his beloved. The evil lover must subject the beloved to his will and in so doing debase him, urge him to become effeminate and eschew activities that would make him a man. The evil lover, then, attempts to make his beloved as unnatural as possible. Clearly his actions are despicable, whereas those of the nonlover have at least the morality of disinterestedness.

The good or noble lover, says Weaver, stands in sharp contrast to the evil lover,

[2] Richard M. Weaver, "The Phaedrus and the Nature of Rhetoric," *The Ethics of Rhetoric* (Chicago: Henry Regnery Company, 1965), p. 6. Excerpts from *The Ethics of Rhetoric* are reprinted with the permission of the publisher.

. . . who, as we have seen, strives to possess and victimize the object of his affections. For once the noble lover has mastered the conflict within his own soul by conquering appetite and fixing his attention upon the intelligible and the divine, he conceives an exalted attitude toward the beloved. The noble lover now "follows the beloved in reverence and awe." So those who are filled with this kind of love "exhibit no jealousy or meanness toward the beloved one, but endeavor by every means in their power to lead him to the likeness of the god whom they honor." Such is the conversion by which love turns from the exploitative to the creative.[3]

As was frequently his habit, Plato is here speaking allegorically, and the allegory concerns the kinds of human discourse. The correspondences that the allegory conveys develop Plato's ideas about the morality of human discourse.

First is the nonlover. In his acts of love, he corresponds to the rhetorician or antirhetorician who would set up as the most desirable goal for human discourse its theoretical and of course unattainable complete lack of suasiveness. We think, here, of the modern Gradgrinds who in effect say that language should give us the facts and nothing but the facts. (Again, an unattainable goal for language.) The disinterested speaker (and here "speaker" is a generic term covering any user of discourse, including the writer) would, like the nonlover, exclude passion from his discourse and would make prudential policy the desideratum of his utterances. That is, this prudential user of language would conscientiously avoid the kind of discourse that, as Longinus said, goes beyond persuasion and transports the auditor:

> At every time and in every way imposing speech, with the spell it throws over us, prevails over that which aims at persuasion and gratification.[4]

It is this very "imposing" speech that the prudential speaker would avoid, in the same way that the nonlover avoids the transports of passion. Disinterested speech, as here defined, then, avoids purely rhetorical elements, as, say, the appeal to pity or lofty style. The disinterested speaker would condemn the "rhetoric" of Hitler, but also that of Winston Churchill. The sorts of discourse that this type of speaker would strive for are represented by the reasoned arguments of a dialectician, not the imaginative and rhetorical arguments of a Plato. In this connection, the difference in the methods of Plato and Aristotle serves as an excellent paradigm. Plato approaches his subject imaginatively and with a degree of moral and artistic

---

[3] Weaver, pp. 13–14.
[4] Longinus, "On the Sublime," trans. W. Rhys Roberts, *The Great Critics*, ed. James Harry Smith and Edd Winfield Parks (New York: W. W. Norton & Company, Inc., 1939), p. 65.

passion. Aristotle argues rationally and, following his own dicta, eliminates passion. Thus, Plato:

> But the region above the heaven was never worthily sung by the earthly poet, nor will it ever be. It is, however, as I shall tell; for I must dare to speak the truth, especially as truth is my theme. For the colourless, formless, and intangible truly existing essence, with which all true knowledge is concerned, holds this region and is visible only to the mind, the pilot of the soul. Now the divine intelligence, since it is nurtured on mind and pure knowledge, and the intelligence of every soul which is capable of receiving that which befits it, rejoices in seeing reality for a space of time and by gazing upon truth is nourished and made happy until the revolution brings it again to the same place. In the revolution it beholds absolute justice, temperance, and knowledge, not such knowledge as has a beginning and varies as it is associated with one or another of the things we call realities, but that which abides in the real eternal absolute; and in the same way it beholds and feeds upon the other eternal verities, after which, passing down again within the heaven, it goes home, and the charioteer puts up the horses at the manger and feeds them with ambrosia and then gives them nectar to drink.[5]

Compare this with Aristotle:

> Again, if you string together a set of speeches expressive of character, and well finished in point of diction and thought, you will not produce the essential tragic effect nearly so well as with a play which, however deficient in these respects, yet has a plot and artistically constructed incidents. Besides which, the most powerful elements of emotional interest in Tragedy—Peripeteia or Reversal of Intention, and Recognition scenes— are parts of the plot. A further proof is, that novices in the art attain to finish of diction and precision of portraiture before they can construct the plot. It is the same with almost all the early poets.[6]

These examples are, I think, representative of the different tones of Plato and Aristotle. Plato is never the nonlover; Aristotle is always the nonlover.

The point is meaningful because of the long-standing reaction against "rhetoric." T. H. Huxley spoke of painting the fair face of truth with the pestilent cosmetic of rhetoric, as though suasiveness toward truth were not a legitimate function of discourse. Somehow the notion is current and deeply imbedded that language should be only prudential. We have seen, of course, that no language is completely devoid of suasiveness, not even

---

[5] Plato, "Phaedrus," trans. Harold North Fowler, *Plato* (8 vols.; Cambridge, Mass.: Harvard University Press, 1947), I, pp. 475–477. This passage is reprinted with the permission of Harvard University Press and the Loeb Classical Library.
[6] Aristotle, *Poetics*, trans. H. S. Butcher, *The Great Critics*, p. 35.

the precise language of mathematics. In the *Phaedrus*, Plato argues in behalf of passionately suasive language.

The evil lover is not prudent; he is simply wicked. But what about the good lover who lets passion sweep him away? Says Weaver,

> Love is often censured as a form of madness, yet not all madness is evil. There is a madness which is simply degeneracy, but on the other hand there are kinds of madness which are really forms of inspiration, from which come the greatest gifts conferred on man. Prophecy is a kind of madness, and so too is poetry. "The poetry of the sane man vanishes into nothingness before that of the inspired madman." Mere sanity, which is of human origin, is inferior to that madness which is inspired by the gods and which is a condition for the highest kind of achievement. In this category goes the madness of the true lover. His is a generous state which confers blessings to the ignoring of self, whereas the conduct of the non-lover displays all the selfishness of business: "the affection of the non-lover, which is alloyed with mortal prudence and follows mortal and parsimonious rules of conduct will beget in the beloved soul the narrowness which common folk praise as virtue; it will cause the soul to be a wanderer upon the earth for nine thousand years and a fool below the earth at last." It is the vulgar who do not realize that the madness of the noble lover is an inspired madness because he has his thoughts turned toward a beauty of divine origin.[7]

Prudential method (the discourse of the nonlover) will carry one only so far. Perhaps the most prudential of all discourse is found in the syllogism, bounded by the strictures of formal and material fallacy, limited in extent, and strictly controlled by a method. Thus,

> All men are divine.
> Jones is a man.
> Therefore, Jones is divine.

This statement has certain virtues in that it is verifiable in its own terms. But it carries certain unavoidable rhetorical implications and rhetorical demands. To convince an audience that men are divine, one needs, perhaps, the inspired discourse of the Bible or of Schweitzer. To prove that the syllogism is valid, one applies only the "rules" for syllogistic reasoning. The nonlover would be adept at the formulation and substantiation of syllogisms; he would lack the "madness" of divine passion to convince an audience that man is divine.

Plato's message is clear. Moral discourse is not necessarily merely prudential discourse. The highest morality frequently demands the dis-

7 Weaver, p. 13.

course of the true lover. In fact, the true lover has no choice; his divine inspiration dictates his type of discourse. It is axiomatic that condemnation of one man's use of a kind of discourse does not condemn that kind of discourse.

The sexual symbolism of the *Phaedrus* is particularly apt, for the sexual act is exactly like the use of discourse in that both must necessarily have consequences and in that both involve moral responsibility. One does not avoid the moral responsibility through eliminating passion.

Finally, language is the unique characteristic of the human being, the talking animal, but more important, it is through language that man must achieve salvation or damnation. All theories of language stop short of complete understanding, but some short-circuit themselves, for they fail to take into account the nature of language as a moral, suasive act—perhaps the only human and humane act of man. Rhetoric focuses on language as suasion, as an act, and as a moral consequence. The rhetorician knows that we can literally talk ourselves to death. Perhaps, in fact, we are doing so.

The Field of Rhetoric

Definition

As groundwork for the pages that are to ensue in this book about rhetoric, it might be well to outline the main concerns of rhetoricians. This outline will be brief, for it is the purpose of the volume to fill in the details —in all their breadth and complexity—of the field of rhetoric.

Aristotle defines rhetoric as *the art or faculty of discovering the best possible means of persuasion in regard to any subject whatever*. He goes on to point out that this is the property of no other discipline, each of which is concerned with its own particular province, as medicine with healing, geometry with the properties of solids, and so forth. But rhetoric impinges on all areas of human concern, for human beings do and must talk about everything within their ken. Aristotle's definition is so basic that it deserves commitment to memory and some discussion here.

Aristotle was thinking of rhetoric primarily as a tool in argumentation, particularly the kind of deliberation or dispute that arose in courts of law or chambers of government. In a sense, his treatise, *The "Art" of Rhetoric*, was basically a handbook for lawyers, diplomats, and politicians, outlining the best methods whereby they might carry their points. But *The "Art" of Rhetoric* is not strictly or even primarily a handbook outlining techniques; if it were, it would have fallen into obscurity. Rather, it is a theoretical treatment of the ways in which man can most effectively persuade. Aristotle argues that ideally logic ought to carry points, but men being what they are, other means must supplement bare dialectic. For human beings act not only on the basis of reason, but also in passion. In effect, Aristotle is saying that rhetoric must gain emotional assent as well as logical assent. Therefore, we can say that Aristotle's definition of rhetoric extends to the ways in which we use discourse to ingratiate ourselves, to arouse sympathy, to evoke indignation, and so forth. And, in fact, we can extend the basic definition of rhetoric posited by Aristotle to include the elicitation of the sympathetic agreement of the reader or auditor, in precisely the way that a lyric poem arouses sympathetic agreement.

What we are here saying—and it is an important point—is that Aristotle's definition serves as a valid and useful basis on which to construct the theory and practice of rhetoric. As the present volume progresses, the reader will begin to understand the possibilities that the Aristotelian definition of rhetoric affords.

The "Departments" of Rhetoric

Rhetoric has five traditional divisions, generally called "departments." They are (1) invention, (2) arrangement, (3) style, (4) memory, and (5) delivery.

Invention is the process whereby subject matter for a discourse is discovered. Aristotle said that arguments could be divided into two categories: the *inartificial* and the *artificial*. In Chapter 2, we shall discuss Aristotle's theories of invention in detail, but for the moment, suffice it to say that inartificial arguments are those that inhere in the nature of the case being argued (Aristotle lists as examples contracts, evidence obtained by torture, witnesses, and the like). Artificial arguments are those that the speaker must invent; they are (1) logical, proceeding inductively from the example or deductively from the enthymeme; (2) ethical, proceeding, roughly speaking, from the hearer's estimate of the speaker's character; and (3) emotional, proceeding from the speaker's appeal to the listener's emotions. It is not here important that we understand this schema in detail; discussion in depth and breadth will come hereafter. It is important, however, that we realize the implications of Aristotle's analysis. He is saying in effect that all proofs are either discoverable (by research?) or that the speaker can invent them by considering the logic of the case, the establishment of his own moral character, and the appeal to the listener's emotions. Aristotle's working out of the methods of appeal is admittedly crude. And why not, considering that, when he wrote, developments in electronic devices for propaganda, depth psychology, brainwashing, and so forth were two millennia away? Nonetheless—and this *is* the important point—Aristotle provides a valid framework on which to build a study of the means of invention. Also, one must in fairness say, Aristotle is seminal;

the hints that he gives and the possibilities that he develops are more important than the actual working out of this doctrine of rhetorical practice.

Arrangement is the department of rhetoric that embraces all theories concerning the ways in which material can be effectively organized in discourse. Rhetorical pronouncements on arrangement run the whole spectrum, from a dogmatic listing of four—and only four—parts for an oration to the oversimplified and basically destructive (but extremely widespread) "law" that the writer or speaker should arrange his points in an ascending order of importance. Cicero, for instance, codified the theory of arrangement when he said that the oration must include these parts: (1) *exordium*, or introduction; (2) *narratio*, the statement of the case; (3) *confirmatio*, proof of the case, and *reprehensio*, refutation of the opponent's case; (4) *peroratio*, the summing up. As we shall see, this rigid outline of organization was so influential that it dictated form in many instances well into the nineteenth century. On the other hand, a modern theorizer, Kenneth Burke, has turned his considerable powers to analysis of the problems of form and has arrived at some of the most exciting insights into rhetoric that have emerged in our century.

Style is the department of rhetoric that embraces all theories about the *manner* of discourse that is effective. Roughly speaking, the history of rhetoric produced two "schools" of thought on style. The first, by various and complicated ways, emerged from Aristotle; this Aristotelian school advocated a plain style, unadorned with "rhetorical flowers." It is best represented by the adherents to the doctrine of perspicuity in the eighteenth century. The second school derives from Cicero; the Ciceronians advocated a richer style than did the Aristotelians. In fact, at its extremes, the stylistic doctrine deriving from Cicero advocates ornateness to the point of eccentricity. Hence, one can speak of Ciceronianism and the Ciceronianistic style. We should be aware, however, that these two mainstreams of style only derive from Aristotle and Cicero. In actual fact, Cicero and Aristotle were not far apart in their attitudes toward style. From a few significant differences, the fabrics of two attitudes were spun out by generations that turned back to the two classical masters. As might be suspected, modern developments in the study of language have provided tremendously useful tools for the meaningful discussion of style, as well as for the understanding of the nature of style. We shall discuss these developments, primarily, in Chapter 5.

Memory and delivery have always received fairly short shrift in discussions of rhetoric. There is little one can say about mnemonic techniques for committing speeches to mind. And techniques of delivery are, finally, the kind of "how to" that is valuable to the speaker, but that must be learned in practice. This book will not deal with the "how to" except by the way. That is, we are concerned with the theory, history, and analytical application of rhetoric, not with details about how to write a better essay or deliver a speech more effectively. The discussion will remain firmly centered on theory, almost to the exclusion of practice. Analogically, this book will be to the course in speech or composition what the psychology text is to the course in teaching methods.

In a field so basically unscientific as rhetoric, one must not expect perfect symmetry. Thus, everything that ensues in the pages to follow will not fit the traditional five-part scheme of rhetoric: invention, arrangement, style, memory, and delivery. But the framework has proved viable and defensible for two thousand years; more important, it serves as a convenient point of reference to keep the traveler oriented. Like all maps, it is but a rough representation of the territory that it charts. Once the traveler, guided by the map, has "been there," his own experience—his memory of the journey—can fill in the details that the map must ignore.

chapter **2**

Aristotle
and Extrapolation

Rhetoric proper starts with Aristotle. All rhetoric is in some way—more or less—derived from Aristotle. Thus, a synthesis of rhetoric must take Aristotle as a point of departure. The discussion in the present chapter will be in part a digest of Aristotle's treatise *The Art of Rhetoric*; but the chapter will also consistently extrapolate, following suggestions, reinterpreting, insofar as possible making Aristotle relevant to the twentieth century.

It is strongly recommended that you read Aristotle's *Rhetoric* before you proceed further with this chapter. The liveliest, most readable translation is that by Lane Cooper, recently issued in a paperback edition.[1] (If and when you do read the *Rhetoric*, keep in mind that it is a pioneering work, and

[1] *The Rhetoric of Aristotle* by Lane Cooper. Copyright, 1932, 1960, by Lane Cooper. Reprinted by permission of Appleton-Century-Crofts. In this chapter, all quotations from *The Rhetoric* are Cooper's translation.

enjoy it with a sense of discovery. It is a thoroughly remarkable book, and it is extremely important in the history of Western thought. Bring to the reading the kind of imaginative, exploratory attitude with which Aristotle wrote it; follow implications. Remember that Aristotle's practical advice both proceeds from and suggests theory and philosophy.)

Aristotle's real ascendancy began in 1619, when Theodore Goulston published his edition of the *Rhetoric*, with, no less, a Latin translation. Of course, between 700 and the third quarter of the sixteenth century, scholastic logic, primarily Aristotelian, was supreme, but for rhetoric, everyone looked to Cicero. When the Aristotelian revival began in the seventeenth century, an antidote against artificiality was sorely needed, and Aristotle provided that antidote.[2]

In 1637, Thomas Hobbes, the great English skeptic, published *A Briefe of the Art of Rhetorique*, in effect a condensation of the Aristotelian work. This turning to Aristotle, as Howell points out, helped give Englishmen confidence in the virtues of plain writing and speaking, with a nice balance between content and style.

In fact, the *Rhetoric* is an extension of the Greek philosophy of the *via media*, of the *edle Einfalt und stille Grösse* of the classical mentality.

Book I

Aristotle's first premise is that rhetoric is the counterpart of dialectic, "for both have to do with such things as fall, in a way, within the realm of common knowledge, things that do not belong to any one science." That is, we use the art of rhetoric to produce discourse on all subjects, just as we use dialectic to determine the validity of propositions concerning any subject whatever. Aristotle goes on to point out that this universality is characteristic of no other art; medicine, for instance, concerns itself only with healing; mathematics, only with the properties of numbers, and so on. Further, rhetoric can be reduced to a method, and hence it is truly an art; that is, its operations can be systematized.

At this point, Aristotle stops short of a conclusion that he implies, namely, that reducing any process to a set of methods or rules gives that process a generative capability. If the art of public speaking (and Aristotle, of course, was speaking almost exclusively of oral discourse) can be reduced *analytically* to a set of rules, these rules can be reapplied to produce or generate other successful discourse. This, as we shall see, is an important

---

[2] For the best discussion of this interesting period in the history of rhetoric, see Wilbur Samuel Howell, *Logic and Rhetoric in England, 1500–1700* (Princeton, N.J.: Princeton University Press, 1956).

point for the current discussion.[3] It is the tacit assumption under which
Aristotle produced his treatise. Aristotle says,

> No art . . . has regard to the individual case. Thus medicine does not
> investigate the question what is a cure for Socrates or for Callias—for
> the individual as such—but asks what will cure a person or persons of
> such and such a type; the latter inquiry comes within the province of
> art, whereas, particulars being infinite, the individual fact cannot be scien-
> tifically known.[4]

The implication here is not that Aristotle produced a generative rhetoric,
but that he perceived an underlying principle that points toward the future.
How, then, does Aristotle define rhetoric? It is *the faculty . . . of
discovering in the particular case what are the available means of persuasion.*[5] An art of "discovery" is also an analytical art; indeed, Aristotle tells
us that "it is the office of one and the same art to discern the genuine means,
and also the spurious means, of persuasion."[6] As we shall see, the means
of persuasion include anything and everything that go to make up effective
discourse: fact, style, arrangement, moral character of speaker, and so on.
And the art of rhetoric is a dual instrument—a means of building effective
discourse, but also a means of systematically dismantling it to gain understanding of how it is constructed. The usefulness of such an art is manifest.
First, it gives us the means to defend truth: "When decisions are not made
as they should be, the speakers with the right on their side have only
themselves to thank for the outcome. Their neglect of the art needs cor-
rection." Second, when "scientific" arguments fail, rhetoric is a valuable
means of instruction. Third, it makes us understand both sides of a case.
Fourth, it gives one a means of defense: "If it is a disgrace to a man when
he cannot defend himself in a bodily way, it would be odd not to think
him disgraced when he cannot defend himself with reason. . . ."[7]
     Aristotle divides rhetorical proofs into two categories, the *nonartistic*
and the *artistic*. Nonartistic proofs are those that are intrinsic to the subject
itself; thus, in legal arguments, witnesses, contracts, confessions under torture, oaths, and so forth are nonartistic proofs. It is on the "invented" or
artistic proofs that Aristotle focuses, of which more will be said later.
     Anticipating what will be a major portion of his treatise, Aristotle
lists three types of artistic proofs: the favorable character (real or assumed)
of the speaker; the adjustment of the speech to a particular audience; the
proving of a point through argument. Thus, the *Rhetoric* will deal with

---

[3] Already the term "generative rhetoric"—an analogy with generative grammar—is
gaining currency.
[4] *Rhetoric*, p. 11.
[5] *Rhetoric*, p. 7.
[6] *Rhetoric*, p. 7.
[7] *Rhetoric*, p. 6.

the three components of any discourse situation: speaker (or writer), hearer (or reader), and the nature of the discourse itself. This speaker-hearer-message equation is fundamental to rhetoric, the kind of insight that ought to be generally available, but which in the actual practice of speaking or writing is often forgotten or submerged. The implications of the equation are far-reaching in some interesting ways. On the most superficial and practical level, we can make this kind of formulation: "That discourse may be totally effective, the audience must be well disposed toward the speaker; hence, the speaker must appear affable, reliable, and the like, and he must adjust his discourse according to his estimate of the audience." With such a practical bit of advice it would be hard to find fault, and yet the admonition sounds callow, even craven. Surely, we feel, the completely ethical man will say what needs to be said, his own predilections and those of the audience be damned. That is, we might feel that in its concentration on efficacy, rhetoric ignores more basic ethical considerations. Some rhetoric, of course, does base itself purely on its ability to effect—whatever. (Examples at this point are unnecessary.) But Aristotelian rhetoric is not of the moment; as we shall see, it is oriented toward time past, time present, and time future and is thus inherently eternal. Moreover, its premise is *identification*, consubstantiality.

If Aristotle had advised the taking of the most expedient means to make discourse effective, his treatise would have been to rhetoric what a cookbook is to cuisine—ancillary and ephemeral. But a deeper motive than the immediately practical underlies Aristotle's speaker-hearer-message equation, and it is this deeper motive that is the *raison d'etre* for all rhetoric. We can begin to understand by thinking of a common metaphor: "That man talks my language." The meaning here has little to do with language as such, but rather with a whole *gestalt*. Anyone who "talks my language" in the metaphorical sense is in some basic ways identical with me, not merely on the level of opinion and overt action, but in fundamental, inchoate, even mystical ways. Anyone who "talks my language" is consubstantial with me. The social intercourse of discourse is an uncannily exact parallel to sexual intercourse, in which two people, momentarily at least, achieve a transcendent unity.[8] Another formulation allows us to say that the rhetorical impulse is toward union. The impulse of the plain dealer is toward disunion. Finally, the *rhetorical* impulse expressed in the speaker-hearer message formula is servile only insofar as the *human* impulse toward union and understanding is servile.

The instruments of persuasion, then, depend upon the *ethos* of the

[8] This is neither the time nor the place for "far-out" speculation, but might it not be possible to build an analytical pattern for rhetoric along Freudian lines? In such a pattern, all rhetorical impulse (the impulse toward identification) would be libidinous; the rhetorician would, in Kenneth Burke's terms, be "wooing" the reader. The process would be "courtship," to borrow from Burke once again.

speaker, the nature of the audience, and the speech itself "in so far as it actually or seemingly demonstrates." And " 'Persuasive' means persuasive to a person. To him, a statement may be persuasive and credible by itself, immediately, or it may become so when it seems to be proved from other statements that he believes."[9]

Rhetoric, says Aristotle, is in a sense a fusion of dialectic and ethics. Dialectic provides a logical or a pseudological means of proof, and it is toward proof of one kind or another that rhetoric aims. (Or we might clarify by saying that rhetoric aims toward the bringing about of conviction in an audience and hence toward some kind of proof.) The ethics of rhetoric are of the public kind and hence can be called, in Walter Lippmann's words, the public philosophy. Rhetoric always goes outward, toward an audience, and its most important uses concern decisions within the body politic; hence, its ethic is identical with the ethic of political science.[10]

The instruments of persuasion by argument are the *example* used inductively and the *enthymeme* used deductively. Aristotle is here saying that one can argue in two ways—on the basis of logical necessity (with the enthymeme) and on the basis of evidence (with the example). The general movement of the two kinds of argument can be illustrated thus:

> All dictatorships are undemocratic.
> All undemocratic governments are unstable.
> All unstable governments are cruel.
> All cruel governments are objects of hate.
> ∴. All dictatorships are objects of hate.[11]

> The dictatorship of Hitler was hated.
> The dictatorship of Mussolini was hated.
> The dictatorship of Franco is hated.
> The dictatorship of Mao is hated.
> ∴. All dictatorships are hated (or, The
> dictatorship of X is—or will be—hated).

Naturally, in a real argument, both modes of proof will be used. It may be that the general form of the piece of discourse will be controlled by the enthymeme and that the individual parts will be developed by the example. We can save ourselves a great deal of trouble if we avoid con-

---

[9] *Rhetoric*, p. 11.

[10] In *De Oratore*, Cicero classified rhetoric as a branch of political science. This classical tendency to orient rhetoric within the realm of politics and public address was a hindrance to the understanding of the art in its widest sense. Nonetheless, Aristotle was thinking primarily about proofs in public matters such as legislative deliberations and law cases.

[11] Morris R. Cohen and Ernest Nagel, *An Introduction to Logic* (New York: Harcourt, Brace & World, Inc., 1962), p. 11.

fusing the rhetorical terms *induction* and *deduction* with their logical counterparts. Aristotle is not—contrary to general opinion—talking about methods of thinking but about methods of developing arguments. As Cohen says, ". . . all inference is deductive and . . . what passes as induction is either disguised deduction or more or less methodical guesswork."[12] The definition of induction formulated by the scholastics was "reasoning from facts or particulars to laws or universals."[13] But even common sense shows that there is no real possibility of such a process. Referring to the "inductive" argument concerning dictatorships (see above), we find that the examples themselves were chosen on the basis of some over-all theory. The "inductive" process in science is also a fiction, for the investigator must proceed experimentally on the basis of a limited number of possibilities in an experimental situation that presupposes a *general* theory on the basis of which work toward a particular result can proceed. And, as Cohen says,

> . . . science never draws any inference from any sense-data except when the latter are viewed as already embodying or illustrating certain universals. It would obviously be impossible to state what happened in a single laboratory experiment except in terms of abstract or universal properties, such as weight, velocity, change, etc. . . . In actual scientific inquiry we start with a number of merely or barely possible explanations. The cause of A may be C, D, or E, or any other number of circumstances. If one of these hypotheses be true certain consequences should follow, and any failure of one of these consequences rules out the hypothesis and thus diminishes the number of alternatives.[14]

In actual fact, then, the difference between *rhetorical* induction and deduction is that induction establishes the general on the basis of examples, while deduction establishes the general on the basis of dialectic; furthermore, the two processes are usually inseparable in any given argument.

Aristotle calls the enthymeme the rhetorical syllogism, but there is some question about the way in which the enthymeme and the syllogism are related. The common definition of enthymeme is a syllogism with one of the terms suppressed; thus, this syllogism:

All men are mortal.
Socrates is a man.
∴ Socrates is mortal.

[12] Morris R. Cohen, *A Preface to Logic* (New York: Holt, Rinehart and Winston, Inc. 1965), pp. 32–33. Excerpts from *A Preface to Logic* are reprinted with the permission of Holt, Rinehart and Winston, Inc., and Routledge & Kegan Paul, Ltd.
[13] Cohen, p. 33.
[14] Cohen, pp. 33–34.

becomes this enthymeme:

> Because Socrates is a man, he is mortal.

from which we can reconstruct the whole syllogism. But Aristotle seems to have a wider meaning for enthymeme than this. Under the general category of enthymeme, he includes the categorical proposition:

> Methinks there is no such wealth as excellent health.

the maxim:

> The mortal should have mortal thoughts, not thoughts immortal.

and the true enthymeme:

> There is none of mankind that is free.
> For each is a slave to money or chance.

From these we can construct the syllogism:

> No one who is a slave to money or chance is free.
> All men are slaves to money and chance.
> ∴. There is none of mankind that is free.

Thus, the enthymeme is a general premise that serves as the basis for argument—as the idea to be proved.

The materials of this enthymeme are *probabilities* and signs. "A 'probability' is that which usually happens or follows . . . yet not (as some would define it) *anything* that so happens, for the thing must belong to the class of things that may turn out this way or that."[15] A *sign*, however, is a proposition that can be or is demonstrated by argument. The focus in rhetoric is on the probable and the possible, not certainty, but by means of the enthymeme we can bring about conviction concerning the probable.

One of the most interesting doctrines of classical rhetoric is that of the *topoi* or *commonplaces.*

> . . . I mean arguments that are applicable in common to the study of justice and physics, to the study of politics—to a large number of inquiries of diverse sorts. Take the topic of *more* and *less:* this is of no greater service when we make a syllogism or utter an enthymeme about matters of right and wrong than when we make one about physics, or about anything else, different though these things are in kind.[16]

15 *Rhetoric*, p. 13.
16 *Rhetoric*, p. 15.

These *topoi* are the "places" where one can find material for argument, the "topics" that are universally applicable in rhetoric. Of course, there are *topoi* that apply only to the subject under consideration, but in order to discover them, the rhetorician must have special knowledge of the subject under consideration.[17] The idea of the *topoi* was actually a whole epistemological theory, one that had wide practical repercussions in pedagogy. The vitiation of the *topoi* theory led to the widespread custom during the Renaissance and after of keeping "commonplace books," namely, notebooks in which the owner recorded pithy sayings for future use. Such a practice was, of course, destructive of originality and led to fustian in writing, but so mendacious a thing as keeping the commonplace book was not in Aristotle's mind.

We can see something of the ramifications of Aristotle's epistemology of *topoi* if we turn to Francis Bacon, who in *The Advancement of Learning* divided logic into *invention, judgment, memory,* and *tradition;* invention into invention of arts and invention of arguments; and invention of arguments into promptuary (places or *topoi* of preparation) and topical (places of suggestion) (see Figure 1).

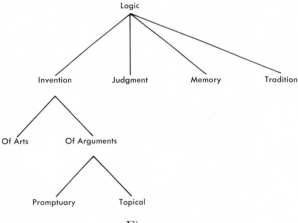

Figure 1

In Bacon's terms, then, the *topoi* have an integral function in one of the two areas of human creativity. That is, man can make things (buildings, pictures, senates), and he can talk about the things that he has made; these represent the limits of human creativity. In the making of arguments, man has two resources: his knowledge of the subject in particular and his knowledge of the way things are in general (or of the general

[17] Later in this chapter, we shall come back to a more detailed and particular discussion of subjects such as the *topoi;* for the moment, it is essential that we gain an overview of what Aristotle is attempting.

laws of the universe). The problem of rhetoric is bringing to bear upon the subject in question one's particular and one's general knowledge. And it is this that Aristotle is suggesting with his doctrine of the *topoi*.[18]

"The kinds of Rhetoric are three in number, corresponding to the three kinds of hearers to which speeches are addressed," namely, "(1) a mere observer [critic] . . . (2) a judge of things past or (3) a judge of things to come." It follows, then, that the three types of speeches are (1) *epideictic* (addressed to a mere observer, such as a participant in a funeral or public celebration), (2) *forensic* (addressed to judges of things past, such as juries), (3) and *deliberative* (addressed to judges of things to come, such as senates). The implications for rhetoric of this tripartite division are (1) that the art is not aimed exclusively at bringing about action and (2) that the art has a temporal orientation.

A widespread misconception is that rhetoric always aims at stirring its audience to action—to the action of acquitting the accused, of voting for X, of buying such and such a brand. But rhetoric also has its moments of repose, when its purpose is *das Ding an sich*, the purely esthetic and tranquil moments when the only action it hopes to bring about is that of the audience's gift of sympathy and understanding. We see, then, that the purposes of rhetoric are in accord with the purposes of art. The focus of art is most often on the tranquil moment of the work for its own sake and the sake of the audience's sympathetic response, but art also enters the arena and attempts to be an overt force for good and truth, perhaps more frequently than we generally realize. Like "pure" art, the epideictic speech steps out of the arena of action and becomes a work for its own sake and that of the audience. Rhetoric praises and blames— and informs, for the epideictic speech is addressed to the critic in the sense that the lyric is addressed to the critic.

Figure 2

Schematically, the three kinds of speeches are shown in Figure 2. But the purposes of the epideictic speech must be interpreted broadly, for "to the epideictic speaker, above all, belongs the present."

---

[18] Bacon has many other interesting things to say about our subject. For instance, he tells us that there are three distempers of learning: "vain affectations, vain disputes, and vain imaginations, or effeminate learning, contentious learning, and fantastical learning." The first of these consists of "luxuriancy of style."

This discussion leads us to a consideration of the way in which each kind of speech is oriented in time as well as toward an audience. The deliberative speech persuades (exhorts) or dissuades concerning a future course of action; the forensic (legal) speech makes accusation or defense concerning past actions. To the epideictic speech belongs the present in exactly the same sense that the present must belong to the lyric. The time of the lyric is the eternal now; hence, its timelessness. Deliberative and forensic oratory—concerning legislation, guilt or innocence, and what-not—are occasional and topical and hence transitory. But, as we shall see, epideictic oratory strives toward eternal verities, the timeless.

Even in an extrapolation, it will not do to *make too much of* our basic document. On the other hand, the tendency has been to take Aristotle at face value, not to follow his many directional signs toward some destination.

Deliberative rhetoric has five chief subjects: ways and means, war and peace, defense of the country, exports and imports, legislation. But all advice, in regard to any subject whatever, concerns happiness:

> Both individually and collectively, we may say, men all have an object at which they aim in whatever they choose and whatever they avoid. This object may be summarily described as Happiness, with its constituent parts.

And

> Happiness may be defined as prosperity conjoined with virtue; or as a self-sufficient existence; or as the pleasantest life, with secure enjoyment thereof; or as a thriving condition of property and persons, with the ability to take care and make use of them.[19]

All of this is rational and straightforward enough. And we should not argue with Aristotle if we had not inherited Freud. We have always known that what normally should bring happiness often brings grief or madness; we know that Richard Cory put a bullet through his head. And as sons and daughters of the twentieth century, we search for hints that at least intuitively Aristotle went beyond his bland rationalism in his view of happiness. In an amazing number of instances, the search for something deeper and more basic in Aristotle pays dividends, as it does in the present case. Later in his treatise (under the discussion of forensic rhetoric), Aristotle gives us the hint that we need. He tells us that men perform actions either by choice or not by choice, for some actions are

[19] *Rhetoric*, p. 24.

dictated by chance or compulsion. Even the actions that men choose to perform come about through either a rational impulse or an irrational impulse such as anger and desire (appetite). In fact, human actions have seven causes: chance, nature, compulsion, habit, reason, passion, and desire. However, a "purposeful wish is an impulse towards . . . a good (for no one wishes a thing unless he conceives it to be a good)." The dialectic of this statement leads us to conclude that all purposeful human wishes are impulses toward some kind of good, and the good is "that which is chosen in and for itself; or . . . that for the sake of which we choose something else; or that which is desired by all beings. . . ."[20] We ask at this point, "What is it that is chosen in and for itself, that is desired by all beings?" Aristotle provides an obvious answer: pleasure, for pleasure "is a certain motion of the soul . . . a perceptible settling of it, all at once, into its rightful nature."[21]

Happiness and pleasure, then, become synonymous, or nearly so; and happiness consists not only in favorable material circumstances but also in a settling of the soul into its rightful nature. If Aristotle is not anticipating the Freudian pleasure principle, he is coming very near to doing so. Thus, Norman O. Brown:

> . . . Freud can say, "Our entire psychical activity is bent upon procuring pleasure and avoiding pain, is automatically regulated by the pleasure-principle." Or, "It is simply the pleasure-principle which draws up the programme of life purpose." At this level of analysis, the pleasure-principle implies no complicated hedonistic theory nor any particular theory as to the sources of pleasure. It is an assumption taken from common sense, and means much the same as Aristotle's dictum that all men seek happiness: Freud says that the goal of the pleasure-principle is happiness.[22]

The pleasure principle, however, is thwarted by the reality principle, or, to translate *out of* psychological jargon: the intense personal motivation for continual pleasure is thwarted by the reality of the society in which the individual must live.

And here, again in Freudian terms, is the function of rhetoric that Aristotle implies: mediation between the pleasure principle and the reality principle. We have already seen that the ideal of rhetoric is consubstantiality, complete sympathetic understanding among men. (The goal of the noisiest of all arts is tranquility.) But the goal of rhetoric is also obviously individual and personal; the goal of rhetoric is mediation between the inexorable demands of the pleasure principle and the equally

---

[20] *Rhetoric*, p. 30.
[21] *Rhetoric*, p. 60.
[22] Norman O. Brown, *Life Against Death* (New York: Vintage Books, 1965), p. 8.

inexorable demands of the reality principle, between the individual and the society in which he lives.

The aim of the deliberative speech, then, is happiness. It aims at establishing the course that will result in good; happiness is the ultimate goal of men. But now we must seek out the differences between happiness and pleasure, for, although deliberative rhetoric's ultimate concern is happiness, the ultimate concern of forensic rhetoric is pleasure. One difference seems to be that pleasure is somehow of the past, whereas happiness is of the future. That is, the deliberative speech, concerned with the future, must take into account man's desire for happiness; the forensic speech, concerned with the past, must take into account man's desire for pleasure. The situation seems enigmatic until we realize that the deliberative speech is concerned with *general* future happiness; the forensic speech, on the other hand, is concerned with *specific* past pleasures (on the theory that criminal motives spring from a desire for pleasure). Of pleasure Aristotle says,

> Everything is pleasant, too, of which the desire exists within us; for desire is an impulse towards the pleasant. Now desires are either irrational or conjoined with reason.[23]

For instance, all "natural" desires are irrational: hunger, thirst, taste, sex. Note again how startlingly congruent Aristotle is with Freud:

> The aim of the theory of instincts is to build a bridge between mental conflict (neurosis) and human biology, and, at least as Freud handled it, it ends by finding the causes of conflict in the biological domain.[24]

Might we not be justified in a reformulation: the aim of forensic rhetoric is to build a bridge between mental conflict (neurosis) and human biology. We must admit, however, that in this instance Aristotle takes with one hand what he gives with the other, for he explains the motives of wrongdoing as completely prudential: the criminal assumes he can "get away with" his act or that the pleasure of the act will be greater than the pain of the punishment.

Such is the outline of Book I of the *Rhetoric*. The lacuna in Aristotle's discussion is glaring; he fails to discuss epideictic rhetoric in detail, and hence his treatise is weighted toward disputation. It is not unlikely to assume that the bent Aristotle gave his subject determined its nature for succeeding centuries. And hence, though our debt to Aristotle

[23] *Rhetoric*, p. 60.
[24] Brown, p. 81.

is immeasurable, on the practical level, he provided theoretical bases for the cacophany of modern pitchmen.

Book II

Book II of the *Rhetoric* deals with means of persuasion by character and emotion, with the common topics, and with logical proofs. Aristotle's prefatory statement:

> Now Rhetoric finds its end in judgement—for the audience [of a deliberative speech] judges the counsels that are given, and [in forensic speaking] the decision [of the jury] is a judgement; and hence the speaker must not merely see to it that his speech [as an argument] shall be convincing and persuasive, but he must [in and by the speech] give the right impression of himself, and get his judge [audience] into the right state of mind. . . . in conducing to persuasion it is highly important that the speaker should evince a certain character, and that the judges should conceive him to be disposed towards them in a certain way. . . .[25]

Thus much of Book II will deal with matters subsumed under the general term *rhetorical stance*.[26] Now, at its lowest level, rhetorical stance becomes a process of servile ingratiation: "Never disagree with the customer!" It becomes a mendacious art. But not necessarily so, because "you persuade a man only insofar as you can talk his language by speech, gesture, tonality, order, image, attitude, idea, *identifying* your ways with his."[27] Kenneth Burke supplies two concepts that are helpful in understanding the theory of rhetorical stance: *courtship* and *consubstantiality*. Courtship is the universal process of overcoming social estrangement, of breaking down the walls of "embarrassment" that stand between men. Many social forms, then, are evidences of courtship: "How are you?" "Lovely weather today." "How's it going?" And so on ad infinitum—even to formal evening wear and use of the proper fork, one assumes. Note, too, that the more familiar the speaker is with those addressed, the less "formal" rhetoric the occasion demands. Thus, when I speak to my wife, I have no problem of overcoming social estrangement, though there are occasions when temporary social estrangement arises between us, and I make automatic adjustments. Whatever the situation, we use courtship

---

[25] *Rhetoric*, p. 91.
[26] See Wayne C. Booth, "The Rhetorical Stance," *College Composition and Communication*, XIV (October, 1963), pp. 139–145.
[27] From the book, *A Rhetoric of Motives* by Kenneth Burke, p. 55. © 1950 by Prentice-Hall, Inc. Published by Prentice-Hall, Inc., Englewood Cliffs, New Jersey. Excerpts from this work are reprinted with the permission of the publisher.

in rhetoric to bring about consubstantiality: insofar as A and B agree on anything (regardless of their countless differences), they are to that extent consubstantial, of the same stuff, of the same flesh. And consubstantiality is the ultimate in overcoming social estrangement.

Aristotle tells us that three elements go into the attempt to achieve consubstantiality (that is, to gain belief): intelligence, character, and good will. Then he immediately launches into a discussion of the emotions, for good will depends upon emotional reactions. It would be easy to say that Aristotle's psychology is "primitive"—that the *Rhetoric* is perhaps the Western world's first major "psychological treatise." However, an unfavorable judgment concerning Aristotle's psychology would overlook two important factors. (1) Aristotle is not attempting a "scientific" inquiry based on laboratory methods; he works from introspection, intuition, and observation. (2) No observation concerning the human psyche can be ontologically false, for the human psyche, by definition, is incapable of conceiving the nonhuman. That is, every observation about the human mind tells us something true about the human mind, even though the observation may be dialectically or scientifically false.[28] But let Aristotle speak for himself, on anger, for instance:

> Anger may be defined as an impulse attended by pain, to a revenge that shall be evident, and caused by an obvious, unjustified slight with respect to the individual or his friends. If the definition is right, then it must be, when a man is angered, that he is always angry with some particular person—Cleon or the like—and not with "man" in general, and is angry because that person has done or meant to do something against him or one of his friends; and it must be that anger is always attended by a certain pleasure arising from the expectation of revenge.[29]

That discussion is well enough as far as it goes—is sound psychology at a given level. But the modern man, whose subconscious has been discovered, will not stop at the rational explanation, and, as usual, Aristotle pays in cash, for he goes on to discuss a kind of anger that is not rational, namely *hubris*, "doing or saying things that cause shame to the victim, not in order that anything may happen to you, nor because anything has happened to you, but merely for your own gratification."[30] Aristotle even advances a good working definition of aggression; it comes about in "those who have any desire that is not being satisfied."[31] Translating into modern psychological jargon, Aristotle's formulation comes out something like

[28] This is why arguments about whether a given piece of literature is "true to life" always proceed from untenable premises.
[29] *Rhetoric*, p. 93.
[30] *Rhetoric*, p. 94.
[31] *Rhetoric*, p. 95.

this: denial of the pleasure principle brings about frustration, and frustration brings about aggression. And the point here is not to argue for Aristotelian psychology; it is outmoded, haphazard, and many times inaccurate. It is also full of uncanny insights.

The emotions—the psychology—of the audience, then, have an important place in rhetoric, as Ernst Dichter and the ad-men have so convincingly demonstrated. It would be beside our purpose here to encapsulate Aristotle's long discussion of the emotions. Suffice it to say that this segment of the *Rhetoric* has an intrinsic historical and philosophical interest and no little practical value. Also, throughout the discussion of emotions, one finds magnificently succinct and clear-sighted formulations, such as the following:

> We like those with whom our relations are such that, without any feeling of contempt, we have no feeling of shame of unconventional behavior before them; and those before whom we should be ashamed to do anything positively wrong.[32]

Aristotle goes on to relate the types of character to the emotions: the young, the old, those in their prime of life. After that discussion, the *Rhetoric* enters an area generally termed *rhetorical invention*, the discovery of subject matter and arguments and the development of the speech: the *topics* (commonplaces) and the *enthymeme*.

Again we can turn to Kenneth Burke for a definition and explanation of the topics:

> The so-called "commonplaces" or "topics" in Aristotle's *Art of Rhetoric* . . . are a quick survey of opinion. . . . Aristotle reviews the purposes, acts, things, conditions, states of mind, personal characteristics, and the like, which people consider promising or formidable, good or evil, useful or dangerous, admirable or loathsome, and so on. All these opinions or assumptions (perhaps today they would be treated under the head of "attitudes" or "values") are catalogued as available means of persuasion. But the important thing, for our purposes, is to note that such types are derived from the principle of persuasion, in that they are but a survey of the things that people generally consider persuasive, and of methods that have persuasive effects.[33]

The topics, then, are rules of thumb, ready ways of finding strategies to achieve consubstantiality with an audience. The logic here is simple: if you can find no common ground on which to begin, discourse cannot proceed, that is, not successfully. The topics provide ways of staking

---

[32] *Rhetoric*, p. 105.
[33] Burke, *A Rhetoric of Motives*, p. 56.

out common ground and hence ways of arguing a given case. Unfortunately, the rhetorical doctrine of topics has been degraded through the centuries, and this degradation manifested itself most clearly in the "commonplace books," collections of witty sayings on various topics, sources to which an author could turn for ready-made rhetoric. (The best modern exemplar is the book of familiar quotations.) For the sake of brevity, but in the interest of completeness, I shall outline the topics.

Four Common Topics

The Possible and the Impossible. "If it is possible for one of a pair of contraries to exist or come to pass, then you may assume that it is possible for the other."[34]

> EXAMPLE: If it is possible for a man to become sick, it should also be possible for him to recover.

Past Fact. If the less probable has happened, the more probable undoubtedly has happened. If the cause has occurred, the result has undoubtedly occurred. (And so on.)

> EXAMPLE: If Socrates understands the ways of God to man, he probably understands the ways of man to man. Or, if an evil man has been tempted, he has undoubtedly succumbed to that temptation.

Future Fact. If the conditions necessary for X to come to pass are present, then X will come to pass also.

> EXAMPLE: If Athens becomes weak, it will be invaded.

Size. We can magnify or minify the fact.

> EXAMPLE: Compared to what A did, B's action is insignificant.

Twenty-eight Topics from Which Enthymemes May Be Drawn

1. *Opposites.* If A and B stand in a given relation to each other, do their opposites, C and D, stand in the same antithetical relation? ("'If war [A] is the cause of our present evils [B], it is peace [C] that we need to correct them [D].'")
2. *Inflections.* These topics involve semantic shifts. ("You may

[34] *Rhetoric*, p. 143.

argue that 'just' does not always mean 'beneficial'; otherwise 'justly' would always mean 'beneficially'; but it is not, in fact, desirable to be justly put to death.")

3. *Correlative Terms.* A is to B as B is to A. (". . . take the trial of Demosthenes . . . and the men who killed Nicanor; since they were held justified in killing him, he was thought to have deserved his death.")

4. *More and Less.* Such arguments concern degrees. (". . . if a thing cannot be found where it is more likely to exist, of course you will not find it where it is less likely.")

5. *Time.* Here chronological relations of events are presented. (If I had demanded payment before I did the work, you would have paid me, but now that I have done the work, you refuse to pay me.)

6. *Use of Opponent's Utterances Against Him.* These topics are self-explanatory.

7. *Definition.* These topics are self-explanatory.

8. *Ambiguous Terms.* Ambiguous terms are used in their most favorable sense. (He was an ambitious man, but only for the good of his country.)

9. *Division.* ("All men do wrong from one of three motives, A, B, C. However, the first two of these motives are out of the question; and as for the third, C, the prosecution itself does not allege this.")

10. *Induction.* Conclusions are drawn from examples. ("If we do not entrust our horses to men who have mishandled other people's horses, nor our ships to those who have capsized the ships of others, and if this is our way with everything else, then beware of employing for the safety of our State men [mercenaries] who have ill protected the safety of others.")

11. *Existing Decisions.* That is, arguments are presented on the basis of precedent. ("Death is an evil; the gods have so judged it, or they would die.")

12. *From the Parts to the Whole.* What is true of the parts must also be true of the whole—a type of argument rich with possibilities for fallaciousness. (All of the parts of this machine, by themselves, are light; therefore, the machine must be light.)

13. *Simple Consequences.* The same thing may have both good and bad consequences; one may argue on the basis of either the good consequences or the bad consequences. (It is good to have money, for money buys comfort, but it is bad to have money, for money brings envy.)

14. *Crisscross Consequences.* Such tactics are used "to urge or dissuade with reference to contrary alternatives." ("For instance, the priestess urged her son not to engage in public speaking: 'For,' she said, 'if you speak honestly, man will hate you; if you speak dishonestly, the gods will hate you.'" But the same circumstances can be reversed: "'Now

you *ought* to engage in public speaking; for if you speak honestly, the gods will love you; if you speak dishonestly, man will love you.' ")

15. *Inward Thoughts and Outward Show.* Arguments of this sort are based on the proposition that what men outwardly approve of they do not inwardly desire; for instance, some men outwardly approve of chastity, but inwardly desire incontinence.

16. *Proportional Results.* "From the proportion between this and that result." ("For example, when they would compel the son of Iphicrates, a youth under the legal age, to discharge a public duty because he was so tall, Iphicrates said: 'If you make big boys count as men, you will have to enact little men into boys.' ")

17. *Identical Results: Identical Antecedents.* ("Xenophon said that to affirm the birth of the gods was as impious as to say that they die; either way, it results that there is a time when they do not exist.")

18. *Altered Choices.* The argument here is based on the knowledge that men often change their minds.

19. *Attributed Motives.* A *possible* motive is presented as the actual motive for something.

20. *Incentive and Deterrents.* The incentives and deterrents to action are considered the motives for action.

21. *Incredible Occurrences.* An attempt is made to convince the audience that the incredible actually did occur.

22. *Conflicting Facts.* The purpose here is to discredit an opponent, seek out discrepancies in his data.

23. *Avoiding Slander.* A person attempts to explain "why the facts appear in a wrong light."

24. *From Cause to Effect.* "If you prove the cause, you at once prove the effect; and, conversely, nothing can exist without its cause."

25. *Course of Action.* "See if it is or was possible to devise a better course than the speaker is recommending."

26. *Actions Compared.* This is a strategy to bring actions together and compare them, for better or for worse.

27. *Previous Mistakes.* An opponent is discredited on the basis of his previous mistakes.

28. *Meaning of Names.* Here we have a play on words. (One might say of Draco that "his laws were 'not the laws of a human being, but of a *dragon*'—so cruel were they.")

These, then, are the common places (or *commonplaces*) to which one can go for the invention of arguments. As Aristotle's section on assessing the audience constituted a practical handbook of psychology, so his list of commonplaces is a compendium of devices for the student of rhetoric. However, it is important to remember that his twenty-eight-item list is a fairly limited example from what amounts to an infinite list of possible commonplaces. The ideal purpose of the commonplaces is to give the student a series from which he can generate other series from which he can generate other series from which he can generate other series. . . . If we view the commonplaces as a finite and comprehensive series—and this is precisely the way that most rhetoricians view them—we then miss precisely their usefulness: they are handy ways of beginning; they imply their own development, transformation, and generation. The situation is somewhat like that found in a "how to write" handbook. Normally such a text presents a series of devices, but if it is a respectable book, it states candidly that the strategies presented are only some of those available and that the combination of writer-audience-situation will (or ought to) generate other devices. The point here is simple but often overlooked: Aristotle is not definitive, nor did he attempt to be. Nor, indeed, could he be. The topics, nonetheless, have a kind of timeless value in illustrating general strategies that are useful.

Now then, as we said before, the means of persuasion in general are *example* and *enthymeme*; in fact, the *Rhetoric* deals with these two subjects before it takes up the commonplaces. For good reasons, which will appear hereafter, the present discussion dealt first with commonplaces.

Aristotle has some interesting—even profound—things to say about the example. First he points out that there are two kinds of examples: historical and invented. Of the invented examples, fables are the most useful. They have wide appeal to popular audiences, and they can point up morals that are difficult to locate in history or actual fact. But examples from history are by far the most convincing, "since in the long run things will turn out in the future as they actually have turned out in the past." What Aristotle is saying is what every reader has sensed: the hypothetical example is unconvincing. Even in the social sciences, the hypothetical construct is always less convincing than the particular case history, and rightly so, for there is actually no such thing as the "norm" or the "typical." The "typical" is a convenient hypothesis with no basis in reality, for the "typical" American male or the "typical" American murder is the sum total of a great many individual instances, all of which probably varied to some degree from the "scientifically" established norm. The hypothetical example in rhetoric has precisely this same note of falseness about it. "Let us take as an example a typical American family, the Smiths." Immediately the reader becomes wary; he would prefer an actual American family, the Kowalskis, perhaps.

Even more important is the consideration of *how* the example proves. Aristotle tells us that "In the absence of Enthymemes [that is, dialectally developed arguments], the speaker must make Examples serve the ends of logical proofs." To do so, one needs a good many sound examples, a piling up of evidence. But when they follow the Enthymeme, Examples function like witnesses—and there is always a tendency to believe a witness. Accordingly, when the speaker puts the Examples before, he must use a good many of them; if he puts them after, one may suffice—on the principle that a single witness, if you have a good one, will serve the purpose.[35]

The single example, then, does not prove; it illustrates. If examples are to prove, they must occur in numbers. (There is something here of the notion of statistical validity.)

The *enthymeme*, the very basis for argument, is the rhetorical syllogism; indeed, it is frequently, as we have noted, a truncated syllogism:

> *Syllogism*
> All men are mortal.
> Socrates is a man.
> .˙. Socrates is mortal.

> *Enthymeme therefrom*
> Since Socrates is a man, he is mortal.

But Aristotle also classifies the *maxim* as an enthymeme: "Take away the syllogistic form, then, and a premise or a conclusion of an Enthymeme is a Maxim."[36] Thus both *All men are mortal* and *Socrates is mortal* are that form of enthymeme known as maxim. The universally overlooked point here is this: Aristotle is telling us that we frequently argue from a generality, a maxim. The maxim needs establishment, either by logic or example. But the rhetorical usefulness of the maxim goes even deeper. In the first place,

> One great advantage of maxims to a speaker arises from the uncultivated mentality of an audience. People are delighted when he succeeds in expressing as a general truth the opinions they entertain about special cases.[37]

The maxim, then, serves as a useful device in achieving consubstantiality with the audience:

> The speaker . . . must feel his way to the subjects on which his audience has prepossessions, and guess how these came about, and then must express the same views, on the same subjects, as general truths.[38]

[35] *Rhetoric*, p. 149.
[36] *Rhetoric*, p. 150.
[37] *Rhetoric*, pp. 153–154.
[38] *Rhetoric*, p. 154.

As we have noted, the enthymeme proper is a truncated syllogism. But in order to make the enthymeme function, the speaker must have broad knowledge of *politics* and *ethics*, as well as extensive knowledge concerning individual subjects. Now, as we have said, politics is to the state as ethics is to the individual—"they have to do with the conduct of men as individuals, and with men in groups." Thus, Aristotle makes the ethical question central to rhetorical theory. For instance, he presents a list of sham enthymemes (logical fallacies) that the rhetorician must be prepared to meet; he recognizes that sophistry is an efficacious device. As an ethical man, the rhetorician must argue on the basis of real knowledge:

> Whatever the subject on which we have to speak or reason—whether the argument concerns public affairs or anything else—we must have some knowledge, if not a complete one, of the facts.[39]

In order to employ the enthymeme effectively, then, the speaker needs a selection of premises, some of which are general (commonplaces or topics) and some of which are particular (facts about the case in question). Thus armed with a method and a subject matter, the moral rhetorician can make truth prevail over falsehood.

Book III

The concluding book of the *Rhetoric* deals with *style* and *arrangement*. It is possible to say, roughly, that the first two books deal with *rhetorical stance* and *rhetorical invention*; the third book deals with the *manner* in which the *matter* is presented. [In effect, then, Aristotle deals with only three of the traditional five departments of rhetoric (invention, arrangement, and style), for rhetorical stance is subsumed under invention. The present book will limit itself pretty much to those same three departments.]

The most unfortunate statement in the rhetoric is Aristotle's justification of a discussion of style. Why study style? Aristotle answers that audiences are such a sorry lot that the merits of the case are not enough to prevail; in addition to truth and justice, one must appeal to the audience's base desire for, I suppose, flamboyance.

> . . . the whole affair of Rhetoric is the impression [to be made upon an audience]; and hence delivery must be cared for, not on grounds of justice, but as something we are bound to do. Strict justice, of course, would lead us, in speaking, to seek no more [of an emotional effect] than that we

[39] *Rhetoric*, p. 156.

should avoid paining the hearer without alluring him; the case should, in justice, be fought on the strength of the facts alone, so that all else besides demonstration of fact is superfluous. Nevertheless, as we have said, external matters do count for much, because of the sorry nature of an audience. Meanwhile attention to style necessarily has some real, if minor, importance in every kind of exposition; it does make a difference in the clearness of an exposition whether you put a thing in this way or that— and yet not so much difference as people think, since all these devices of style and the like are of the imagination, and meant for the ear. No one uses them in teaching mathematics![40]

This statement by Aristotle is the grandsire—or at least the *spiritual* grand-sire—of the periodic revolts against the copious style, revolts that occur regularly in the history of rhetoric. The argument of the plain versus the grand style is so important to rhetoric—its theory and its practice—that a rather lengthy case history is in order.

The masters of Renaissance prose in English viewed the instrument of their art as one of infinite variety, a copious field adorned with every attraction. In their writing was a kind of unrestrained *jeu d'esprit* that often bordered on the artificial but that always opened new vistas of expression. Any device to make prose more elegant was fair game. And the results were, of course, spectacular. Here is Roger Ascham speaking in a fairly typical passage:

> Learning teacheth more in one year than experience in twenty; and learning teacheth safely, when experience maketh mo [sic] miserable, than wise. He hazardeth sore that waxeth wise by experience. An unhappy master he is that is made cunning by many shipwrecks; a miserable merchant, that is neither rich nor wise but after some bankrouts. It is costly wisdom that is bought by experience. We know by experience itself, that it is a marvellous pain to find out but a short way by long wandering. And surely, he that would prove wise by experience, he may be witty indeed, but even like a swift runner, that runneth fast out of his way, and upon the night, he knoweth not whither. And verily they be fewest in number that be happy or wise by unlearned experience. . . .

It hardly takes detailed analysis to sense the cadences and richness of this prose—or to perceive that in many important ways it is different from a mystical entity that we might call "the plain style." Even in the sentence "He hazardeth sore that waxeth wise by experience," we sense a "strangeness" that labels the utterance passé. In fact, Ascham and other Renaissance prose stylists were logical results of a stylistic doctrine that had evolved directly from Cicero, who stands at the opposite pole from

[40] *Rhetoric*, pp. 183–184.

Aristotle. To oversimplify just a bit, one might say Aristotle's theory advanced the plain, unadorned style; Cicero's theory advanced copiousness, ornament, style for its own sake. In *Elizabethan and Metaphysical Imagery*, Rosemond Tuve has shown that the ornament—the image—in Renaissance prose and poetry was not a mere superaddition for the sake of beauty, but functioned to illuminate the nature of the whole work; that is, the individual image was, in a sense, the work in miniature or an integral part of the theme and structure of the work. The "beauties" of Renaissance style were not "mere" beauties; they had a workmanlike purpose. In a society that believed in analogy as a means of arriving at truth, such a theory functioned well; the image was legitimate "since its ultimate impact would lie in revealing the forming and 'informing' 'cause' of a literary work."[41]

But there was a turn from the luxuriance of Renaissance prose. The stylistic doctrine that developed during the end of the seventeenth century was one "which discovers a mean between brevity and prolixity. . . . It developed, insofar as it derived from classical models, out of the loose unexpected period of Seneca rather than out of the formal expected period of Cicero."[42] This reaction was brought about by many factors, but primarily by the neo-Aristotelian doctrine that any adornment is excrescence. Somehow, the argument runs, everything that is not necessary to convey the bare message is immoral, for it is the message that counts, not the symphonic nature of language; furthermore, the beauties of language can be devices for making untruthfulness prevail. The luxuriant style, the feeling goes, may well be the device of the sophist. Thus, in 1667, in *History of the Royal Society*, Sprat can say,

> The Style perhaps in which it is written, is larger and more contentious than becomes that purity and shortness which are the chief beauties of Historical Writings: But the blame of this ought not so much to be laid upon me, as upon the Detractors of so noble an Institution: For their Objections and Cavils against it, did make it necessary for me to write of it, not altogether in the way of a plain history, but sometimes of an Apology.

Sprat vigorously attacks the Ciceronianism of his age, and the passage in which he does so most vigorously is worth quoting, for it shows something of the neo-Aristotelian revolt against the Ciceronianism of the Renaissance:

---

[41] Jackson I. Cope, *Joseph Glanvill* (Saint Louis: Washington University Studies, 1956), p. 145.
[42] George Williamson, *The Senecan Amble* (Chicago: University of Chicago Press, 1951), p. 336.

Who can behold, without indignation, how many mists and uncertainties, these specious *Tropes* and *Figures* have brought on our Knowledge? How many rewards, which are due to more profitable, and difficult Arts, have been still snatch'd away by the easie vanity of *fine speaking*? For now I am warm'd with just Anger, I cannot with-hold my self, from betraying the shallowness of all these seeming Mysteries; upon which, *we Writers* and *Speakers*, look so bigg. And, in few words, I dare say; that of all the Studies of men, nothing may be sooner obtain'd, than this vicious abundance of *Tongue*, which makes so great a noise in the World.

Sprat longed "to return back to the primitive purity, and shortness, when men deliver'd so many *things*, in almost an equal number of words."

Here, then, is a case study in miniature of the clash between the stylistic doctrine that can be traced back to Aristotle and the stylistic doctrine that can be traced back to Cicero. By and large, all arguments about style and all doctrines of style fall into one or the other camp. (Such is the historical necessity of rhetoric.) The oversimplified formulation that resulted was this: Aristotle represents plainness and simplicity; Cicero represents ornateness and copiousness.

The question before us now, however, is Aristotle's doctrine of style. Aristotle tells us that style ought to be merely clear, that its ideal is a vehicle that will carry reason without arousing either pleasure or pain in and of itself. He recognizes the rhetorical necessity for ornament, but he decries that necessity. What Aristotle fails to realize is the nexus between rhetoric and esthetics. Beyond its suasiveness, style also has an esthetic function. One should remember that Coleridge objected to Wordsworth's proposition that "the proper diction for poetry in general consists altogether in a language taken, with due exceptions, from the mouths of real men in real life." Coleridge says (1) this holds true only in certain classes of poetry; (2) the poet might choose low and rustic life for a subject, but that does not necessitate his using such language for the representation. Much the same objection can be raised against Aristotle's doctrine. Only one of the functions of style is the conveyance of information or ideas. Justifying the other function carries us into the arguments for the beautiful, and the beautiful cannot be justified on merely pragmatic grounds. As Walter Ong points out, rhetoric and poetry have this in common: the truth that they convey does not exist independently of the language in which it is conveyed. Philosophy, on the other hand, directed to the speculative intellect, "has its existence independently of the words used to communicate it."[43] The "messages" of rhetoric and poetic are not

[43] Walter J. Ong, "The Province of Rhetoric and Poetic," *The Province of Rhetoric*, ed. Joseph Schwartz and John A. Rycenga (New York: The Ronald Press Company, 1965), p. 53.

only deeply embedded in the words but are part and parcel of the style. The difference between rhetoric and poetic lies in the ends to which they are directed: poetic is directed to the speculative intellect (contemplation), whereas rhetoric is directed in some sense toward action. This idea is most clearly grasped in the analogy between rhetoric and some modern architecture, in which design is subordinate to function. Architecture that pays no attention to esthetic design is mere engineering.

Aristotle's theory of style is, then, Gradgrindian.

But there are extenuating circumstances! In the first place, Aristotle opts for naturalness:

> . . . since the poets were thought to have won their fame by their fine language, when their thoughts were not profound, so the language of prose at first took on a poetical cast—for example, that of Gorgias. Even now the uneducated mostly think such discourses very fine. But it is not so. On the contrary, the language of prose is distinct from that of poetry. . . . it is absurd to imitate the poets in a fashion which the poets themselves have dropped.[44]

The "natural" style, by Aristotle's definition, is one which eschews the devices of poetry or uses them sparingly: figures, images, symbols. But such a difference can be only a matter of degree. This natural, good style is *clear* and *appropriate*, but "it is well to give the ordinary idiom an air of remoteness; the hearers are struck by what is out of the way, and like what strikes them." We conclude that Aristotle advises a "rhetorical" diction that is only apparently natural ("the language of common men," in Wordsworth's sense), but that actually is structured and conceived differently from the language of everyday life.

> . . . the speaker should use rare words, compound words, and coined words, but sparingly and seldom. On what occasions they may be used we shall state by and by; why they should be sparingly used has already been explained—they diverge too far from custom toward the extreme of excess. In the language of spoken prose, only the current term, the distinctive name, and metaphors can be used to advantage; we so infer because these, and these alone, are what every one used in ordinary conversation. Every one does use metaphors, as well as distinctive names and current terms. So it is plain that good composition will have an air of novelty [remoteness], while the art can escape notice and the style is clear.[45]

Aristotle is saying that the structure of prose and prepared spoken discourse is a good deal different from that of conversation, a principle that

[44] *Rhetoric*, pp. 184–185.
[45] *Rhetoric*, p. 186.

is generally recognized. In this sense, the language of "rhetoric" will have a remoteness about it. To determine wherein that remoteness consists, one can compare, for instance, the extemporaneous answers of John F. Kennedy at a press conference with the prepared speeches that he delivered or with his writings.

This is all that we will say at this point about Aristotle's doctrine of style. Subsequent chapters will deal with style in detail and will fully discuss the metaphor ("It is metaphor above all else that gives clearness, charm, and distinction to the style. . . .")[46]

Aristotle's final consideration is *arrangement*. Theories of arrangement have been perhaps the least satisfactory aspects of rhetoric—from the time of Aristotle to the present day, with its proliferation of freshman handbooks. The following is typical:

> While you are deciding how you will use your material in developing your subject, you will also be thinking about how you will organize your paper. Grouping related material into blocks and then arranging these blocks in a sensible order constitutes the fourth stage in writing. From this stage should emerge a plan for the paper—whether in your mind or in scribble notes or in a formally prepared outline.[47]

The next step in the handbook is inevitably a discussion of orders of development and then the outline. As we shall see hereafter, such discussions falsify the complexity of the act of writing or speaking, and they make impossible the perceptive analysis of the act of discourse. The infinitely complex process of putting ideas into coherent discourse simply is not amenable to such handy and superficial formulations.

Aristotle divides the speech into the following parts: *proem, narration, arguments pro and con,* and *epilogue*. That is, one introduces his subject and gains the good will of his audience (proem); one outlines the case or subject (narration); one advances arguments in behalf of the case and against the opponent's case (arguments); and one sums up and makes a final attempt to win the audience's good will (epilogue). Aristotle hints at something of the flexibility required to make a description of arrangement accurate; for instance, he tells us that the narration may not form a section of the speech, but should be distributed throughout the speech, so that the audience does not know the whole case until the argument is concluded.

Of the classical doctrine of arrangement, Kenneth Burke has this to say:

[46] *Rhetoric*, p. 187.
[47] Porter G. Perrin, *The Writer's Guide and Index to English* (4th ed.; Glenview, Ill.: Scott, Foresman and Company, 1965), p. 47.

There is also persuasive form in the larger sense, formulated as a progression of steps that begins with an exordium designed to secure the good will of one's audience, next states one's own position, then points up the nature of the dispute, then builds up one's own case at length, then refutes the claims of the adversary, and in a final peroration expands and reinforces all points in one's favor, while seeking to discredit whatever had favored the adversary (vituperation, irony, and appeal to the emotions also being drawn upon here).[48]

That is a fair summary of what Aristotle has to say about form. With further detail we need not at this point be concerned.

The *Rhetoric* somehow—if one searches deeply enough—lies at the basis of all discussions of the subject. It is seminal and exciting. And it has served the Western world from ancient times to the present.

[48] Burke, A *Rhetoric of Motives*, p. 69.

chapter 3

The Neoclassical Age–
Force and Counterforce: A
Rhetorical Case History*

Some Basic Assumptions

From the time of Aristotle to the time of the Royal
Society in England (1660), much happened to rhetoric, developments that a history of our subject
would need to examine with some care. If Aristotle
is the Alpha of rhetoric and, say, Kenneth Burke the
Omega, the neoclassical age represents the Mu. But
the neoclassical age is also a period in which we can
speak of the beginnings of a "new" rhetoric that

---

* Some of the materials in this chapter appeared in an altered
and abbreviated form in *The Relevance of Rhetoric*, ed. E. V.
Stackpoole and W. Ross Winterowd (Boston: Allyn and
Bacon, Inc., 1966); used here by permission of Allyn and
Bacon, Inc.

sprang from forces and counterforces in the intellectual history of the Western world.

In the first place, two kinds of rhetorical attitudes had evolved. One, stemming from Aristotle, advocated the plain, unadorned style; the other, stemming via a circuitous route from Cicero, was committed to the "grand" style. And it was in the eighteenth century that these two almost diametrically opposed viewpoints confronted one another in the arena of both theory and practice. The result of the confrontation was a significant new philosophy of rhetoric.

But the eighteenth century was truly the age in which rhetoric became "popular" in a very broad sense of that word. Public speaking—and to a lesser extent elegant writing—were viewed as the ways by which societies might be conquered.

It was in the eighteenth century that, for the first time, the manifold possibilities of rhetoric in all their richness and complexity fully emerged.

As early as 1661, the poet Cowley had said that scholars in his proposed academy might turn to Aristotle, Hermogenes, and Longinus for instruction in morals and rhetoric. But Hermogenes was past history long before the 1660s, and Longinus was yet to come into his own. In fact, neoclassical rhetoric, based on Aristotle and Cicero, was the result of interaction among three diverse intellectual and popular movements that early in the century took hold of the bourgeois imagination on the one hand and of the artistic imagination on the other. First, Longinus was "discovered"; second, the tremendously influential elocutionary movement got under way; and third, a new school of rhetoricians set forth the doctrine of perspicuity. Longinus came via France and gave the theorizer about art a fascinating hint concerning the effects of poetry. The elocutionary movement arose from the widespread faith that through effective oratory one could conquer worlds—or at least societies. The doctrine of perspicuity was a logical result of the rationalistic attitude toward human discourse.

Tracing these three diverse movements, and discovering their tendencies and countertendencies, is a fascinating but difficult enterprise. Yet the effort is worthwhile, for the neoclassical period provides a "classic" instance of the war between the plain, unadorned method of human discourse and the elegant and ornate.

The Sublime

Longinus

With the translation into French by Boileau in 1674, the modern life of *Peri Hupsous* began. We are not certain that the author of this third-century treatise was Longinus, but long tradition attributes the work to him. Certainly, until 1674 the work was virtually unknown, though it had been translated into English as early as 1652. The first translation to use the word "sublime" in the title appeared in 1698: John Hall's *An Essay on the Sublime: Translated from the Greek of Dionysius Longinus Cassius the Rhetorician.* Hall's title, then, for the first time gave prominence to the word that was to act as a kind of talisman for discussions about art. But, according to Charles Sears Baldwin, the rendering of *Peri Hupsous* as "On the Sublime" (the most common English title for the work) is an inadequate translation of the original Greek. Even though the Latin *sublimitas* is an accurate translation of the Greek, the English word "sublime" is a bad translation of the Latin. "But though the meaning is clear, an equivalent English term is still to seek. *Elevation* has unfortunate suggestions of the rhetorical; *height* is too vague; *heightening*, though nearer, is not generally used in this sense."[1] Baldwin concludes that the English word "style" is as near to Longinus' intention as we can come. Because Longinus was talking about a style that transports, "On the Style That Transports" probably conveys Longinus' meaning adequately, and because the discussion of the grand versus Longinus' conception of the sublime turns on the point of suasion as opposed to involuntary response, an exact understanding of the title of the treatise is crucial. Early in the essay (1.4), the distinction is clarified: "Our persuasions we can usually control, but the influences of the sublime bring power and irresistible might to bear, and reign supreme over every hearer."

Baldwin points out that the unique Longinian contribution lies in showing the relation of poetic and rhetoric. First, thought and emotion are not to be separated; thus, for instance, *inventio* is a twofold process. Second, the orator, like the poet, "gives us the truth of life by bringing into organic continuity what is revealing and significant." Third, where poetry compresses, oratory "iterates and enlarges."[2] The sublime comes about through five excellences: "the power of forming great conceptions," "vehement and inspired passion," "the due formation of figures" of thought and expression (that is, tropes and schemes), "noble diction," and "dignified and elevated composition."[3] Thus, three of the five sources of sublimity are strictly rhetorical; one (the power of forming great conceptions) is rhetorical in the sense that Crassus in Cicero's *De Oratore* claimed that substance was essential to style.[4]

[1] Charles Sears Baldwin, *Ancient Rhetoric and Poetic* (New York: Crowell-Collier and Macmillan, Inc., 1924), p. 123.
[2] Baldwin, pp. 126–127.
[3] Longinus, "On the Sublime," *The Great Critics*, ed. James Harry Smith and Edd Winfield Parks (New York: W. W. Norton & Company, Inc., 1959), p. 71.
[4] One should note, however, that Cicero's *inventio* differs considerably from Longinus' "power of forming great conceptions." Cicero speaks of intellectual substance brought about through learning, specifically the law. Longinus, however, says, ". . . it is abso-

The important point is this: the sublime comes about through elevation of mind expressed in the proper style. And now Longinus turns to rhetorical analysis to determine the technique of the sublime style. *Peri Hupsous* is admirably sensible and to the point, particularly in the discussion of the metaphor. The treatise takes a sublime style—a style that transports—for granted, and then goes about describing and analyzing that style. As we saw, there are five sources of excellence, but Longinus says, "Let us next consider whether we can point to anything further that contributes to sublimity of style." One such element is amplification, even though amplification is not sublimity:

> The point of distinction between them seems to me to be that sublimity consists in elevation, while amplification embraces a multitude of details. Consequently, sublimity is often comprised in a single thought, while amplification is universally associated with a certain magnitude and abundance. Amplification (to sum the matter up in a general way) is an aggregation of all the constituent parts and topics of a subject, lending strength to argument by dwelling upon it. . . .[5]

Next, Longinus recommends imitation of "previous great poets and writers":[6]

> . . . from the great natures of the men of old there are borne in upon the souls of those who emulate them (as from sacred caves) what we may describe as *effluences*, so that even those who seem little likely to be possessed are thereby inspired and succumb to the spell of others' greatness.

There follows a brief discussion of rhetorical stance, which in Cicero and particularly Aristotle, as we have seen, is a paramount consideration in the suasiveness of rhetoric. But Longinus goes beyond the two classical masters. Though both Aristotle and Cicero advocated a shrewd summing up of the audience to be addressed, Longinus advises asking this question: "In what spirit will each succeeding age listen to me who have written thus?"[7] Hence, Longinus sidesteps the issue of pragmatic suasiveness to action.

He next deals with the following figures (both of speech and of thought, for he does not differentiate tropes and schemes): questions and

---

lutely necessary to indicate the source of this elevation, namely, that the truly eloquent must be free from low and ignoble thoughts" (IX.3). And again: "Sublimity is the echo of a great soul."
[5] Longinus, p. 79.
[6] Longinus, p. 80.
[7] Longinus, p. 81.

interrogations, asyndeton, polysyndeton, hyperbaton, the periodic sentence, polyptota, historical present, periphrasis, hyperbole, irony, and, of course, the metaphor. For Longinus, the metaphor is an instrument for arousing the emotions, to be used "when the passions roll like a torrent and sweep a multitude of them down their resistless flood."[8] The implication is that metaphorical style will inevitably be what later ages were to call the Ciceronian. Indeed, the hearer is incapable of criticizing the profusion of metaphors, for he is so carried away by the passion that they convey that he is incapable of "rational" criticism.

As the last section of "On the Sublime" makes clear, Longinus stands at the opposite pole from the rationalists:

> Summing up, I maintained that among the banes of the natures which our age produces must be reckoned that half-heartedness in which the life of all of us with few exceptions is passed, for we do not exert ourselves except for the sake of praise and pleasure, never for those solid benefits which are a worthy object of our own efforts and the respect of others. But " 'tis best to leave these riddles unresolved," and to proceed with what next presents itself, namely the subject of the Passions, about which I previously undertook to write in a separate treatise. These form, as it seems to me, a material part of discourse generally and the Sublime itself. . . .[9]

So stand the last remaining words in *Peri Hupsous*.

Now, a problem presents itself: how do eighteenth-century thinkers amalgamate accepted doctrine of the perspicuous, plain style, the "flowers" of elocutionary style, and Longinus' concept of the sublime? Monk points out that Boileau "had made it possible to consider the sublime apart from high style, and it was this that the English began to do."[10] Copernican science put man into a quandary. Apparently the universe was infinite and incomprehensible, but heretofore infinity had been the exclusive attribute of God. Locke must reconcile the concept of the infinite with the verity of God, and his thesis that space is a concept distinct from solidity is such an attempt. Says Ernest Tuveson, "Extension must then have an existence independent of that of bodies." God fills the unlimited immensity. The natural result of these trends of thought was to transfer the idea of the infinity of empty space to whatever objects were even apparently limitless, for instance, the sea. Tuveson contends that in "The Pleasures of the Imagination," Addison first stated the theory of the natural sublime:

---

[8] Longinus, p. 96.
[9] Longinus, pp. 110–111.
[10] Samuel Holt Monk, *The Sublime: A Study of Critical Theories in XVIII-Century England* (New York: Modern Language Association of American, 1935), p. 84.

The central theme of these essays is the universe as God's own theater, in which are presented spectacles designed to improve and divert men's souls. Since the imagination is the agency by which God produces these effects, there is a new importance and dignity assigned to the imagining faculty.[11]

Peri Hupsous provided hints about the torrential nature of passions aroused by sublimity, a sublimity that frequently arose from a single idea and was independent of rhetorical devices. Nonetheless, the treatise did go on to define a "sublime" style, in which the metaphor would be the main rhetorical device for bringing about the unthinking response that constitutes Longinus' idea of a sublime reaction. As we shall see, Longinus served as a stimulus to diverse theories of the sublime, he provided fascinating hints to theorizers about art, and he was the subject of numerous interpretations, reinterpretations, and misinterpretations. Somehow, finally, theory transferred the sublime from the work of art, to the subject of that work, to the "natural sublime." The jump from *Peri Hupsous* to a sublimity residing in natural objects, in immensity, and in noble flashes of thought takes place via the distinction between figures of speech and figures of thought. The figure of speech is a structurally recognizable device of rhetoric. For instance, on the most elementary level, we recognize polysyndeton on the basis of the "particles" in a construction. Asyndeton is the opposite. Thus, "the sound and fury and the storm and the stress" employs polysyndeton, while "the sound, fury, storm, stress" employs asyndeton. This distinction, then, classified metaphor as a figure of thought; simile, on the other hand, is structurally recognizable and is hence a figure of speech. As has been pointed out, *Peri Hupsous* classes metaphor as the primary figure for conveying sublimity. The result is that the Longinian treatise in effect places the sublime in thought or conception, not in the expression.

In a discussion of "On the Sublime," Elder Olson points out, uniquely, it appears, that *Peri Hupsous* must be viewed as a "reasoned structure." Longinus himself set forth the two rules for composition of a treatise on a subject such as the sublime. The writer may deal with ends or means or, I suppose, both. But Longinus chose to deal with means; he took Caecilius to task for iterating the obvious, namely, that there is a sublime effect. The important question, it seems, was the means thereto. Olson goes on to show that Longinus developed a "triadic" relation for these means. The "order of composition" concerns an *author* who composes a *work* that affects its *audience,* but the order of inquiry into the technique of composition is the exact opposite of this, "for we begin with

[11] Ernest Tuveson, "Space, Deity, and the 'Natural Sublime,'" *Modern Language Quarterly,* XII (March 1951), 20–38.

a sensation in ourselves, as audience."[12] It is the second element of this triad, the work and the means it employs, that *Peri Hupsous* focuses upon. The treatise as a discussion of means emphasizes conception and figures of thought. Thus, it would tend to devalue figures of speech as devices for creating the lofty style. This tendency is a direct reversal of the Ciceronianistic trend during the Renaissance, and for this reason, "On the Sublime" provided a direct stimulus toward the plain, perspicuous style of the eighteenth century and was probably essential to developments in neoclassical rhetorical doctrine.

Neoclassical Longinians

Though Addison was the first clear enunciator of a principle of natural sublimity, John Dennis in "The Grounds of Criticism in Poetry" (1704) pointed the way. Dennis' purpose in the essay was to show that religion is the most fitting and noble subject for poetry and, conversely, that poetry is religion's most necessary instrument. Dennis defines poetry as "the art by which a poet excites passion (and for that very cause entertains sense) in order to satisfy and improve, to delight and reform, the mind, and so to make mankind happier and better." Dennis avows that he is able to supply the definition of the sublime that Longinus avoided: ". . . the sublime is nothing else but a great thought, or great thoughts, moving the soul from its ordinary situation by the enthusiasm which naturally attends them." Longinus, says Dennis, had some idea of this, for he said that the sublime does not convince us; it transports or ravishes us. However, Longinus contradicts himself when he says that the sublime may be achieved independent of passion as well as enthusiasm.

For Dennis, the distinction between passion and enthusiasm was of the utmost importance. Passion arises from the everyday events of the world; enthusiasm, however, comes from contemplation or meditation, usually on ideas that do not belong to common life. Hence, enthusiasm is the nobler emotion and is identified with such responses as admiration, terror, horror, joy, sadness, desire. So far, Dennis has defined what might be called a sublime of contemplation or of concept or of idea. But because God (as in the poetry of Milton or Tasso) is the most lofty subject for poetry, it is obvious that the greatest enthusiastic passions are produced by contemplation of God and His works. The works of God are, of course, natural sublimity, though Dennis is not as specific in listing the objects of natural sublimity as is Addison. Strangely enough, Dennis says that in its function as an instrument to bring about piety among men, poetry is

---

[12] Elder Olson, "The Argument of Longinus on the Sublime," *Critics and Criticism*, ed. R. S. Crane (Chicago: University of Chicago Press, 1952), p. 239.

best served by the "vulgar" passions rather than by lofty enthusiasms, for only the noble-minded are capable of enthusiasms, whereas the great generality of mankind is subject to passion. Nonetheless, proper subjects to produce the

> enthusiasm of admiration are the great phenomena of the material world, because they too lead to the soul of its Maker, and show, as the Apostle says, His eternal power and Godhead: as the heavens and heavenly bodies, the sun, the moon, the stars, and the immensity of the universe, and the motions of the heaven and earth.

Given his premise, Dennis' argument is unexceptionable. His one error, of course, is his failure to understand the nature of the Longinian argument concerning the sublime. If he had understood that argument, he could have accepted the proposition that the sublime effect is a known quantity, to be taken for granted. However, if the sublime effect of enthusiasm arises from the contemplation of the most sublime ideas, and if the most sublime ideas are those concerning God, true sublimity arises in poetry that deals with God and His works. Such, in brief, is what Dennis is saying. The significance of his idea is that it provides a basis for the complete separation of matter and manner. Thus, if we say for the sake of illustration that Longinus provided a stimulus to theorizing, Dennis carried the Longinian argument to one of its conclusions.

In 1711, Addison provided a theory of the sublime that extended Dennis' concept and in so doing, removed the sublime yet another step from the Longinian definition. The sense of sight, says Addison,

> furnishes the imagination with its ideas; so that by the pleasures of the imagination or fancy . . . I here mean such as arise from visible objects, either when we have them actually in our view or when we call up their ideas into our minds by paintings, statues, descriptions, or any the like occasion.[13]

Imagination concerns "only such pleasures as arise originally from sight," either immediately or from memory. The *fancy*, apparently, is anything else. Nowhere in his essays does Addison use the term "the natural sublime," but his implications are clear. Where Dennis would attribute the sublime to the contemplation of God and His works, Addison would limit it to contemplation of God's works, the visual objects of the universe. This is not to say that Addison excluded the idea of divinity from his theory, for the pleasures of the imagination have a theological basis. Because men should delight in the contemplation of His being, God has

---

[13] ["The Pleasures of the Imagination"], *The Spectator*, Nos. 411–421.

made them take delight in viewing whatever is vast or unlimited. Nature is infinitely greater than art.

> The one may be as polite and delicate as the other but can never show herself so august and magnificent in the design. There is something more bold and masterly in the rough, careless strokes of nature than in the nice touches and embellishments of art.

Here, however, a paradox arises, for works of nature please more as they resemble art and vice versa. This is because our pleasure arises from a double principle: "from the agreeableness of the objects to the eye, and from their similitude to other objects." For this reason, well-chosen words give us more pleasure than does the sight of the objects they describe. The words stir the imagination, and the scene is painted more vividly in the imagination than in actuality.

The limitations of Addison's theory are apparent. His implication is that only descriptive poetry can bring the highest pleasures of the imagination, though, of course, he contends that the pleasures of understanding are really superior to those of the imagination, even though those of the imagination have the advantage of being more obvious and more readily acquired. Addison the stylist would find it difficult not to require that the natural sublime be described in well-chosen words, but Dennis' failure to deal with style is undoubtedly nothing more than a sin of omission. *The fact is, by 1711 the tendency to look for the sublime outside of style or manner was firmly established.* It remained for treatise after treatise to attempt to isolate the nature of sublimity.

In 1739, John Holmes appended "On the Sublime" to his formidably titled *The Art of Rhetoric Made Easy: or, the Elements of Oratory Briefly Stated, and Fitted for the Practice of the Studious Youth of Great-Britain and Ireland: In Two Books.* A fairly detailed treatment of Holmes's elocutionary treatise will be in order subsequently. At this point, however, his pronouncements are important because they show a development in the theory of sublimity. Dignity, says Holmes, is one of the prime requisites of successful oratory, and *"Dignity* is that which *adorns* Language with *sublime Thoughts,* and *Rhetorical Flowers,* such as noble *Tropes,* moving *Figures,* and beautiful *Turns."* For Holmes, then, achievement of the best utterance depended on the Ciceronian concept of noble thoughts well expressed. But, clearly, the sublimity reposed in thoughts; the *Rhetorical Flowers* adorned these thoughts to bring about excellence, not in style, but in the total utterance. Thus, noble thoughts without "rhetorical" excellence would fall short of the highest achievement, as would the "prettiest" style without the substance of sublime thoughts. Holmes the practical elocutionist dealt with the sublime only by the way, but in 1747 Dr. John Baillie set himself the task of explaining the sublime once and for all.

Baillie's *Essay on the Sublime* is one of those discussions that largely ignore Longinus' emphasis of stylistic matters and turn to "an analysis of the effects of sublimity in nature on the 'soul' of man."[14] Baillie starts with a reiteration of Dennis' complaint:

> . . . *Longinus* has entirely passed over the Inquiry of what the *Sublime* is, as a thing perfectly well known, and is principally intent upon giving *Rules* to arrive at the elevated *Turn* and *Manner.*

Baillie concludes that sublimity is inward. It comes from the "Effort of the Soul to extend its *Being.*" The very nature of our minds, says Baillie, responds to magnitude, and it is this quality in objects that causes the soul to respond. Thus, because the soul in its vastness has a natural affinity for magnitude, the human psyche responds immediately and automatically to the high, the wide, and the immense. That is the nature of the Sublime response, though Baillie does not elaborate the mental or physical symptoms of the response and hence is more Longinian than he admits. Baillie assumes with *Peri Hupsous* that the reader must of necessity know the nature of the sublime reaction. But perfect sublimity has two concomitants: uniformity and strangeness. That is, objects familiar to the imagination will not arouse a sublime reaction. And, says Baillie, reason convinces us that uniformity is necessary, for by glimpsing the part, we can perceive the whole. "Where an object is *vast*, and at the same Time *uniform*, there is to the Imagination No Limits of its Vastness, and the Mind runs out into *Infinity*, continually *creating* as it were from the *Pattern.*"[15]

Dennis had termed enthusiasm a contemplative passion, and Baillie felt that the sublime composes the mind, in contrast to the pathetic, which agitates. Filling the mind with "one vast and uniform Idea," the sublime brings about a sedateness and calm. One does not scurry from object to object, but contemplates the whole. Nonetheless, the beholder of lofty passion experiences sublimity in the same way as does the beholder of vastness, "for the *Sublime* of the *Passions* must influence the *Mind* in

[14] Samuel Holt Monk, "Introduction," John Baillie, *Essay on the Sublime*, ed. Samuel Holt Monk (Augustan Reprint Society, No. 43; Los Angeles: 1953), p. 1.
[15] In his *Sacred Theory of the Earth*, Thomas Burnet had considered the world a "mighty ruin" of a perfect original. " 'If the Sea had been drawn round the Earth in regular figures and borders, it might have been a great Beauty to our Globe, and we should have reasonably concluded it a work of the first Creation; but finding on the contrary all the marks of disorder and disproportion in it, we may as reasonably conclude, that it did not belong to the first order of things, but was something succedaneous, when the degeneracy of mankind, and the judgments of God had destroy'd the first World, and subjected the Creation to some kind of Vanity.' " Quoted in Basil Willey, *The Eighteenth Century Background* (New York: Columbia University Press, 1941), p. 29.

the same manner as the *Sublime* of *natural Objects,* and must produce the same *Exaltedness* of *Disposition.*"

In the same year (1747) that Baillie's *Essay on the Sublime* appeared, Edmund Burke completed the first draft of his *A Philosophical Enquiry into Our Ideas of the Sublime and Beautiful,* which was not published until a decade later.[16] Burke is of extreme importance to the present discussion because he brings us to the nexus of sublimity and perspicuity. Burke defintively classes the sublime as a kind of esthetic experience that can be found both in art and in "nature" in the broadest sense of that term. Harking back to a hint that appeared in Dennis' work, Burke presents a straightforward definition of the sublime:

> Whatever is fitted in any sort to excite the ideas of pain, and danger, that is to say, whatever is any sort terrible, or is conversant about terrible objects, or operates in a manner analogous to terror, is the source of the *sublime;* that is, it is productive of the strongest emotion which the mind is capable of feeling, because I am satisfied the ideas of pain are much more powerful than those which enter on the part of pleasure.

Undoubtedly Baillie's idea of uniformity influenced Burke's idea of the beautiful.[17] The beautiful, said Burke, is "no creature of our reason"; its influence does not depend on its usefulness.

> . . . since the order and method of nature is generally very different from our measures and proportions, we must conclude that beauty is, for the greater part, some quality in bodies, acting mechanically upon the human mind by the intervention of the senses.

Theoretically at least, Burke's idea of the beautiful should have prepared the way for a beautiful style independent of, or in conjunction with, sublime matter. In fact, the dignified style that John Holmes described would be very near to Burke's concept of the beautiful as a quality in bodies. In this one respect, then, Burke and Holmes coincide. But Holmes stands a good deal nearer to *Peri Hupsous* than does Burke, for Holmes felt that the "flowers" of speech were a necessary element in the dignified style; that is, he recognized the power of purely rhetorical devices. Burke, however, theorized that the emotional power of language was not necessarily dependent on its capacity for presenting images. Burke said,

> I find it very hard to persuade several that their passions are affected by words from whence they have no ideas; and yet harder to convince them,

---

[16] J. T. Boulton, "Introduction," Edmund Burke, *A Philosophical Enquiry into the Origin of Our Ideas of the Sublime and Beautiful,* ed. J. T. Boulton (New York: Columbia University Press, 1958), p. xvii.

[17] Boulton, p. liii.

that in the ordinary course of conversation we are sufficiently understood
without raising any images of the things concerning which we speak.

Clear expression appeals to the understanding; yet strong expression appeals
to the emotions, and apparently both the clear and the strong are independent of beauty with its essential regularity.

Although Holmes's flowers of speech are something quite different
from Burke's concept of language's capacity to raise images, the tenor of
both arguments is clear. Holmes would argue for a literally "flowery" style;
Burke, in contrast, would imply that regularity in style brings about beauty.
Furthermore, Burke effectively separates matter from manner, for language, he says, is capable of conveying ideas without the intermediary
effect of the image. Had Burke used examples more frequently, one could
gain a better idea of his exact meaning than his actual method of treating
his subject makes possible. For instance, he speaks of "strong expression" and means perhaps expression characterized by certain rhetorical
devices, but one has no way of determining. Nevertheless, according to
J. T. Boulton, Burke's influence was minimal.[18] Were it not that Hugh
Blair turned to Burke, A Philosophical Enquiry would have little importance for the present discussion.

The year 1759 seems to be a turning point in theories of the sublime
and of the good style. In that year, Blair started his influential Lectures
on Rhetoric and Belles Lettres, which was to carry stylistic and rhetorical
theory to a conclusion posited in the seventeenth century by Bishop Sprat,
Bishop Wilkins, and a bevy of rationalists. At the same time, however,
one sees the influence of an elocutionary attitude such as that expressed
by Holmes making itself felt. The sublime was to serve well. It was all
things to all men. It seemed to be the sine qua non of any discussion of
rhetoric or style, and hence both the "perspicuous" stylists and the elocutionists took up the concept, used it for their own ends, and developed
from it two disparate attitudes toward human discourse.

Characteristic of what was happening to the concept of the sublime
is Goldsmith's essay "Of Eloquence," which also appeared in 1759. "Of
all the kinds of success," said Goldsmith, "that of an orator is the most
pleasing"—namely, because the orator gets his applause immediately. Subsequently, we will discuss Goldsmith's essay as a statement of the attitude
of the elocutionist. For the moment, it is necessary to determine what
Goldsmith had to say about sublimity. It is nothing more than elevation
of mind. And because "no discourse can be eloquent that does not elevate
the mind," eloquence and sublimity are the same thing. Goldsmith's
straightforward statement of the relation between sublimity and style is

---

[18] Boulton, p. lxxxii.

an oversimplification, and yet it summarizes an attitude that had been growing for half a century:

> . . . we may be eloquent in any language, since no language refuses to paint those sentiments with which we are thoroughly impressed. What is usually called sublimity of style, seems to be only an error. *Eloquence is not in the words, but in the subject; and in great concerns, the more simply any thing is expressed it is generally the more sublime.* True eloquence does not consist, as the rhetoricians assure us, in saying great things in a sublime style, but in a simple style; the sublimity lies only in the things; and when they are not so, the language may be turgid, affected, metaphorical,—but not affecting. [Italics mine.]

Exactly contemporaneous with Goldsmith's essay (1759) is A *System of Oratory*, by John Ward. Ward could not ignore the question of the sublime, but he had to make it square with his doctrine as a practical elocutionist. Ward is of extreme interest because his theory contradicts his practice. In the year that Blair began his lectures, the same year in which Goldsmith published his essay, and only two years after the composition of Burke's treatise, the general attitude toward the sublime was clearly fixed. Said Ward, "lofty and grand sentiments" are the basis of the sublime. Where this loftiness exists, expression will not be wanting. The speaker with lofty sentiments will find his metaphors and images, by which he will be able to convey his message. But true sublimity is perfectly consistent with simplicity and plainness. In order to keep Ward's discussion in perspective, however, one should turn to what he says about the language necessary to express sublime thoughts. Elegance is an absolute necessity to such language, and elegance is found in words and phrases that are "sonorous, splendid, forceful and dignified." Lecture XXXIX of his book is a case in point: in general, he argues that a highly "rhetorical" style, replete with apostrophes and other figures, is proper for the conveying of sublimity. As a theorist about the effects of language, he could not beg the question of the sublime; as an elocutionist, he could not escape the popular doctrine of oratory. Because he elected to present the conventional view of each subject, he was forced into a contradiction that exemplifies the basic contradiction between the doctrine of perspicuity and its contemporaneous elocutionary movement.

By 1764, the date of Thomas Leland's A *Dissertation on the Principles of Human Eloquence*, the attitude toward the relation of style to the sublime seems to have become fairly well fixed. Leland was replying to a treatise by the Bishop of Gloucester in which the Bishop had said that inspired language is not eloquent and that eloquence is not natural to human speech, but is an abuse thereof. Leland replied that pathos is a necessary constituent of sublimity, which can certainly exist without figurative language. The sublime effect might also arise where "an extraordinary dignity of character is indicated." Some subjects are in themselves "greater and more elevated than others"; for instance, ocean is more elevated than rivulet, serious actions than amusements, battles than calmer occupations of social life, and "the works and dispensations of the Deity, still more august and aweful than the most striking actions of the Creature." But simplicity and sublimity go together, and hence a simple style, one that does not show artifice or affectation, "is the true and proper garb of the sublime sentiments."

In the last quarter of the century, Anselm Bayly was to assert laconically that "the Sublime is introduced on certain occasions only, to add dignity, and to attract admiration."[19] It was in mid-century that the logomachy about the sublime raged hottest. S. H. Monk pointed out that the influence of "On the Sublime" had made it possible to consider sublimity as a quality independent of the high style.[20] The elocutionists, however, were not ready to make such admission. With few exceptions, their whole doctrine centers around the proposition that the grand style is essential to human discourse. Granted, they were speaking of oral, not written, discourse; nonetheless, their theories were applied to discourse in general, and they developed an eighteenth-century Ciceronianism that stands in sharp contrast to the dicta of, say, Hugh Blair and George Campbell, who were products of a rationalistic philosophy of language.

The Elocutionary Movement

The elocutionary movement is

the historical trend in which rhetoric as a formal discipline not only renounced her previous interest in the classical doctrines of invention, arrangement, and style, but undertook also to confine herself to the study of oratorical delivery and its twin aspect of voice and gesture.[21]

Howell places the inception of the elocutionary movement at the beginning of the eighteenth century. By 1750, certainly, the movement was vigorous and far reaching—and it stood at the opposite pole from the strong trend toward perspicuity.

One of the first landmarks in the elocutionary movement is *An Introduction to the Art of Rhetoric* (1671), by John Newton. In his

---

[19] Anselm Bayly, *The Alliance of Musick, Poetry, and Oratory* (London: 1789), p. 322.
[20] Monk, *The Sublime*, p. 47.
[21] Wilbur Samuel Howell, "The Sources of the Elocutionary Movement in England: 1700–1748," *Historical Studies of Rhetoric and Rhetoricians*, ed. Raymond F. Howes (Ithaca, N.Y.: Cornell University Press, 1961), p. 43.

definition of rhetoric, Newton makes a radical departure from Aristotle and Cicero: it is, he says, "the Art or faculty of eloquent and delightful speaking." The ends of rhetoric, said Newton, are (1) "to tickle and delight the ears of the Auditors that they may be willing to hear that which is intended to be delivered"; (2) to inform and convince; and (3) to move their "affections so that they will act." Writing four years after Sprat had defined the new perspicuous style of science (see below), Newton was able to give clear enunciation to a principle of discourse that his followers in the elocutionary movement were to develop, reiterate, and refine. With Newton, a clear Ciceronianism emerged, to capture the popular imagination and to provide wares for a great many booksellers who supplied the demand for treatises on discourse that would "tickle the ear" and hence persuade.

Nearly seventy years later, in 1739, John Holmes presented a detailed explanation of the means whereby the speaker might achieve his ends through the sort of discourse that Newton advocated. Holmes's book, *The Art of Rhetoric Made Easy*, was apparently influential, for in 1788, John Sterling appended it to his *A System of Rhetorick in a Method Entirely New*. We have already seen what Holmes had to say about the sublime. But what advice did he give the orator?

He listed the parts of rhetoric as invention, disposition, elocution, and pronunciation,

> because all that an orator has to do is, *Argumenta Invenire, Inventa disponere, Disposita exornare, & Exornata pronunciare*, viz. To *Invent* proper arguments; to *Dispose* of 'em in a right Method; To *Adorn* 'em with beautiful *Tropes, Figures*, and fine *Turns*; and To *Pronounce* 'em with the ornaments of *Utterance* and *Action*.

He goes on to say that elocution is proper, polite, and ornamental. Thus, it occurs in highly figurative language. Indeed, a figure, says Holmes, "is the Fashioning and *Dress of Speech*." More important, however, a figure of speech is always different from the "ordinary and natural," and it always contains either a "*Passion*" or a "*Beauty*."

Holmes is representative of the elocutionists in general: the elocutionary movement advocated a literally unnatural style, for eloquence reposed in figures, and figures were different from the "natural" way of expressing ideas. Like other elocutionists, Holmes also made a clear division between logic and rhetoric, the same kind of division that Ramus had made two hundred years earlier. To the elocutionists, manner was virtually the all. Pronunciation became "the very Soul of all Rhetoric," and the old Ramistic stress on gesture appeared once again. Holmes admonishes the putative orator that he should pay close attention to the "due Management of the *Voice* and Countenance, as well as the proper *Gesture* of the Body and Hands, according to the Nature of the Passion or Thing spoken of." He concludes with this bit of advice:

> Adorn with *Tropes* and *Figures* your *Oration*,
> By *Voice* and *Action* grace *Pronunciation*.

And we see the identical theme with variations in other elocutionists. Twenty years after Holmes, *A System of Oratory* (1759), by John Ward, lists the parts of rhetoric as invention, disposition, elocution, and pronunciation, and defines elocution as elegance, composition, and dignity. Composition, says Ward, is the "turn and harmony of the periods," dignity comes from "various kinds of tropes and figures," and elegance consists of "purity and perspicuity." It is perhaps inevitable that by 1759 even an elocutionist would list perspicuity as an important element of style. When Ward summarizes his idea of style, he says that it is imaginative and passionate, but ruled by good sense. Because style comes from a vigorous, even passionate nature, young men frequently have better style than have old men. It has even been said, Ward points out, that Cicero's style degenerated as he grew older. In his long treatise, Ward does not mention Aristotle, though he turns to Cicero and Quintilian, as, for instance, when he refers to Cicero as a basis for the discussion of perspicuity. Ward, of course, took a less extreme position than did Holmes. But twenty years separated their works, and in those twenty years, the elocutionary movement had come into its own; however, the countertendency of the doctrine of perspicuity was gaining importance in theories of discourse.

The next elocutionary pronouncement with which we must concern ourselves is John Lawson's *Lectures Concerning Oratory* (1759), which is exactly contemporaneous with Ward's work. Lawson says that the end of language is to "communicate our Sentiments for the Instruction or persuasion of other men." Therefore, the "most necessary Property" of style is clearness. But the orator also has the task of gaining a listener, and thus he must please and move; to accomplish these ends he adds ornament to perspicuity. Lecture III is an abstract of Aristotle's *Rhetoric* and Cicero's *De Oratore*, about which Lawson makes this comment: Cicero is superior for the person who has the genius to become an orator, but for someone without that genius he is of little value; on the other hand, anyone can profit from the good sense and wisdom of Aristotle. The implication is that Ciceronian doctrine is the basis for the highest achievement in elocution. *Lectures Concerning Oratory* lists three styles: "the Concise and Nervous"; "the Copious and Sweet"; and "the Vehement and Sublime." The last, of course, represents the highest accomplishment. In its use, the pulpit orators of England stand unrivaled.

Even Goldsmith, with "Of Eloquence" (1759), made his way into the elocutionary movement; in fact, he echoed Lawson's sentiments about the pulpit orators of England. Goldsmith had said that an orator's success is the most pleasing, for it is attended by immediate applause. In fact,

> the rewards which attend excellence in this way are so pleasing, that numbers have written professed treatises to teach us the art; schools have been established with no other intent; rhetoric has taken its place among the institutions; and pedants have ranged under proper heads, and distinguished with long learned names, *some* of the strokes of nature, or of passion, which orators have used. I say only *some*, for a folio volume could not contain all the figures which have been used by the truly eloquent; and scarce a good speaker or writer but makes use of some that are peculiar or new.

Nonetheless, Goldsmith goes on to say, English pulpit oratory leaves much to be desired; English divines, with their cold rationality, simply do not move the hearers. The Anglicans would indeed do well to emulate their Methodist brethren. Furthermore,

> enthusiasm in religion, which prevails among the vulgar, should be the chief object of politics. A society of enthusiasts, governed by reason, among the great, is the most indissoluble, the most virtuous, and the most efficient of its own decrees that can be imagined.

As we have seen, Goldsmith said that "there is, properly speaking, no such thing as a sublime style; the sublimity lies only in the things." It seems, then, that proper subjects coupled with enthusiastic delivery will bring about the excellence that Goldsmith desires.

The elocutionary movement continued until after the end of the eighteenth century. In the seventies and eighties, the indefatigable John Walker was advancing elocutionary doctrine in book after book.[22] In *Elements of Elocution* he gave extensive treatment to the pronunciation of words in sentences, for, he stressed, elocution is not the pronunciation of single words. In *Exercises for Improvement in Elocution,* he presented passages suitable for exercises, for example, from *The Spectator,* Sterne, Milton, Akenside, Young, Dryden, Gray, Pope, Ambrose Philips, Addison, Shakespeare, Steele, Aeschines, Demosthenes, Cicero, and Livy. His *Hints for Improving in the Art of Reading* is an extensive treatise on how to

---

[22] *The Elements of Elocution; Exercises for Improvement in Elocution; Hints for Improving in the Art of Reading; The Melody of Speaking Delineated; A Rhetorical Grammar, or Course of Lessons in Elocution; The Teacher's Assistant in English Composition: or, Easy Rules for Writing Themes and Composing Exercises on Subjects Proper for the Improvement of Both Sexes at School.*

read aloud effectively; the more we sound extemporaneous in reading, he says, the better we succeed. And so with the rest of his works. They are extraordinarily pedestrian and must have been less than exciting even for the aspiring public speaker. But they represent the logical extension of the elocutionary movement, the tendency, which became more and more clear, to focus on manner to the exclusion of matter.

Late in the century, John Sterling, in A *System of Rhetorick in a Method Entirely New* (1788), even went so far as to versify the rules of elocutionary rhetoric as a mnemonic aid:

The Four Proper Tropes

A *Metaphor*, in place of proper Words,
Resemblance puts; and Dress to Speech affords.
A *Metonymy* does new names impose,
And Things for Things by near Relation shews,
Synecdoche the Whole for Part doth take;
Or, of a Part for Whole, Exchange doth make.
And *Irony*, dissembling with an Air,
Thinks otherwise than what the words declare.

Walker had been concerned with pure elocution; Sterling, like Ramus, concentrated on the figures. In fact, he tells us that he took his definitions from Farnaby's *Index Rhetoricus* (1625). A year after Sterling's work, there appeared the anomalous *The Alliance of Musick, Poetry, and Oratory* (1789), by Anselm Bayly. In it, Bayly says that music "softens the passions" and poetry "illumines the understanding," but oratory rules over both, for it "calls forth to action." With Bayly, the sublime enters only as an afterthought: "The sublime is introduced on certain occasions only, to add dignity, and to attract admiration." In a sense, Bayly's work epitomizes the result of seventy-five or more years of theorizing about eloquence.[23]

At the same time that the elocutionary movement was flooding book stalls with treatises on the art of oratory, a great number of opportunistic writers were producing books of model letters after which the great unwashed could pattern their own epistles. Katherine Gee Hornbeak's study documents the vendibility and wide use of the letter book; she says that

---

[23] Any discussion of the elocutionary movement must take note of Orator Henley, who appears in Fielding's *The True Patriot* (February 13, 1746) as Mr. McHenly. Henley's extraordinary career would attest to the general interest in and subscription to the importance of public speaking. In 1726, Henley established The Oratory, an institution devoted to the "legal right of private judgment in religion" and "declared to be an academy of the sciences and languages to supply the want of a university in London." Henley created enough stir to be relieved of his clerical duties in London and to be rusticated to a country benefice. See Howell, "Sources of the Elocutionary Movement in England: 1700–1748."

this "homely genre . . . immortalizes the life of the submerged, anonymous, inarticulate millions, as the letters of Lord Chesterfield and Horace Walpole do that of the beau monde."[24] The letter book was a series of isolated models, designed to provide the masses with paradigms of felicitous epistles for all occasions; thus such subjects as these were likely to appear: "A Letter from an Apprentice to his Father," "A Letter of Reproof from an Uncle to a Nephew," "A Letter from one Maid-Servant to another, inviting her to come to London," "A Letter from an Apprentice, in excuse of himself to his Master," and so forth.[25]

The submerged masses would turn to the letter book as an example of elegance and gentility, and like the confession magazine of today or the pulp western of yore, it would be quite likely to avoid great refinement in favor of a readily perceivable manner that would not tax the unsophisticated. A public unaccustomed to dealing with the nuances of a fine style would respond to an exaggerated style, one that a perspicuous, chaste writer would rebel against. In this sense, the Ciceronianistic style is completely plebian. *The Secretary's Guide*, by John Hill, has many examples of the kind of rhetoric that would appeal to the initiated:

A Letter from one Maid-Servant to another, inviting her to come to London

Dear Nancy,

It was your request, when I left the Countrey [sic], that I should give you an account of how I liked the Town; and that has occasion'd my giving you the trouble of this letter, by which I assure you, my fears of speeding well, which, if you remember, were not a few, were altogether needless, tho', as 'tis wisely said, we ought at all times to fear for the worst; for I was no sooner arrived, but I was settl'd in a credible [sic] Place, and not long after discover'd those pretended Dangers and Ill-conveniences, with which we Country Lasses were frequently discourag'd prov'd only Bugbears to fright us from the pursuit of our better Fortunes & Advantages, that we might become perpetual Drudges to others, by being kept in ignorance to what Preferment we might arise by our Industry. Therefore be not discouraged, but make it your Business to come up with the first opportunity, where you shall find me ready to assist you in all I can, as to your Settlement. . . .[26]

The letter was, in a sense, the popular art form of the eighteenth century, and apparently letter books were an excellent investment for publishers,

[24] Katherine Gee Hornbeak, *The Complete Letter-Writer in English 1568–1800* (Smith College Studies in Modern Languages, vol. XV, nos. 3–4; Northampton, Mass.: 1934), p. viii.
[25] Hornbeak, pp. 86–91.
[26] Hornbeak, pp. 89–90.

for we find dozens of exemplars appearing, starting as early as 1592, when Angel Day added A *Declaracion of al such Tropes or Schemes* to his *The English Secretary*. Gabriel Harvey also published a letter book, as did many others in the seventeenth century. Samuel Richardson's *Familiar Letters* (1741) went through six editions, the last appearing in 1755. Richardson's immensely popular novels, *Pamela* and *Clarissă*, are basically letter books with plots, and their appeal undoubtedly derived in large part from the public's general fondness for the epistolary form.

The Doctrine of Perspicuity

Thomas Sprat and the Royal Society

Theories of the sublime, stemming from *Peri Hupsous* and carried on in numerous eighteenth-century treatises, and the elocutionary movement were, then, two significant forces in the shaping of neoclassical rhetoric. The third force was the doctrine of perspicuity. The code of mathematics is "pure." The code of language is "corrupt." How can one convey pure idea in a code that is rife with ambiguity, appeals to supra-rational human drives, and affords possibilities for misuse? These were the questions that bothered a group of language theorists from 1667 on, when Sprat's *History of the Royal Society* was published.

Sprat, it may be recalled, proposed an English Academy, to be modeled after the French Academy. England, he said, was ready for such a group. Greatness of empire and purity of speech always meet together, and certainly England was on the threshold of greatness. This imminent and destined greatness, coupled with the necessity of purifying the language of "fantastical" elements brought to it by religious enthusiasm, made the institution of an academy most necessary.[27] There can be no doubt that Sprat had classical rhetoric—particularly that of Aristotle—in the back of his mind. We hear him echoing Aristotle's argument when, in "An Advertisement to the Reader," he says,

> The Style perhaps in which it is written, is larger and more contentious than becomes that purity and shortness which are the chief beauties of Historical Writings: But the blame of this ought not so much to be laid upon me, as upon the Detractors of so noble an Institution: For their Objections and Cavils against it, did make it necessary for me to write of it, not altogether in the way of a plain history, but sometimes of an Apology.

[27] Thomas Sprat, *History of the Royal Society*, ed. Jackson I. Cope and Harold Whitmore Jones (Washington University Studies; Saint Louis: 1958), pp. 40–45.

Sprat argues that the Greeks were masters of the art of *speaking*, an art that he felt would be destructive of science. Because they were consummate public speakers, says Sprat, they sought subjects "which could be elegantly expressed." As a result, they looked for the sort of lofty subject matter for lofty discourse that Demetrius had spoken of; hence, they avoided the drudgery of minute observation, which serves as the very basis of science. And that, concludes Sprat, is why science was so long in getting a real start! In Sprat's frame of reference, "rhetoric" could hardly be more roundly condemned.

The manner of discourse of the Society would be to "reject all amplifications, digressions, and swellings of style: to return back to the primitive purity, and shortness, when men deliver'd so many *things*, in almost an equal number of words." If the Society had not paid close attention to its manner of discourse, "the whole spirit and vigour of their *Design*, had been soon eaten away, by the luxury and redundance of *speech*." Sprat waxes warm indeed, expressing moral indignation at the Ciceronianism of his age:

> Who can behold, without indignation, how many mists and uncertainties, these specious *Tropes* and *Figures* have brought on our Knowledge? How many rewards, which are due to more profitable, and difficult *Arts*, have been still snatch'd away by the easie vanity of *fine speaking*? For now I am warm'd with just Anger, I cannot with-hold my self, from betraying the shallowness of all these seeming Mysteries; upon which, *we Writers* and *Speakers*, look so bigg. And, in few words, I dare say; that of all the Studies of men, nothing may be sooner obtain'd, than this vicious abundance of *Phrase*, this trick of *Metaphors*, this volubility of *Tongue*, which makes so great a noise in the World.

What place does such discourse have in a nation of people distinguished by "an unaffected sincerity," a people who "have the middle qualities, between the reserv'd and subtle southern, and the rough unhewn Northern people"?

Sprat and the Royal Society were serious enough about their aphorism ("so many things, almost in an equal number of words") that in 1668 they published surely one of the strangest books ever to appear, Wilkins' *An Essay Toward a Real Character and a Philosophical Language*. Wilkins' proposition is that only the first language (that is, Hebrew) was "established according to the rules of Art." Other languages, like Topsy, have just grown up, and in the course of their uncontrolled development have become riddled with the kinds of imperfections that the rules of art might have obviated. "Nor," says Wilkins, "could this otherwise be, because that very Art by which Language should be regulated, viz. *Grammar*, is of much *later* invention *than Languages themselves*, being adapted to what was already in being, rather than the Rules of making it so." Now, says Wilkins, because all men perceive alike, and an idea is but a mental image, the confusion of tongues comes from the variety of ways of expressing that notion. One way to overcome the confusion is to adopt a universal language. The other and more practical suggestion, according to Wilkins, is to devise a system of "language" that "by its facility and usefulness, (without the imposition of Authority) might *invite* and ingage men to the learning of it; which is the thing here attempted." The great bulk of the book (pages 22–288) is devoted to a long table that supposedly classifies all concepts according to genus, for example, "transcendentals general," "transcendentals mixt," "herbs according to their flowers," "herbs according to their leaves," "parts general," "sickness," "oeconomical relation," "civil relation," and so on. The result of the system, then, is a philosophical language with an ideograph for each genus. The combination of these ideographs (the "real characters") brings about a "philosophical language" of so many things in so many words. At the conclusion of the book, Wilkins, with unbelievable optimism, says, "Though I have not as yet had opportunity of making any trials, yet I doubt not, but that one of a good Capacity and Memory, may in one Months space attain to a good readiness of expressing his mind this way, either in the Character or Language."

Bunyan provides another good example of the rationalistic trend away from Ciceronianism that began in the last half of the seventeenth century. In 1666, he said (incidentally in the most "rhetorical" of terms),

> I could have enlarged much in this my Discourse, of my Temptations and Troubles for Sin; as also the Merciful Kindness and Working of God with my Soul. I could also have stepped in a Style much higher than this in which I have Discoursed, and could have adorned all things more than here I have seemed to do; but I dare not. God did not play in convincing of me; the Devil did not play in tempting of me; neither did I play when sunk as into a bottomless pit, when *the pangs of hell caught hold upon me*: wherefore I may not play in my relating of them, but be plain and simple and lay down the thing as it was. He that liketh it, let him receive it; and he that does not, let him produce a better.

When we remember that rhetoric is the element in discourse that woos the reader, we can see that Sprat, Wilkins, and Bunyan reach a point of philosophic agreement. The point that they reach is several steps removed from Aristotle, who had wished that discourse could be stripped of suasive devices, at a great distance from Cicero, who defended suasive devices per se, and at a complete remove from the elocutionists. Bunyan said, in effect, "Take it or leave it!" Sprat wanted discourse to strip itself of "rhetorical" suasiveness, and Wilkins devised a real character and philosophic language that would at once say so many things in so many words.

Whether the Royal Society was the force that shaped Joseph Glanvill's stylistic theory,[28] in *An Essay Concerning Preaching: Written for the Direction of a Young Divine* (1678) he nonetheless added his voice to the movement away from "rhetoric." His target was "enthusiasm" in preaching, defined by Nathaniel Ingelo as " 'the apish imitation of . . . [divine inspiration] by which Device Religious Mountebanks have often abus'd the credulous world.' "[29] The logic was that the Anglican divine, through moral exhortation, could avoid the hate mongering of enthusiastic preachers.[30]

Rationalism and Perspicuity

The rationalistic revolt began in the seventeenth century; in the eighteenth, it had gained force and, like the sublime and elocutionary doctrine, became a trend to be reckoned with. In 1711, we find Joseph Addison explaining that passions are pleasant, but only because we can see them in art without being caught up in their turmoil. We find delight in reflecting on dangers that are past or on pictures of hideous scenes. "In short, we look upon the terrors of a description with the same curiosity and satisfaction that we survey a dead monster. . . ." Fénelon's *Dialogues* (1717) advocate natural inspiration but inveigh against enthusiasm. Fénelon says that the ancients might have stamped their feet and struck their foreheads, but only in extraordinary situations. Then he points out that even Cicero "does not make mention of continuous gesture." It is unnatural to be "forever moving the arms in speaking."[31] And as late as 1828, we find Richard Whately attacking the enthusiastic theological style. Only when subject matter carries no weight, says Whately, does the "theological" style supply "in some degree the deficiencies of matter."[32]

By the close of the seventeenth century, "the controversy about style was settled in favour neither of the scholar nor of the artisan, but

---

[28] Albert C. Baugh *et al.*, *A Literary History of England* (New York: Appleton-Century-Crofts, 1948), p. 811.

[29] Quoted in Cope, *Joseph Glanvill* (Washington University Studies; Saint Louis: 1956), p. 73.

[30] Cope, p. 76. See also George Williamson, "The Restoration Revolt against Enthusiasm," *Studies in Philology*, XXX (October 1933), 571–603. Cope (pp. 73–86) presents a full discussion of the revolt.

[31] François de la Mothe Fénelon, *Fénelon's Dialogues on Eloquence*, trans. Wilbur Samuel Howell (Princeton, N.J.: Princeton University Press, 1951), pp. 97–98.

[32] Richard Whately, *Elements of Rhetoric* (stereotyped ed.; Boston: 1852), pp. 209–210.

of the gentleman."[33] For instance, in 1698 John Hughes said that elegance of style comes about through the use of the figures of rhetoric; however,

> . . . a Man may write *Metaphors, Tropes, Hyperboles,* and all the other Figures, without the Trouble of studying a System of Rhetorick; and I believe better too, for to attend to a great many Rules whilst you are writing, is the way to make your Style stiff and constrain'd, whereas Elegance consists very much in a genteel Ease and Freedom of Expression; it is like a coy mistress, of so nice a Humour, that to court her too much, is the surest way to lose her. . . .[34]

When Hughes's essay appeared, "the reign of the plain style was over and the reign of the correct, just, or accurate style had begun."[35] Thus, there was a fairly clear settling of an attitude toward style and rhetoric on the one hand, and on the other, as in Goldsmith, a plea for enthusiasm.

Hugh Blair

Perhaps the culmination of the rhetorical tendencies of which Sprat, Wilkins, Hughes, and other seventeenth-century theorizers are representative is the impressive and influential work of Hugh Blair and George Campbell, for these two rhetoricians encyclopedically and intelligently set forth the doctrine of perspicuity. Boswell reports that Sir Joshua Reynolds once praised the sermons of Mudge, to which Dr. Johnson replied,

> "Mudge's sermons are good, but not practical. He grasps more sense than he can hold; he takes more corn than he can make into meal; he opens a wide prospect, but it is so distant, it is indistinct. I love 'Blair's Sermons.' Though the dog is a Scotchman, and a Presbyterian, and everything he should not be, I was the first to praise them. Such was my candour."[36]

According to Boswell, it was Dr. Johnson who convinced the London printer Strahan that Hugh Blair's sermons were worthy of publication; nonetheless, Johnson predicted that within seven years they would have

---

[33] George Williamson, *The Senecan Amble* (Chicago: University of Chicago Press, 1951), p. 336.
[34] John Hughes, "Of Style," *Critical Essays of the Eighteenth Century,* ed. Willard Higley Durham (New York: Russel & Russel, Inc., 1961), I, 82.
[35] Williamson, p. 354.
[36] James Boswell, *The Life of Samuel Johnson,* (2 vols.; London: J. M. Dent & Co., 1907), II, 383.

run their course as profitable books. Not only was Blair a successful sermonizer; he produced the "classical" neoclassical rhetoric, and in it he removed sublimity from style and placed it definitively in nature, a process aided, in one way or another, by the burst of the Ossianic poems on the literary horizon.[37]

Blair's main importance lies in his definitive—even brilliant—discussion of the style par excellence. He first complains that most critics have completely missed the point about sublimity:

> I distinguish these two things from one another, the Grandeur of the objects themselves when they are presented to the eye, and the description of the Grandeur in discourse or writing; though most critics, inaccurately I think, blend them together; and I consider Grandeur and Sublimity as terms synonymous, or nearly so.[38]

The effect upon one of beholding sublime objects is "a sort of internal elevation and expansion." The sublime "raises the mind much above its ordinary state; and fills it with a degree of wonder and astonishment, which it cannot well express." The emotion that the sublime creates has about it an awfulness and solemnity.[39] Obviously Blair attributes sublimity to magnitude, though not to that alone. For instance, length is not so sublime as depth or height; thus, a plain is not so sublime as a mountain. "Wherever space is concerned," says Blair,

> it is clear, that amplitude or greatness of extent, in one dimension or other, is necessary to Grandeur. Remove all bounds from any object, and you presently render it sublime. Hence infinite space, endless numbers, and eternal duration fill the mind with great ideas.

Vastness is not the basis of sublimity, but only an aspect thereof, for loud sounds (thunder, roaring waves, a chorused Allelujah) also create the sublime effect. Furthermore, "ideas of the solemn kind, and even bordering on the terrible" are conducive to sublimity, as are obscurity and disorder. The list extends itself, to include, for instance, moral grandeur.

If, then, there is sublimity in objects, what about sublimity in writing? In the fourth lecture,[40] Blair answers the question. He imme-

---

[37] Monk, *The Sublime*, pp. 120–129.
[38] Hugh Blair, *Lectures on Rhetoric and Belles Lettres*, (7th ed.; 3 vols.; London: 1798), I, 52. Though they were not published until 1783, Blair started his *Lectures* in 1759. Thus Blair began his work two years after the publication of Burke's *A Philosophical Enquiry*. As we shall see, Burke influenced Blair. See Boulton's "Introduction" to Burke's work, p. lxxxvii.
[39] The discussion of the natural sublime appears in Blair on pp. 53 ff. of vol. I.
[40] Blair, I, 65–90.

diately takes Longinus to task. Of the five sources that Longinus claims for the sublime, the Scot dourly admits only two as valid: elevated or noble thought and passion. The "rhetorical" elements that Longinus lists have perhaps less relation to the sublime than to any other type of writing, for sublimity needs no help from ornamentation; it reposes in matter. Among examples of sublimity in writing appears *Ossian;*[41] the selection that Blair quotes is worth repeating here, for it serves as a touchstone to the sublime:

> As autumn's dark storms pour from two echoing hills, toward each other approached the two heroes. As two dark streams from high rocks meet and mix, and roar on the plain: loud, rough, and dark, in battle, met Lochli and Inisfail; chief mixed his strokes with chief, and man with man. Steel clanging founded on steel. Helmets are cleft on high; blood bursts, and smokes around. As the troubled noise of the ocean when roll the waves on high; as the last peal of thunder of heaven; such is the noise of the battle. The groan of the thunder of night, when the cloud bursts on Cona, and a thousand ghosts shriek at once on the hollow wind.

"Never," says Blair ecstatically, "were images of more awful Sublimity employed to heighten the terror of battle." Then, quite unhumorously, he says,

> I have produced these instances, in order to demonstrate that conciseness and simplicity are essential to Sublime Writing. Simplicity, I place in opposition to studied and profuse ornament; and conciseness to superfluous expression.

The so-called sublime style is usually "a very bad one." The idea that ornamentation of any kind adds to sublimity is completely false.

> "God said, Let there be light, and there was light." This is striking and Sublime. Put it into what is commonly called the Sublime Style: "The Sovereign Arbiter of nature, by potent energy of a single word, commanded light to exist;" and, as Boileau has well observed, the style indeed is raised, but the thought is fallen. In general, in all good writing, the Sublime lies in the thought, not in the words; and when the thought is truly noble, it will, for the most part, clothe itself in a native dignity of language.

And that constitutes a fair summary of Blair's thinking on the subject of matter and manner.

[41] A literary forgery by James MacPherson. MacPherson claimed that he had discovered an ancient British text.

His treatise is long, some 1200 or 1300 pages in the seventh edition. His discursiveness, however, provides a comprehensive treatise on rhetoric, both in writing and speaking, for Blair stands as a monument in the elocutionary movement. He discusses both theory and practice, including a philosophy of language in general and of grammar in particular. A good deal of condensation and summary, however, will present his theory of style with manageable brevity.[42] Though perspicuity is the greatest quality of style, a certain amount of ornamentation is allowable. And this perspicuity is not merely "a negative virtue"; rather, it lends beauty to style. The elements of perspicuity (which hardly need explanation) are purity, propriety, and precision. In order to illustrate imprecision in language, Blair presents a fairly long list of near synonyms that he claims are frequently misused. For instance,

> To invent, to discover. We invent things that are new; we discover what was before hidden. Galileo invented the telescope; Harvey discovered the circulation of the blood.[43]

Or, more subtly,

> Entire, complete. A thing is entire by wanting none of its parts; complete, by wanting none of the appendages that belong to it. A man may have an entire house to himself; and yet not have one complete apartment.[44]

There are, says Blair, two kinds of style, the periodic and the coupé. His definition of the periodic is conventional: "several members linked together, and hanging upon one another, so that the sense of the whole is not brought out till the close." The coupé, on the other hand, is the sort of style in which

> the sense is formed into short independent propositions, each complete within itself; as in the following of Mr. Pope: "I confess, it was want of consideration that made me an author. I wrote, because it amused me. I corrected, because it was as pleasant to me to correct as to write. I published, because, I was told, I might please such as it was a credit to please."

The periodic style, says Blair, is grave and dignified, whereas the coupé is "more lively and striking." However, a good writer will seldom use only one or the other, but will rather mix them, suiting manner to matter, style to mood.

[42] Blair, Lectures X–XVII.
[43] Blair, p. 230.
[44] Blair, p. 230.

Unique in its completeness, *Lectures on Rhetoric and Belles Lettres* descends from theory into practice, so that, in effect, Blair gives a point-by-point description of the style that he considers best. For instance, he discusses the position of adverbs, interrupters, relative pronouns, and so on. Volume II (Lectures XX–XXIV) contains detailed "critical examinations" of the style of Addison and Swift, specifically Addison's "Pleasures of the Imagination" papers and Swift's "A Proposal for Correcting, Improving, and Ascertaining the English Tongue." Blair's comments on style are both perspicuous and penetrating, but he suffers from a lack of a system whereby he can objectify his pronouncements. An example will suffice to make his methods clear:

> *Our sight is the most perfect, and most delightful of all our senses.*

> This is an excellent introductory sentence. It is clear, precise, and simple. The author lays down in a few plain words, the proposition which he is going to illustrate throughout the rest of the paragraph. A first sentence should seldom be long, and never an intricate one.

Then Blair goes into detail and defines the desiderata of the ideal neo-classical style.

George Campbell

In 1776, George Campbell published *The Philosophy of Rhetoric*. It is the second important treatise bearing on the doctrine of perspicuity. Though Blair's work was not published until seven years after Campbell's, he had begun his lectures in 1759.[45] When the *Lectures* were finally printed, Blair acknowledged a debt to Campbell "In Dr. Campbell's Philosophy of Rhetoric . . . [the reader] will likewise find many acute observations, both on the English Language, and on Style in general."[46] In the first part of the nineteenth century, Richard Whately attacked Campbell's lack of knowledge of logic, but this attack had ignored the characteristic attitude of *The Philosophy of Rhetoric*, namely, that logic and rhetoric name the tools, whereas common sense supplies them:

> It is long since I was first convinced, by what Mr. Locke hath said on the subject, that the syllogistic art, with its figures and moods, serves more to display the ingenuity of the inventor, and to exercise the address and fluency of the learner, than to assist the diligent inquirer in his researches after truth. The method of proving by syllogism, appears, even

---

[45] Boulton, p. lxxxvii.
[46] Blair, I, 211n.

on a superficial review, both unnatural and prolix. The rules laid down
for distinguishing the conclusive from the inconclusive forms of argument,
the true syllogism from the various kinds of sophism, are at once comber-
some to the memory and unnecssary in practice. No person, one may
venture to pronounce, will ever be made a reasoner, who stands in need
of them. In a word, the whole bears the manifest indications of an artificial and ostentatious parade of learning, calculated for giving the
appearance of great profundity, to what in fact is very shallow.[47]

And Campbell may have "given the death blow to the pale retreating
forces of 'universal grammar' and of 'language as an entity.' Though these
are again and again reaffirmed, the statements are little regarded after
Campbell's time."[48]

As the works of Blair and Campbell are roughly contemporaneous,
their differences serve as an illuminating commentary on rhetorical doctrine after mid-century.

Campbell divides the arts into elegant and useful; eloquence, like
architecture, is at once beautiful and useful.[49] He ascribes four ends to
eloquence, only one of which any discourse may aim at. For instance, a
discourse addressed to the understanding will admit metaphor and comparison, but hardly the bolder figures, and certainly not an address to the
passions. Then, interestingly enough, he says, "There is indeed one kind
of address to the understanding, and only one, which, it may not be
improper to observe, disdains all assistance whatever from the fancy. The
address I mean is mathematical demonstration." Mathematical demonstration is the most perspicuous of "eloquence"; it has "propriety and
simplicity of diction," "accuracy of method," and "no one unnecessary
word or idea." According to Campbell's psychology, however, the passions have a rhetorical (that is, suasive) function: "Knowledge, the object
of the intellect, furnisheth materials for the fancy; the fancy culls, com-
pounds and, by her mimic art, disposes these materials so as to affect the
passions; the passions are the natural spurs to volition or action, and so
need only to be right directed." The four ends of eloquence according
to Campbell, then, are to "enlighten the understanding, to please the
imagination, to move the passions, or to influence the will." When the
orator addresses himself to the understanding, his end is *information*
through *perspicuity* or *conviction* through *argument*.

Campbell's dicta on the sublime are interestingly ambiguous. First,
the sublime is inherent in magnitude or "whatever is great and stupendous

[47] George Campbell, *The Philosophy of Rhetoric* (2 vols.; London: 1776), I, 164.
[48] Sterling Andrus Leonard, *The Doctrine of Correctness in English* (University of Wisconsin Studies in Language and Literature, No. 25; Madison: 1929), p. 161.
[49] Campbell, I, 7–8.

in its kind." Campbell separates admiration from sublimity; admiration is a function of taste and is completely external. Discourse addressed to the understanding, as we have noted, may either inform or convince, and when the orator attempts to bring about conviction he must use a method analogous to that of the painter; he must give a dignified "picture" of a dignified "object," and he must obtain a high degree of resemblance. Obviously, Campbell points out, two modes of discourse achieve these ends: narration and description. Poetry, especially the epic, he calls a kind of oratory that relies upon these two modes of discourse; tragedy, on the other hand, works upon the passions. Consequently, we have what Anselm Bayly called an alliance between poetry and oratory, whereas tragedy falls into another class altogether. The class to which eloquence and its subdivision poetry belong

> attains the summit of perfection in the *sublime*, or those great and noble images, which, when in suitable colouring presented to the mind, do, as it were, distend the imagination with some vast conception, and quite ravish the soul.[50]

Now, says Campbell, because the sublime evokes admiration, we might consider it an address to the passions, but it is not. It is only that "pleasurable sensation which instantly ariseth on the perception of magnitude, or of whatever is great and stupendous of its kind." What Campbell is saying, of course, is that sublimity is twofold, thus, an external state of magnitude or vastness or an external state of their representation in style; or admiration or the instantaneous response to sublimity. In a way, then, through equivocation Campbell solves the matter-manner problem.

With Blair and Campbell's enunciation of the doctrine of perspicuity, eighteenth-century theories of rhetoric received their copestone. To be sure, what the *Lectures on Rhetoric and Belles Lettres* and *The Philosophy of Rhetoric* had to say was almost directly contrary to elocutionary theory and practice, but Blair's and Campbell's pronouncements were the culmination of the rationalistic attitude toward discourse which began, roughly, in 1667.

Together, the Aristotelianism of the rationalists and the Ciceronianism of the elocutionists constituted the scene from which a modern rhetoric might emerge. Longinus had provided the doctrine of the sublime, the viaticum whereby matter and manner could be separated. Rationalism posited psychological theories that gave philosophical credence of the doctrine of perspicuity and the plain style. And the elocutionists had

---

[50] Campbell, I, p. 30.

brought a kind of rhetoric to the masses—a kind of rhetoric that concerned itself largely with the "flowers" of discourse.

In no other period are the main problems of rhetoric so clearly defined as in the eighteenth century. To understand the forces and counterforces of the neoclassical tradition is largely to understand the rhetorical problems of our age.

chapter **4**

The New Rhetoric: Desiderata

The pressing need to develop curricula in literature and language—curricula for both high school and college—has brought about a complaint that is becoming more and more common. Says Robert Gorrell:

> I think . . . that there is more than enough subject matter on the art of writing to justify a separate course, a course that can be made interesting and challenging enough for college students and one that works directly toward the purposes for which freshman English [and he might have added, high school English] is usually required. This subject matter is difficult and not readily defined, and about many parts of it we know much less than we should. *There is, for example, no new rhetoric to parallel the new criticism and the new grammar.*[1]

[1] Robert M. Gorrell, "Freshman English," *The College Teaching of English*, ed. John C. Gerber *et al.* (NCTE Curriculum Series; New York: Appleton-Century-Crofts, 1965), pp. 111–112. Italics mine.

We recognize that studies initiated by I. A. Richards and John Crowe Ransom, Northrop Frye, Leonard Bloomfield, Alfred Korzybski, and Noam Chomsky have brought about relatively sudden and dramatic changes in the attitudes toward literature and language, and apparently many of us wait hopefully for the Messiah in rhetoric. But if he does come, he will almost necessarily be a false prophet.

In the first place, there *is* a new rhetoric. However, this new rhetoric will never find utterance in a single book or in the corpus of one man's works. Even the importance of Kenneth Burke's studies does not constitute Burke the prophet of the new rhetoric. The reason for this paradox—that there is a new rhetoric but that it never has been and never will be enunciated in the manner of the new grammar or the new criticism—lies in the nature of rhetoric itself. From Aristotle onward, systems of literary criticism and attitudes toward literature and criticism have been amenable to formulation in relatively narrow compass; in fact, it is striking that Richards, Ransom, Frye, Leavis, and Fiedler can say such a great deal—so many fundamental things—in so very few words. This the rhetorician can never do, at least not if he approaches his subject humbly and with understanding, because rhetoric, as Aristotle said, is the art of discovering the possible means of persuasion with regard to any subject whatever; it is the art that has no autonomous subject matter but that concerns all of the suasive arts. This is an important point—and one that modern scholars find too easy to forget.

Now, rhetoric should not stop with Aristotle (as it does in some modern textbooks), but the study of rhetoric can justifiably and conveniently begin with him; in fact, his definition—discovering the possible means of persuasion with regard to any subject whatever—remains the basis for all subsequent rhetorical studies. And rightly so. Rhetoric is not *only* the persuasive art, perhaps not *primarily* the persuasive art; rather, it is the art that studies means of suasion. This sort of "art" is obviously a good deal different from the "art" of linguistics or the "art" of criticism. In the first place, the new grammar and the new criticism began in large part by pruning away or ignoring or debunking "old" criticism and "old" grammar. Note, for instance, how Chomsky takes care of the structural linguists, as well as Jespersen, Curme, Kruisinga, and Poutsma. Says Chomsky: "First, it is obvious that the set of grammatical sentences cannot be identified with any particular corpus of utterances obtained by the linguist in field work."[2] Or again, note the iconoclastic but justified brashness of I. A. Richards:

> I have set three aims before me in constructing this book. First, to introduce a new kind of documentation to those who are interested

[2] Noam Chomsky, *Syntactic Structures* (The Hague: Mouton & Cie, 1957), p. 15.

in the contemporary state of culture whether as critics, as philosophers, as teachers, as psychologists, or merely as curious persons. Secondly, to provide a new technique for those who wish to discover for themselves what they think and feel about poetry (and cognate matters) and why they should like or dislike it. Thirdly, to prepare the way for educational methods more efficient than those we use now in developing discrimination and the power to understand what we hear and read.[3]

The point is this: it has been and will continue to be productive for literary and linguistic studies to start largely from new premises that are self-contained within a given canon. This rhetoric cannot do.

The "new" rhetoric of our age—if and when it comes—will not be iconoclastic; it will be developed and written in the spirit of Quintilian. That is, it will be an attempt to centralize and organize our knowledge about rhetoric, because the components of the "new" rhetoric are all about us; they merely need to be gathered and organized.

The "new" rhetoric—and perhaps it has already been written—will be a disappointment for those who await the rhetorical Messiah. Nevertheless, this new rhetoric will probably start with Aristotle, and it will undoubtedly be in large part a compendium. If it does its job for this age as well as *Institutio Oratoria* did its job for Quintilian's age, it will be forced to treat extensively of what Kenneth Burke calls "the lugubrious region of malice and the lie." This new rhetoric, now fragmented and awaiting synthesis, is emanating in part from ad agencies, governments, the political fringe. And not only do these groups practice a rhetoric; they actively study rhetoric. What must motivational research be if not a study of the possible means of persuasion with regard to any subject whatever?

Because rhetoric does not and cannot have an autonomous subject matter, it cannot make a dramatic departure that will leave the old behind. But this statement does not mean that new theory and practice cannot accrue to it, thus, in effect, bringing about a revision to make the subject meaningful—even vital—for the here-and-now. I have said that the new rhetoric exists, awaiting only the accessibility that a Quintilian could give it. And I would propose that the putative twentieth-century Quintilian, who I hope is already well under way with his project, will be looking at certain areas in his effort to bring us up to date and thus give us a new rhetoric.

Kenneth Burke

First, he will be looking at Kenneth Burke, whose genius lies primarily, it seems to me, in his showing the relevance of rhetoric in litera-

[3] I. A. Richards, *Practical Criticism* (New York: Harcourt, Brace & World, Inc., 1950), p. 3.

ture. But the plain fact is that Burke is largely inaccessible to anyone but the most serious student. The nature of "Boikwoiks," as he calls them, is intricate, profound, and monumental. Because we are talking about the kind of new rhetoric that will provide materials for a general curriculum or, as far as that goes, for the general public, we need to see a serious effort to make Burke teachable. Two books on Burke attempt to bring him within reach of the reader who is less than totally dedicated, but they do not show how Burke's theory can function in the practice of rhetoric. (The two books are George Knox, *Critical Moments: Kenneth Burke's Categories and Critiques* (Seattle: University of Washington Press, 1957), and William H. Rueckert, *Kenneth Burke and the Drama of Human Relations* (Minneapolis: University of Minnesota Press, 1963). Of the two, Rueckert's is, in my opinion, inestimably the better. Two brief and exceedingly general synoptic essays are included in Daniel John Fogarty, *Roots for a New Rhetoric* (New York: Bureau of Publications, Teachers College, Columbia University, 1959), and Marie Hochmuth Nichols, *Rhetoric and Criticism* (Baton Rouge: Louisiana State University Press, 1963). We need someone to do for Burke what Paul Roberts and Owen Thomas, among others, did for transformational grammar.

Linguistics and Psycholinguistics

The next area of investigation for the new rhetoric is linguistics and psycholinguistics. These fields are opening—in fact, have already opened—immense possibilities for the rhetorician. First, then, linguistics. What might be its contributions? Studies of style have always been unsatisfactory. The lack of any system by which the manifold nuances of prose could be dealt with has meant that stylistic analysis would necessarily be fragmented. Probably no one applied himself more rigorously to the job of analyzing prose style than did Hugh Blair in the eighteenth century, or, for that matter, W. K. Wimsatt in the twentieth, but in the absence of a comprehensive theory and description of language, even the most perceptive stylistic analyst must resort to searching out the particularities of one style with no very precise idea of what constitutes the norm. To illustrate this point, we can turn to many sources: to Ramus in the sixteenth century, Blair in the eighteenth, or Wimsatt in the twentieth. Or to illustrate the lack of viability of "programs" for stylistic analysis, we can look at Dobrée, Read, or Lucas. Lucas, for instance, says,

> Literary style is simply a means by which one personality moves others. The problems of style, therefore, are really problems of personality —of practical psychology. Therefore this psychological foundation should come first; for on it the rules of rhetoric are logically based. These are *not* (when they are sound) arbitrary or capricious. And when they are

seen to be neither arbitrary nor capricious, but rational and logical, they may then cease to be irritating or boring.[4]

This is exactly the point, unfortunately, where we came in many centuries ago. An approach such as that of Lucas will never provide a *descriptive system* for style, just as the venerable lists of tropes and schemes failed to provide a workable mechanism for the description of style. In fact, so far the rhetorician has not been able to provide himself with a systematic and comprehensive program of style on the basis of which he might make judgments. The system of tropes and schemes has always been too specific and too unsystematic to provide even a meaningful set of terms (but the whole effort of the rhetorical analysis of style from Cicero onward has been taxonomic). We can illustrate this problem by stating that the rhetorical effect of, say, Johnson's prose takes place only in a wide context. One sentence from *The Lives of the Poets* functions rhetorically only insofar as it "blends in with" or differentiates itself from its immediate context, the context of the passage, the context of all Johnson's work, and the context of that mystical entity, eighteenth-century prose style. The analyst relying on traditional means, then, faces an almost insuperable problem. The method that he must use is unbelievably cumbersome and is characterized by lack of coherent system. A vivid illustration of this difficulty is Sister Miriam Joseph's *Shakespeare's Use of Language* (New York: Columbia University Press, 1947). One must be impressed by her painstaking and intelligent work; it is a milestone in both rhetorical and Shakespearian scholarship. But one has the sense that it does not, finally, say anything coherent about its subject. That failing— if failing it be—results from the inherent deficiency of the traditional prevailing tools of rhetorical analysis. Sister Miriam Joseph has done all that she could do. Like other rhetoricians, she undoubtedly awaits the "new" rhetoric. Studies of prose style have been notable in their reliance on totally subjective criteria emanating from what the Germans call *Sprachgefühl* (either you have it or you do not). Herbert Read, for instance, tells us,

> These two examples of eloquence (one from William Drummond of Hawthornden and one from Henry James) are extremely different in inspiration, but agree in their rhetorical characteristics—in their sustained periods and long rhythmical cadences, in their intense or lyrical phrases . . . and in "the general sense of *glory*" which each passage radiates. Eloquence is, indeed, closely related to glory, for one is the expression in deeds, as the other is in words, of the same animating principle of human conduct.[5]

---

[4] F. L. Lucas, *Style* (New York: Crowell-Collier and Macmillan, Inc., 1962), p. 47.
[5] Herbert Read, *English Prose Style* (Boston: The Beacon Press, 1952), p. 179.

Or another discussion of style, this one in some respects far better than Read's:

> How then, it will be asked, do we come into contact with the man? The answer seems to be "By the sound of his voice." For whenever we read a book, although we do not read it aloud, or even consciously form the words in our minds, we are aware of a voice. It is as though someone had been speaking to us, telling us something, or working upon our feelings. It is this voice which we roughly call style, and however much a writer may ignore his personality, even seek to conceal it, he cannot disguise his voice, his style, unless he is deliberately writing a parody. It is here that the truth will out: *Le style, c'est l'homme même*; and if we know a writer of any note, it is extraordinary how we seem to hear the inflexions of his living voice as we read what he has written. Moreover it is ultimately by his style that a writer is great, and remains great, for only books that are well-written survive, though that is not to say that all well-written books do: it is by his style that we recognize a writer.[6]

Thus Bonamy Dobrée.

Of course, countless other definitions of style (or kinds of style) are readily available. In varying degrees most of them rely upon criteria more nebulous than would be allowed in criticism and certainly a good deal less objective than linguistics would admit of. In one way or another, the traditional studies of style tell us that *Le style, c'est l'homme même* or *Le style, c'est que l'homme même dit.*

Modern studies in linguistics, however, are making tentative but hopeful efforts to present a system whereby style can meaningfully be discussed—and, through discussion, taught. Typical of the direction in which the scientific study of language is moving is this definition: ". . . style is defined as an individual's deviations from norms for the situation in which he is encoding, these deviations being in the statistical properties of those structural features for which there exists some degree of choice in his code."[7] Stripped of its jargon, this statement tells us that style is the choices in expression that a writer can and does make. Insofar as he has no choices, he is writing English; insofar as he makes a choice, either consciously or unconsciously, he is expressing his style. Thus, in analyzing style, we can begin to systematize and describe *the strictly linguistic features* of prose until we arrive at an accurate statement of what has been done visibly on the printed page (or orally, for that matter). A statement such as the following by Chomsky is highly suggestive about the possibilities for a new rhetoric of the sentence, a rhetoric that will obviate the difficulties of the "old" rhetoric:

[6] Bonamy Dobrée, *Modern Prose Style* (Oxford: The Clarendon Press, 1964), p. 3.
[7] Charles E. Osgood, "Some Effects of Motivation on Style of Encoding," *Style in Language*, ed. Thomas A. Sebeok (New York: John Wiley & Sons, Inc., 1960).

In producing a sentence, the speaker begins in the initial state, produces the first word of the sentence, thereby switching into a second state which limits the choice of the second word, etc. Each state through which he passes represents the grammatical restrictions that limit the choice of the next word at this point in the utterance.[8]

To an amazing degree, transformational grammarians have begun to set forth the system of rules that describes the limitation of choices. The rhetorician of the new rhetoric will undoubtedly use the tools provided by linguistics and thereby annex for himself a systematic description of style that will really define the periodic or the *coupé* or the exalted or the sublime. (Be it understood, however, that the linguist, if he maintains his current state of mind, will never talk about exalted or sublime style. However, *I* will be able to describe to *you* exactly what *I* mean by a sublime style; I will be able to avoid the vagueness and circumlocution of the terminological concepts that are now at my command as a rhetorician steeped in the tradition.)

The linguist, then, will provide the rhetorician with a system of analysis and a viable taxonomy. There are hints that the psycholinguist (who, by the way, is not a crazy grammarian) may go well beyond categorizing and naming. There are some hints that he will provide relatively objective criteria for calling a passage or a work pathetic or exalted or bombastic. As examples, I will briefly discuss two fairly recent studies. The first, by Dr. Arnold Miller,[9] handles the relation between physical movements and the meaning of words. The author finds that "word meanings last longer accompanied by action than unaccompanied by action. . . . When the organism is able to perceive a relation between its activity and the word with which it is engaged, that activity becomes meaningfully related to the word." The suggestions for rhetoric that one finds in Dr. Miller's paper apply more readily to speech than to writing; in fact, on the basis of his study, the whole business of *actio* in rhetoric gains new meaning. But I wonder if perhaps the meaning-action relation might not begin to explain one of the oldest and most frequently repeated truisms in rhetoric: "Use action verbs, not 'to be' verbs."

In another interesting (though inconclusive) study, John B. Carroll applied the principles of factor analysis to prose style.[10] It is interesting that he found high coefficients for purely subjective ratings on his adjective scale. Briefly, here is what Carroll did. He selected 150 diverse passages of prose, each of which was more or less self-contained within the area

[8] Chomsky, p. 20.
[9] Arnold Miller, "Verbal Satiation and the Role of Concurrent Activity," *Journal of Abnormal and Social Psychology*, LXVI (1963), 206–212.
[10] John B. Carroll, "Vectors of Prose Style," *Style in Language*, pp. 283–292.

of slightly more than 300 words. These passages were chosen for their diversity: essays, newspaper material, novels, scientific papers, textbooks, speeches, legal documents, personal letters, and so forth. Then twenty-nine adjective scales were chosen (Carroll does not say by whom), for example, *profound-superficial, graceful-awkward, vigorous-placid, lush-austere, earnest-flippant,* and so forth. Eight "expert" judges rated each of the 150 passages on the twenty-nine scales. All of these judges, supposedly, had "interest and training in English literature." The very fact that Carroll's study showed a meaningful consensus indicates that subjective reactions can be objectified, systematized, and named.

Now, we should hope that the new rhetorician, the twentieth-century Cicero, will be aware of developments in linguistics and psycholinguistics. In fact, this space-age Quintilian, acting the compleat rhetor, will undoubtedly use a system such as Carroll's to classify styles, and then to these classifications, he will apply linguistic analysis to describe the classes of styles arrived at through application of a subjective adjective rating scale or some more refined device. At this point, rhetoricians strolling in the garden for discussion of their favorite subject can have a meeting of minds such as Cicero or any other rhetorician since never dreamed of. That is, the student of rhetoric will have something definite and systematic to work with. And this is a state of affairs devoutly to be desired, particularly in the high schools.

Logic

Heretofore, rhetoricians have been woeful atavists, clinging tenaciously to scholastic logic. Logic and rhetoric have always been sister subjects, as Thomas Wilson said in 1551:

> Rethorique at large paintes wel the cause,
> And makes that seme right gay,
> Whiche Logique spake but at a Worde,
> And taught as by the way.

However, rhetoric's sisterhood with the scholastic variety of logic makes both arts seem rusty. For instance, in *Rhetoric, Principles and Usage,* an otherwise admirable book, Richard E. Hughes and P. Albert Duhamel devote their entire chapter on deduction and fallacy to the syllogism, as if Whitehead, Russell, Langer, and Cohen had never written. This book is typical rather than exceptional. I suspect that the allegiance to Catholicism of many rhetoricians—perhaps the majority of today's rhetoricians—at least in part explains the failure of symbolic logic to make significant inroads in the study of rhetoric as a discipline, particularly on the lower levels (as in high school English classes). Modern logic is pregnant with concepts for the rhetorician, but fortunately for the new rhetoric, the establishment of "ties," of lines of force and counterforce, between logic and rhetoric is unnecessary. Since the death of Ramism, the subjoining of logic in its totality to rhetoric in its totality has been accepted practice. In the rhetorical view, logic is a part of the whole discipline. Aristotle, it will be remembered, argued that rhetoric should merely supply the failings of logic; the logical argument, stripped of its rhetoric, remained the *sine qua non* of human discourse, the Platonic ideal which the practical Aristotle knew that man would never reach. If man were completely rational, said Aristotle, rhetoric would have no function. There are many arguments against the Aristotelian viewpoint, not the least of which is the esthetic elements that rhetoric brings to discourse. However, that is a story beyond the scope of the present discussion.

To get back to the point about modern logic and rhetoric: while the author of the "new" rhetoric will concentrate on making MR, linguistics, and psycholinguistics relevant to this subject, he will merely present the new logic in an intelligible form, pointing out here and there pertinent interconnections between the two subjects, showing, for instance, that, as Morris R. Cohen says,

> The attempt to make logic a matter of syntax of words assumes the primacy of words as essential language. This obviously is false. We can convey information without the use of words in any way, for example, through the derisive laugh, or other forms of non-verbal expression. This may be illustrated by a story current at Harvard University. Students who regarded themselves as budding literary geniuses were in the habit of reading their papers to Professor C. One student made an appointment with Professor C to read him an essay of which he was very proud. After a short while Professor C fell asleep. The student waited awhile, and then seeing no sign of Professor C awakening, he put the paper into his pocket and started to walk out. Just then Professor C woke up. The student remarked, "I am sorry I did not have the benefit of your criticism." "Why," Professor C remarked, "is not sleeping a criticism?"[11]

Jargon

These, then, are some of the areas that the rhetor of the "new" rhetoric will set forth. But he needs to be aware of a grave hazard that

---

[11] Morris R. Cohen, A *Preface to Logic* (New York: Holt, Rinehart and Winston, Inc., 1965), pp. 63–64. This and other excerpts from A *Preface to Logic* are reprinted with the permission of Holt, Rinehart and Winston, and Routledge & Kegan Paul, Ltd.

could well take him into the most lugubrious of lugubrious regions: the modern tendency for specialists to talk to specialists and to be virtually inchoate outside the pages of the learned journals or the various departments of the various universities. Commentator after commentator tells us that we are in the age of jargon just as surely as we are in the atomic age. The danger of our jargonism is not that it prevents communication. In fact, I suspect that the learned jargons serve the rhetorical purpose of catching the listener's ear. The sociologist responds to his own particular cherished language when he hears it, as do the linguist, the critic, the physicist, and the educationalist to theirs. Jargon does, however, tend to isolate scholars in their own specialized cells of learnedness, and isolation has always been antirhetorical. The symbol of rhetoric is the open hand, beckoning to understanding; the rhetorician has always been a citizen of the *agora*, in most senses a real democrat. Thus, this paragon of men, this "new" rhetorician, will speak, like Matthew Arnold, to all who will listen. And the multifarious critics who find it fashionable to attack rhetoric will not be able to say with Petronius—by the way, in William Arrowsmith's translation—

> . . . it was you rhetoricians who more than anything else strangled true eloquence. By reducing everything to sound, you concocted this bloated puffpaste of pretty drivel whose only real purpose is the pleasure of punning and the thrill of ambiguity. Result? Language lost its sinew, its nerve. Eloquence died.[12]

[12] *The Satyricon of Petronius*, trans. William Arrowsmith (Ann Arbor: University of Michigan Press, 1962), pp. 3–4.

chapter 5

New Rhetoric:
Style

Definition

In rhetoric, style should be the manifestation of a conscious adjustment to the reality principle, to the audience addressed, to the extrinsic world. "Proper words in proper places makes the true definition of style," said Swift. And Buffon: *Le style c'est l'homme même.* But whatever else style is, in rhetoric it should represent an attempt to adjust to an audience.

Following the principle of first things first, we should establish some analytical basis for a discussion of style, a rubric and a vocabulary whereby we can talk about this style, that style, or style in general. This task demands close attention and no small amount of patience, for analysis of style is predicated on attention to a great number of details. From the very specific come limited but valuable generalities.

Even the most cursory and superficial remarks about style attempt some kind of classification; that is, they work toward a system. Thus, in classical rhetoric, we hear about the elevated, the middle, and the plain style. Styles are sublime, perspicuous, ornate, clear, intricate, simple, complex, fluid, cursive, crabbed, eccentric bombastic, humble, free-flowing, open, abrupt, languid. . . . In fact, the list of descriptive adjectives that have been applied to style is endless. And yet whenever we apply such a term to style, we are making an impressionistic judgment, valid to the degree that our taste does not mislead and our experience gives us basis for comparison. The problem arises when we attempt to go beyond the impression into the difficult area of analysis and description. Anyone who has ever attempted a detailed analysis of prose realizes how elusive is that quality called style.

The ideal is an analytical method that will describe and identify the style of any writer (or speaker). In theory, style should be as distinguishable as, say, the fingerprints or the voice—and should be as precisely describable as the fingerprints. These premises may seem to need a bit—even quite a bit—of substantiation, and it will come hereafter. For the moment, however, we must explore methods of analysis and description.

Impressionism

As Professor Louis T. Milic has pointed out, "Stylistics . . . has for most scholars still no method beyond the method of impressionistic description and a vague use of rhetoric."[1] In his essay, Milic cites some typical examples of the impressionistic approach to prose:

> Snow's prose, as well, is marked by plainness, an innocuous prose that rarely does more than indicate essentials. His style is, as it were, virtually an absence of style when we use the word to signify something distinctive. There is also, a curious lack ,of development in his power of expression from first novel to last, as though Snow refused to tamper with something that he considered adequate.   —FREDERICK R. KARL, C. P. Snow: The Politics of Conscience

> Wordsworth's prose is admirable. It is seldom magnificent. "It does not sparkle," said Nowell C. Smith justly. As a prose stylist, Wordsworth lacks the clarity of Dryden, the force of Hazlitt, the passion of Milton, the metaphorical daring of Coleridge, the simultaneous levels of either Swift or Lamb, and the opulence of an admirer who borrowed power from Wordsworth, De Quincey. And yet Wordsworth practiced to a viable

[1] "Metaphysics in the Criticism of Style," *College Composition and Communication*, XVII (October 1966), 124.

degree clarity, force, passion, strength of metaphor, levels at least of scorn, and richness if not opulence. He achieved what he most wanted, the signature of personal conviction.   —CARL R. WOODRING, *Wordsworth*

Milic's essay has other such examples, and specimens like them abound wherever prose comes up for discussion. The trouble with impressionistic descriptions is not that they are inaccurate per se, but rather that they finally do not tell us much about style. On the face of it, it seems strange that so clear-cut a matter as proper words in proper places should be so elusive a subject for systematic objective discussion. Such a quality as "the signature of personal conviction" in style, if it exists at all, must reside in the way words from the English lexicon are put into various structural combinations determined by the possibilities and limitations of the system known as the English language. In fact, we have no quarrel with the impressionistic descriptive value judgments concerning style as long as they do not emerge under the false colors of descriptive analysis.

Stylistics and Metastylistics

It will be helpful, then, in the construction of a theory of style, to talk about *stylistics* and *metastylistics*. Under stylistic auspices come all of the objectively verifiable data concerning style. Under the auspices of metastylistics come semantic and esthetic considerations as well as value judgments. It is extremely important that in the study of style we keep the two kinds of procedures separate. Mixing them leads only to confusion.

A *stylistic* statement: Five percent of X's sentences are in the passive.
A *metastylistic* statement: X's prose is passionate.

Both kinds of statements have their value; they are not, however, interchangeable.

Because I intend to say very little about *metastylistics*, I shall turn to this subject first. Metastylistics is concerned with a number of topics, among them semantics, esthetics, and appropriateness. Unfortunately, very little has been done in the way of providing theory or a *modus operandi* whereby really meaningful statements about these subjects can be made. General semantics has provided valuable insights concerning meaning. Rhetoric, of course, traditionally takes appropriateness into account. And discussions of the esthetics of style are rife. The present discussion will leave semantics to the semanticists and refer anyone who is curious to two sources: Hayakawa's popular *Language in Thought and Action* and the article, "Semantics," in the *Encyclopaedia Britannica*, the latter of which is difficult reading but an admirable compact survey of the field. Appropriateness, belonging as it does to the field of rhetoric, will be dealt with later. However, in the field of metastylistics there are certain hints pointing toward the future, and these deserve some mention.

If we think carefully of Buffon's famous aphorism, *Le style c'est l'homme même*, we perceive that it contains impeccably simple logic: whatever the talking animal produces in the way of talk must mirror him who produced it. Freud's preoccupation with slips of the tongue helps us here. Freud says,

> When it happens that I make a mistake in a word I could obviously do this in an infinite number of ways, in place of the right word substitute any one of a thousand others, or make innumerable distortions of the right word. Now, is there anything which forces upon me in a specific instance just this one slip, out of all those which are possible, or does that remain accidental and arbitrary, and can nothing rational be found in answer to this question?[2]

Freud's answer, of course, is that something indeed does force the "mistake" on the speaker, namely, the speaker's own psychic equipment, so that a Freudian reformulation of Buffon's aphorism would say, *The mistake is the man himself*. In other words, to follow the logic to its conclusion, all verbal activity is the result of psychic determinism. Thus, we ought to be able to predict style on the basis of personality and analyze personality on the basis of style. Such a situation lies perhaps in the future.

The present leaves us with only the visible manifestations of style from which we can draw few justifiable conclusions about the stylist. We can be certain that style does mirror the inner man, that *Le style c'est l'homme même*, but we can make our most valuable observations about the extrinsic style that consists in words in sequence. We present ourselves with unnecessary difficulties when we try to second-guess the stylist.

Grammar and Style

In order to have a theory of style from which we can work, we must have a theory of grammar, and clearly the most viable theory of grammar is that developed by Noam Chomsky.[3] We shall proceed on the basis of Chomsky's theory of transformational grammar; a brief summary is therefore in order. Chomsky says,

[2] Sigmund Freud, *A General Introduction to Psychoanalysis*, trans. Joan Riviere (Garden City, N.Y.: Permabooks, 1953), p. 36.
[3] Noam Chomsky, *Syntactic Structures* (The Hague: Mouton & Cie, 1957).

The fundamental aim in the linguistic analysis of a language L is to separate the *grammatical* sequences which are the sentences of L from the *ungrammatical* sequences which are not sentences of L and to study the structure of the grammatical sequences. The grammar of L will thus be a device that generates all of the grammatical sequences of L and none of the ungrammatical ones.[4]

In every language, there are two kinds of meaning, structural and semantic. What we are saying here is that a perfectly grammatical English sentence may be meaningless, or nearly so, as in Chomsky's famous *Colorless green ideas sleep furiously.* Structure and meaning are to a great degree separable. This is demonstrated in even the most primitive analysis of style when the analyst comments on the length of sentences, the occurrence of the passive, the degree of subordination, and so on. It is also demonstrated by the fact that we can talk impressionistically about "jerky" or "choppy" or "free-flowing" style. And it is in the area of structural analysis that we are on the safest ground.

It is time, then, to posit a working definition of style on the basis of which we can proceed. The following seems to be workable and accurate:

> Some elements of language do not allow choice: *He hit the dog,* but not *The dog he hit* (though *The dog he hit yelped* works). When one has no choice, he is merely using the language; when one has a choice and makes it, he is expressing style.[5]

Style, then, is the composite result of choices made, either consciously or unconsciously.

Texture

A good starting point for a discussion of style is the work done by my colleague, Professor Francis Christensen.[6] Christensen says that in their discussion of the sentence modern textbooks falsify the reality of prose structure. Most textbooks talk about *loose, balanced,* and *periodic* sentences. Furthermore, traditional grammar is an inadequate analytical and pedagogical tool. Thus, Christensen begins by attacking the most common procedures of analysis and pedagogy in style. His alternative, it would

---

[4] Chomsky, p. 13.
[5] *The Relevance of Rhetoric,* ed. E. V. Stackpoole and W. Ross Winterowd (Boston: Allyn and Bacon, Inc., 1966), p. 545. Reprinted with the permission of the publishers.
[6] Francis Christensen, "A Generative Rhetoric of the Sentence," *Notes Toward a New Rhetoric* (New York: Harper & Row, Publishers, 1967), pp. 1–22. The excerpts from Professor Christensen's work are reprinted with the permission of the author.

seem, is eminently workable; furthermore, it provides a good deal of stylistic insight. (Because his discussion is widely reprinted and readily available, I shall summarize as briefly as possible.) The style of a sentence depends on the principle of *addition*, on *direction of modification*, on *levels of generality*, and on *texture* brought about by addition. "When you write," said John Erskine, "you make a point, not by subtracting as though you sharpened a pencil, but by adding." Thus, *We try to withdraw from the embrace of the future* becomes

> Now, stunned, puzzled and dismayed, we try to withdraw from the embrace, not of a necessary tomorrow, but of that future which we have invited and of which, at last, we have grown perceptibly afraid.
> —LOREN EISELEY[7]

Sentences come about by addition.[8] Modification is directed:

$$\rightarrow$$
During the summer of 1963, I was in Oregon.
$$\leftarrow$$
The sheets on the line were white flags flapping in the wind.

And so on. "When you add a modifier, whether to the noun, the verb or the main clause, you must add it either before the head or after it."

The main clause of a sentence will probably be a fairly high-level generality; the additions will be on lower levels of generality.

> When I speak of Knowledge, I mean something intellectual, something which grasps what it perceives through the senses; something which takes a view of things; which sees more than the senses convey; which reasons upon what it sees, and while it sees; which invests it with an idea.   —JOHN HENRY NEWMAN

In this respect, sentence and paragraph are frequently alike in their movement.

The texture of a sentence depends on the number of additions. Few additions make for thin texture. This term is both descriptive and evaluative, a thin-textured sentence being (to use a common term) anemic. In the *cumulative sentence*, "The additions stay with the same idea, probing its bearings and implications, exemplifying it or seeking an analogy or metaphor for it, or reducing it to details." The best way of seeing the

---

[7] Excerpts from *The Firmament of Time* by Loren Eiseley. © 1960 by Loren Eiseley. Reprinted by permission of Atheneum Publishers and Victor Gollancz, Ltd.
[8] Those familiar with generative grammar will immediately remember $N \rightarrow N(S)$.

texture of the sentence, says Christensen, is to write it out schematically
thus:

   1 He dipped his hands in the bichloride solution and shook them,
      2 a quick shake,
         3 fingers down
           4 like a pianist.   —SINCLAIR LEWIS

The grammatical nature of the sentence additions that Christensen
identifies will provide the first analytical rubric that we shall employ for
stylistic analysis. These additions are subordinate clause (SC), relative
clause (RC), noun cluster (NC), verb cluster (VC), adjective cluster
(AC), adjective series (A + A), absolute (Abs), and prepositional phrase
(PP). Analysis of prose according to its use of these additions should make
possible a stylistic profile. For instance, here is a paragraph from Emerson's
"The American Scholar":

The first
    (PP) in time
and the first
    (PP) in importance
        (PP) of the influences
           (PP) upon the mind
is that
        (PP) of nature.
Every day, the sun;
and, /   / Night and her stars.
    (PP) after sunset,
Ever the winds blow, ever the grass grows.
Every day, men and women,
    (VC) conversing—beholding and beholden.
The scholar is he
    (PP) of all men
    (RC) whom this spectacle most engages.
He must settle its values
    (PP) in his mind.
What is nature
    (PP) to him?
There is never a beginning, there is never an end,
    (PP) to the inexplicable continuity
        (PP) of this web
           (PP) of God,
but always circular power
    (VC) returning
        (PP) into itself.

Therein it resembles his own spirit,
    (RC) whose beginning, whose ending, he never can find.
    (RC) Far too as her splendors shine,
        (Abs) system on system shooting like rays, upward, downward,
            (PP) without centre
            (PP) without circumference,—
    (PP) in the mass
    (PP) and in the particle
nature hastens to render account
    (PP) of herself
        (PP) to the mind.
Classification begins.
    (PP) To the young mind
every thing is individual, stands
    (PP) by itself.
By and by, it finds how to join two things and see in them one nature; then
three, then three thousand;
and so, /
    (VC) tyrannized over
        (PP) by its own unifying instinct,
/ it goes on
    (VC) tying things together,
    (VC) diminishing anomalies,
    (VC) discovering roots
        (VC) running under ground
        (RC) whereby contrary and remote things cohere and flower out
            (PP) from one stem.

Now compare the following passage from "The Disadvantages of Being Educated," by Albert Jay Nock:

The difference seemed to be
    (RC) that /
            (SC) while education was still spoken of
            (NC) as "a preparation for life,"
    / the preparation was
    (PP) of a kind
        (RC) which bore less directly
            (PP) on intellect and character
        (SC) than [it did]
            (PP) in former times
      and more directly
        (PP) on proficiency.
It aimed
    (PP) at
        (RC) what we used to call training rather than education

and it not only did very little
    (PP) with education,
but seemed to assume
    (SC) that training *was* education,
        (VC) thus overriding a distinction
            (RC) that formerly was quite clear.
Forty years ago a man /
    (VC) trained
        (PP) to proficiency
        (PP) in anything
/ was respected accordingly, but was not regarded
    (NC) as an educated man
    (AC) or "just as good,"
        (PP) on the strength
        (PP) of it.
A trained mechanic, banker, dentist or man of business got all due credit
    (PP) for his proficiency
but his education, /
            (SC) if he had any,
/ lay
    (PP) behind that
and was not confused
    (PP) with it.
His training, /   / bore directly
        (PP) in a word,
    (PP) upon
        (RC) what he could do or get
    (SC) while his education bore directly
        (PP) on neither;
it bore
    (PP) upon
        (RC) what he could become and be.

A table of the additions in each of the passages looks like this:

	PP	VC	RC	Abs	SC	NC	AC	A + A
Emerson								
Total words: 215								
Total additions: 35	23	7	4	1	0	0	0	0
Nock								
Total words: 170								
Total additions: 33	17	2	6	0	5	2	1	0

Because they are so limited, these samples do not necessarily say anything about Nock's or Emerson's style in general; a much more extensive analysis would be necessary before one could make such a generalization as "Emerson appears to rely more heavily on the prepositional phrase for expansion of his sentences." But speaking only of the two passages under consideration, we can derive some principles that are applicable to more extensive expanses of prose. A typical statement concerning Emerson's style underlines the necessity for discussion in terms of actual constructions:

> A notable writer, his essays are compounded of metaphors, quotations, illustrations, allusions, and applications of his doctrines. He learned to write in "the old school" where eloquence (Dr. Ripley called it "the diction of the ages") and rhetoric were preferred. Consequently, his personality pervades the phrasing rather than italicizes it as in the sharp, brittle, repertorial style of contemporary writing. His unit was the sentence, for he seemed to think in Delphic statements that are tipped with light.[9]

Such an evaluation, just though it may be in the main, overlooks the structural features that make Emerson's prose what it is, and if style is indeed proper words in proper places, we must have some method of analyzing these places before we can judge their propriety.

From the paragraph by Emerson that we analyzed we can develop an accurate description of the structural style of the paragraph. Emerson relies heavily on prepositional phrases and verb clusters. The variety of additions that he uses is limited. (He employs only four kinds, compared to Nock's seven.) Because of the dearth of relative clauses and the absence of subordinate clauses, he cannot qualify ideas through predication and he cannot employ the standard tool of argument, the enthymeme. (In fact, one notes that Emerson's sentences tend to be maxims in the Aristotelian sense.) We also find an interesting paradox: at first glance we would say that the *texture* of Emerson's prose is *denser* than that of Nock's. But, in fact, Nock uses thirty-three additions in 170 words, whereas Emerson uses thirty-five additions in 215 words, and the implication is that Nock's prose is denser and more varied than Emerson's. It seems that the facts of the analysis contradict what intuition tells us.

We are brought to the point, then, that we need to ask whether or not our analytical tool has been probing enough to get us at basic explanations. The answer is "no."[10] The rubric by which we have been guided does not set out to be inclusive enough to provide a complete analysis. Among stylistic devices that the rubric overlooks are figures of grammar, coordination, figures of thought, and so on.[11]

---

[9] Ralph Waldo Emerson, *Selected Prose and Poetry*, ed. Reginald L. Cook (New York: Holt, Rinehart and Winston, Inc., 1963), p. lx.

[10] Nor did professor Christensen intend to supply an analytical device that would be reliable in the discussion of this style versus that style. His purpose, as the name of his article implies, was to work toward a generative rhetoric of the sentence that would explain the ways in which sentences gain density of texture so that students might build their own sentences to maturity.

[11] See the discussion of figures below.

In other words, style is much too complex to be satisfactorily explicable in terms that we so far have employed.

Idiosyncratic Analysis

Another angle of attack sheds a bit of light on the mystery of style and provides a handy method for "instant analysis." We can take as our starting point the view that there are two methods to studying style: (a) the *idiosyncratic*, "concerned with describing and interpreting the necessarily unique features of style," and (b) *nomothetic*, "the discovery and validation of general dependency relations between message indicators and variables in communicators."[12] We shall here concentrate on the *idiosyncratic*. When we say, offhand, that a person has style, we probably mean that he has recognizable idiosyncrasies that we immediately, though perhaps intuitively, recognize as his "style." The most unsophisticated observer, for instance, can easily identify a passage by Faulkner or Lyly. Hemingway and Mark Twain, and perhaps Thoreau, are virtually as easy to spot. Our question, then, should ask why some stylists are so individual (or idiosyncratic) that they can be identified nearly at first glance. A spectrum of styles will illustrate what we are here getting at:

> 1. His day came at last. In the surrey with his cousin and Major de Spain and General Compson he saw the wilderness through a slow drizzle of November rain just above the ice point as it seemed to him later he always saw or at least always remembered it—the tall and endless wall of dense November woods under the dissolving afternoon and the year's death, sombre, impenetrable (he could not even discern yet how, at what point they could possibly hope to enter it even though he knew that Sam Fathers was waiting there in the wagon), the surrey moving through the skeleton stalks of cotton and corn in the last of open country, the last trace of man's puny gnawing at the immemorial flank, until, dwarfed by that perspective into an almost ridiculous diminishment, the surrey itself seemed to have ceased to move (this too to be completed later, years later, after he had grown to a man and had seen the sea) as a solitary small boat hangs in lonely immobility, merely tossing up and down in the infinite waste of the ocean while the water and then the apparently impenetrable land which it nears without appreciable progress, swings slowly and opens the widening inlet which is the anchorage. He entered it. Sam was waiting, wrapped in a quilt on the wagon seat behind the patient and steaming mules. He entered his novitiate to the true wilderness with Sam beside him as he had begun his apprenticeship in miniature to manhood after the rabbits and such with Sam beside him, the two of them wrapped in the damp, warm, negro-rank quilt while the wilderness

---

[12] Charles E. Osgood, "Some Effects of Motivation on Style of Encoding," *Style in Language*, ed. Thomas Sebeok (New York: John Wiley & Sons, Inc., 1960), p. 295.

closed behind his entrance as it had opened momentarily to accept him, opening before his advancement as it closed behind his progress, no fixed path the wagon followed but a channel nonexistent ten yards ahead of it and ceasing to exist ten yards after it had passed, the wagon progressing not by its own volition but attrition of their intact yet fluid circumambience, drowsing, earless, almost lightless.

2. "I for mine own part am brought into a paradise by the only imagination of women's virtues, and were I persuaded that all the devils in hell were women, I would never live devoutly to inherit heaven, or that they were all saints in heaven, I would live more strictly for fear of hell. What could Adam have done in his paradise before his fall without a woman, or how could he have risen again after his fall without a woman? Artificers are wont in their last works to excel themselves, yea, God when he had made all things, at the last, made man as most perfect, thinking nothing could be framed more excellent, yet after him he created a woman, the express image of eternity, the lively picture of nature, the only steel glass for a man to behold his infirmities, by comparing them with women's perfections. Are they not more gentle, more witty, more beautiful than men? Are not men so bewitched with their qualities that they become mad for love, and women so wise that they detest lust."

3. Jack started training out at Danny Hogan's health farm over in Jersey. It was nice out there but Jack didn't like it much. He didn't like being away from his wife and the kids, and he was sore and grouchy most of the time. He liked me and we got along fine together; and he liked Hogan, but after a while Soldier Bartlett commenced to get on his nerves. A kidder gets to be an awful thing around a camp if his stuff goes sort of sour. Soldier was always kidding Jack, just sort of kidding him all the time. It wasn't very funny and it wasn't very good, and it began to get to Jack.

4. We found a small skiff belonging to the Brigade boys, and without loss of time set out across a deep bend of the lake toward the landmarks that signified the locality of the camp. I got Johnny to row—not because I mind exertion myself, but because it makes me sick to ride backwards when I am at work. But I steered. A three-mile pull brought us to the camp just as the night fell, and we stepped ashore very tired and wolfishly hungry. In a "cache" among the rocks we found the provisions and the cooking utensils, and then, all fatigued as I was, I sat down on a boulder and superintended while Johnny gathered wood and cooked supper. Many a man who had gone through what I had, would have wanted a rest.

It does not demand a thoroughgoing analysis to sense immediately that we are dealing here with four diverse styles—those of (1) Faulkner,[13]

[13] William Faulkner, "The Bear," Go Down, Moses (Modern Library Edition; New York: Random House, Inc., 1942), pp. 194–195. Reprinted with the permission of the publisher.

(2) Lyly, (3) Hemingway, and (4) Mark Twain—and yet, amazingly, it is a difficult thing to translate that style sense into an adequate formulation. The dearth of satisfactory analyses of style is one evidence of this difficulty, and another is the experience of anyone who has had a literary education: teachers and critics analyze metaphor, idea, symbol, and so on in great detail, but on style they seldom give more than a few random impressionistic comments supplemented by examples. However, viewed as *idiosyncrasy*, style becomes amenable to a kind of "instant analysis" that allows us to make valid statements about the *reasons* for stylistic effects.

The logic here is this: there are styles that we sense as "undifferentiatable," that is, as having no apparent idiosyncrasies that identify them and set them apart from the "general" or "ordinary" style. We need not concern ourselves with the important theoretical question of what constitutes the "general" or "ordinary," for, in fact, we rely upon our own intuition to determine this. Sometimes we talk about style in this sense: "Now so and so really has *a style*." And it is when we use the word "style" in that sense that we can begin to look for idiosyncrasies in the prose. (As we shall see, analysis in depth reveals that all styles have idiosyncrasies, but in the loosely defined general style, these idiosyncrasies are not readily apparent and hence do not set the styles apart readily.)

On the level of analysis at which we are now working, then, we will search for the idiosyncratic and then analyze that. We will define the idiosyncratic as those features of the style that strike us most obviously; hence, they will all be surface features; the analysis will, in this sense, be surface analysis.

The Faulkner passage, for instance: most noticeable is the length of the second sentence (207 words) and the last sentence (113 words). The second sentence contains two included-sentences in parentheses, and the 163 words after the dash in the second sentence are an addition that explains "he saw the wilderness . . . as . . . he always saw it or at least remembered it." The dash, then, separates the main part of the sentence from its development, and that development is accomplished largely through verbal constructions: "the surrey moving through the skeleton stalks of cotton and corn," "dwarfed by that perspective," "merely tossing up and down," and so on. Both long sentences from the Faulkner passage are loose in the rhetorical sense; they establish their main points and then elaborate extensively. More could be said—a great deal more. However, with the brief surface analysis here presented, we have arrived at a kind of thumbnail sketch of Faulkner's prose, for the patterns that we find in the quoted paragraph appear repeatedly in his writings.

It is a cliché to state that the particular effect of Lyly's prose results from carefully constructed balance. The "simplicity" of Hemingway's prose is much more difficult to get at than is the elaborateness of Lyly's, and yet "instant analysis" provides some insights. For instance, in the Hemingway passage, note the recurrence of personal pronouns in short sentences. Note also the colloquial use of double prepositions: "*out at* Danny Hogan's health farm *over in* Jersey." Other colloquialisms: "we got along *fine* together"; "his stuff goes *sort of* sour"; "*sort of kidding* him"; "it began *to get to* Jack." Notable in the Mark Twain passage is the anticlimactic, self-depreciatory humor: "I got Johnny to row—not because I mind exertion myself, but because it makes me sick to ride backwards when I am at work."

This sort of "instant analysis" based on the most ovious idiosyncrasies of style is "unscientific" and basically unsystematic, but it does provide a way of saying *demonstrable* things about style. Applied rigorously enough, it reveals the nature of a style with remarkable clarity.

Loren Eiseley is an admirable stylist and thinker. His essay "How Human Is Man?" from *The Firmament of Time* is an excellent example of how much analysis of the idiosyncratic can reveal about a rich style. The *modus operandi* of the analysis is simple enough. One merely reads the passage to be analyzed with some care, noting in the margin idiosyncrasies, the features that "stand out," that seem to "make" the style. One sentence from Eiseley's essay will illustrate:

> It is with the coming of man that a vast hole seems to open in nature, a vast black whirlpool spinning faster and faster, consuming flesh, stones, soil, minerals, sucking down the lightning, wrenching power from the atom, until the ancient sounds of nature are drowned in the cacophony of something which is no longer nature, something instead which is loose and knocking at the world's heart, something demonic and no longer planned—escaped it may be—spewed out of nature, contending in a final giant's game against its master.

It so happens that this sentence is a microcosm of Eiseley's style; the devices in the sentence appear again and again throughout the essay:

1. What I choose to call the *adjusted appositive*:

It is with the coming of man that a *vast hole* seems to open in nature, a *vast* black *whirlpool*

> They had an *old contract*, an *old promise*. . . .

2. *Asyndeton,* or the deletion of particles in a series:

spinning faster and faster, consuming flesh, stones, soil, minerals, sucking down the lightning, wrenching power from the atom

> . . . the enemy is known, the contingency prepared for . . . but the games were each one known, the rules ancient and observed. . . .

3. *The repetition of words, in the same sentence, in adjusted contexts*:

until the ancient sounds of *nature* are drowned in something which is no longer *nature*,

> Perhaps, in a sense, the *great* play is actually a *great* magic. . . .
> Scarcely had he stepped across the border of the old instinctive *world* when he began to create the *world* of custom.

4. *The parenthetical remark in dashes*:

something instead which is loose and knocking at the world's heart, something demonic and no longer planned—escaped, it may be—spewed out of nature. . . .

> Not long ago, a young man—I hope not a forerunner of the coming race of men on the planet—remarked to me. . . .

These constitute, it seems to me, a fair summary of the idiosyncrasies that make Eiseley's style readily identifiable.

In summary, aspects of style are not so mysterious. With a little insight and patience, one can arrive at an objective analysis of what constitutes the proper words in the proper places of a given passage. Of course, it must be stressed here that the analysis so far has been superficial (not in the pejorative sense of that word) and that below the surface lie stylistic features that one can get at with more thoroughgoing, systematic procedures.

Tropes and Schemes

Stylistic analysis inherited from the Ancients—particularly Cicero and Quintilian—was based on *tropes* and *schemes* and, hence, in effect, on the idiosyncratic. As one scholar says,

> According to the ancient conception, expressed by Cicero and Quintilian, figurative language includes any deviation, either in thought or expression, from the ordinary and simple modes of speaking. This would include the language of ordinary persons moved by excitement to adopt short cuts and turns of expression which give their speech liveliness and vividness not ordinarily found in it.[14]

The fallacy in such analysis based on the *unusual* or idiosyncratic is that it proceeds without defining the usual or ordinary; it has no general theory

[14] Sister Miriam Joseph, *The Trivium in College Composition and Reading* (South Bend, Ind.: McClave Printing Company, 1948), p. 262.

and thus cannot lead to a coherent philosophy of style or method of stylistic analysis.[15] Nonetheless, by the time of the Renaissance, scholars had found and classified some 200 figures and schemes.[16] At this point in history, it is futile to urge the utility of the ancient categories of figures and schemes; they are anachronisms. And yet Sheridan Baker says, "You can indeed increase your power by making these venerable devices your own, by having them ready, by learning through them the fair and beautiful play of language."[17] Baker here raises an interesting point that must be dealt with. How does one go about increasing his stylistic power? In *Ramus*, Walter Ong argues that the result of intensive analysis of figures and schemes was Renaissance prose and poetry; the Renaissance schoolboy, devoting almost one third of his time to a rhetoric of figures, naturally developed a highly figurative style! With a slight shift, Rosemond Tuve (in *Elizabethan and Metaphysical Imagery*, Chicago: University of Chicago Press, 1947) argues substantially the same point. And both are undisputably right. Intensive work with a given kind of prose or a given aspect of prose brings about inevitable—even automatic—imitation. So that in this sense, to paraphrase Francis Christensen, the old rhetoric of figures did give texture and density to prose. But imitation works on many levels—not necessarily on the conscious level of analysis and then reproduction. Any writer unconsciously imitates the other writers that he reads intensively; his own style results from amalgamation and superaddition. This, perhaps, is what Hemingway meant when he attributed American prose to one book: *Huckleberry Finn*.

A second point is that the systems of figures and schemes were analytical devices, employed after the fact, to classify the effects of a given writing. It is inconceivable that any writer thought in terms of a given figure to express a given idea, just as it is inconceivable that any writer thinks in terms of a given grammatical construction. In fact, in this sense, grammar too is an analytical device.

There is some confusion about the definition of *figure, trope, scheme*. In general, *figure* is a generic term embracing both tropes and schemes. *Schemes*, in general, are deviations from the ordinary, in either thought or expression. *Tropes* are in the modern sense figurative uses of language. It is handy to divide schemes into *figures of thought* and *figures of grammar*; thus, in effect, they embrace tropes. But tropes, as a matter of fact, usually signify the figures of speech that we call metaphors. Thus, to clear up the confusion, the classical system of figures looks like this:

[15] See Walter J. Ong, *Ramus: Method and the Decay of Dialogue; From the Art of Discourse to the Art of Reason* (Cambridge, Mass.: Harvard University Press, 1958).
[16] Sheridan Baker, *The Complete Stylist* (New York: Thomas Y. Crowell Company, 1966), lists sixty-two.
[17] Baker, p. 320. Reprinted with the permission of the publisher, Thomas Y. Crowell Company.

Schemes:
>   Figures of thought (EXAMPLE: litotes, or understatement—*Einstein was a fairly bright man.*)
>   Figures of grammar (EXAMPLE: asyndeton—*The storm, stress, sound, fury,* as compared to polysyndeton—*The storm and the stress and the sound and the fury.*)
>Tropes (EXAMPLE: metaphor—*He was a lion in battle.*)

Frequently, *scheme* is synonymous with *figure of grammar,* and *trope* is synonymous with *figure of speech.* For the sake of clarity, we shall here generally use *figure of speech* and *figure of grammar.*

The same criticism that applies to much of traditional grammar also applies to the system of tropes and schemes. That is, traditional grammar was an attempt to make discrete comments on items in an infinite series. Because it is easily demonstrable, for instance, that the English language is capable of generating an infinite number of sentences, no grammar that attempts to classify and analyze these sentences *as produced* can be a complete grammar. What is needed is a grammar that will generate all the sentences in the language and no ungrammatical sentences, in just the same way that a system of mathematics is finite in its conception but infinite in its application. As long as stylistic analysis relied on picking out and classfying the unusual without addressing itself to the basic system of the language, such analysis was doomed to muddle around in an unworkable system. To be sure, some patterns seem to be recurrent and prevalent in language. Baker classifies the figures thus, according to their function:

Alluding to the Familiar. EXAMPLE: paroemia (applying proverbs to a new situation): "Man shall not live by bread alone. [He has just ordered steak.]"

Building to Climax. EXAMPLE: synonymy (using synonyms for emphasis): "A miserable, wretched, depressed neighborhood."

Intensifying. EXAMPLE: aposiopesis (stopping in midsentence): "And in the name of common sense———"

Irony. EXAMPLE: oxymoron (emphasizing a point by the irony of an apparent contradiction): "A wise fool, a fearful joy, a sweet sadness, a quiet orgy."

Overstating, Understating. EXAMPLE: hypothesis (illustrating with an impossible supposition): "If salt lose its savor, wherewith shall it be salted?"

Posing Contrasts. EXAMPLE: chiasmus (crossing the terms of one clause by reversing their order in the next): "Ask not what your country can do for you: ask what you can do for your country."

Refining, Elaborating. EXAMPLE: hirmos (heaping appositives together): "All men, rich, poor, tall, short, young, old, love it."

Repeating. EXAMPLE: epistrophe (ending several sentences alike for emphasis): "They loved football. They ate football. They slept football."

Substituting. EXAMPLE: prosopopoeia (personifying an inanimate object): "The stadium settled back for a lonely week."[18]

This classification according to function obviously overlooks the difference between figures of thought and figures of grammar. Furthermore, Sheridan Baker's last classification is "Miscellaneous"—and that tips the hand concerning the figures, for the "miscellaneous" list indicates that the figures are theoretically infinite in number and thus of little value in the systematic analysis of style.

Finally, the best way to discover the shortcoming of figures as devices for stylistic analysis is to attempt an analysis of prose with them. Take, for instance, the two hundred or so figures that Peacham lists in *The Garden of Eloquence* and attempt to use them to arrive at the whereby and wherefore of Faulkner's prose. It will soon become apparent that a better system is necessary.

Generative Grammar

This better system, apparently, lies in generative grammar. Style functions on many levels, and we might with justice speak of *structure, words,* and *content.* That is, style consists in the grammatical structures that one uses, the words that one puts into these grammatical structures, and the ideas that these words and structures express. One, indeed, might go a step further and speak of style in the form of organization of the whole piece (essay, book, novel, poem, and the like). Generative grammar gives us the most precise instrument—perhaps the only precise instrument—for analysis of grammatical structure and thus for the analysis of that aspect of style. This premise leads to the inevitable conclusion that the rhetorician must also be a generative grammarian—or, if not, ignore that department of rhetoric that includes style. However, rhetoric cannot afford to overlook style as the prime device of achieving consubstantiality in written discourse.

The problem that we now encounter is this: a thoroughgoing discussion of the application of generative grammar to style presupposes a knowledge of generative grammar—and would demand a substantial volume in itself. However, it is fairly easy to outline some principles and illustrate some basic processes. The rhetorician's obligation to understand generative grammar should become clear.

[18] Baker, pp. 320–332.

It is axiomatic with generative grammar that every sentence can be traced back to this simple formula: S→NP + VP. (Read: Sentence is rewritten as Noun Phrase plus Verb Phrase.) Or, roughly, every sentence represents what can be done with a subject and a predicate, so that S→NP + VP represents the "kernel" form of any of the following:

John	sings.
The little boy	sings in the choir.
The little boy who lives next door	sings in the choir of the church that I attend.

Generative grammar systematically describes the ways in which any sentence develops from an irreducible kernel such as *John sings*. Hence, the rules of generative grammar provide a descriptive system for the structural style of any writer. At the beginning of this chapter, we said that style is the linguistic choices that a writer can and does make. Every time a writer exercises an option—either consciously or unconsciously—he is creating his style. Concisely stated, a tabulation of the grammatical rules that a writer employs (in other words, of the choices that he makes) will constitute an extremely exact description of his style at its most basic level, the structural. A brief illustration will clarify. One of the most powerful rules in English grammar is that every noun can be followed by a sentence (that is, clause). The rule is written thus: N(S)

N   S

The airplane—the airplane flies above my house—is a jet.

This locution in actual usage comes out

The airplane which flies above my house is a jet.

But note the transformations that his basic structure can now undergo:

The airplane which is flying above my house is a jet.
The airplane flying above my house is a jet.

And these represent but a fraction of the possible transformations that come about because of N(S).

A complete generative grammar is basically nothing but a list of rules, both obligatory and optional, whereby structures in a language come about. The rubric of generative grammar systematizes what native speakers know about their language: if they did not have a highly sophisticated "internal" generative grammar, they could not communicate in the language. In order to demonstrate stylistic analysis via generative grammar, then, we shall cut free of the specialized notation and vocabulary, but apply the principles systematically in order to discover how the style in two passages of prose came into being. The analyses will not, by any means, be complete; they will concentrate on fairly obvious aspects of style and on narrow bands in the spectrum of possibilities. Specifically, the analyses will concentrate on (1) the verb system, (2) the rule $N(S)$, (3) the rule $(Sub)S$, and (4) co-ordination.

Vi_1: intransitive verbs like *see* in *I see* that take no particle or complement.

Vi_2: intransitive verbs like *lie* that take a particle, as in *I lie down*.

Vi_3: intransitive verbs like *stay* that take a complement as in *I am staying in a hotel*.

Vt_1: transitive verbs that take no particle or complement, as *bite* in *I bite the dog*.

Vt_2: transitive verbs that take a particle, as *look* in *I looked up the word* or *I looked the word up*.

Vt_3: intransitive verbs that take a complement, as *elect* in *We elected him president*.

Vt_{to}: transitive verbs that take infinitives as objects, as *hate* in *I hate to go*.

Vt_{ing}: transitive verbs that take gerunds as objects, as *enjoy* in *I enjoy swimming*.

Vb: verbs like *become* that take either a substantive or an adjective as complement: *He suddenly became brave. He suddenly became a hero.*

Vh: verbs like *have* that take a direct object, but that cannot be modified by an adverb of manner: *I have plenty of money*, but not *I have plenty of money quickly*.

Vs: verbs like *seem* that take an adjective as complement: *He seems brave.*

Be: Any form of the verb *to be*.

Psv: Any VT in passive voice.

The syntactic features that we shall examine are those that come about through

Coord: We will note only coordinate clauses.

$N(S)Adj$: This is a shorthand way of expressing a basic principle of language, namely, that any noun may be followed by a sentence that ultimately, in actual discourse, turns into an adjective clause: *The man—I saw the man—is my uncle* becomes *The man whom I saw is my uncle.*

N(S)AdjDel: From structures generated by N(S), certain elements may be deleted: *The man whom I saw is my uncle* becomes *The man I saw is my uncle; The man who is swimming in my pool is my uncle* becomes *The man swimming in my pool is my uncle.*

N(S)V: Verbal constructions (such as *People owning property* must pay taxes) result from the powerful N(S) rule: *People who own property must pay taxes* becomes *People owning property must pay taxes.*

(Sub)SAdv: Every sentence may be subordinated as an adverb clause: *I went* and *I had the urge* become *I went whenever I had the urge.*

(Sub)SN: Every sentence may be subordinated as a noun clause: *I knew X* and *I had the urge* become *I knew that I had the urge.*

A Passage from Thoreau's Walden
(223 words)

Verbs		Structures
	Sentence 1 (abbreviated) I have discerned a matchless and indescribable light blue, such as watered or changeable silks and sword blades suggest, more cerulean than the sky itself, alternating with the original dark green on the opposite sides of the waves, which last appeared but muddy in comparison.	
Vt₁	I have *discerned* a matchless and indescribable light blue	Base
Vt₁	such as watered or changeable silks and sword blades *suggest*	N(S)Adj
Be	[that is] more cerulean	N(S)AdjDel
Be	than the sky itself [*is* cerulean]	(Sub)SAdv
Vi₃	*alternating* with the original dark green on the opposite sides of the waves [< the light blue alternates with the original dark green. . . .]	N(S)V
Vs	which last *appeared* but muddy in comparison	N(S)Adj
	Sentence 2 It is a vitreous greenish blue, as I remember it, like those patches of the winter sky seen through cloud vistas in the west before sundown.	
Be	It *is* a vitreous greenish blue	Base
Vt₁	as I *remember* it	(Sub)SAdv

Verbs		*Structures*
Be	[which *is*] like those patches of the winter sky	N(S)AdjDel
Vt₁Psv	[which *are*] *seen* through cloud vistas in the west before sundown	N(S)V

Sentence 3
Yet a single glass of its water held up to the light is as colorless as an equal quantity of air.

Be	Yet a single glass of its water / / *is* as colorless	Base
Vt₂Psv	/ [which *is*] *held* up to the light /	N(S)V
Be	as an equal quantity of air [*is* colorless]	(Sub)SAdv

Sentence 4
It is well known that a large plate of glass will have a green tint, owing as the makers say, to its "body," but a small piece of the same will be colorless.

Be	It *is* well known	Base
Vh	that a large plate of glass *will have* a green tint	(Sub)SN
	owing / / to its "body"	
Vt₁	/ as the makers *say* /	(Sub)SAdv
Be	but a small piece of the same *will be* colorless	Coord

Sentence 5
How large a body of Walden water would be required to reflect a green tint I have never proved.

Vt_to Psv	How large a body of Walden water *would be required* to reflect a green tint	(Sub)SN
Vt₁	I *have* never *proved.*	Base

Sentence 6
The water of our river is black or a very dark brown to one looking directly down on it, and, like that of most ponds, imparts to the body of one bathing in it a yellowish tinge; but this water is of such crystalline purity that the body of the bather appears of an alabaster whiteness, still more unnatural, which, as the limbs are magnified and distorted withal, produces a monstrous effect making fit studies for a Michael Angelo.

Be	The water of our river *is* black or a very dark brown to one	Base
Vi₂	[who *is*] *looking* directly down on it	N(S)V
Vt₃	and like that of most ponds *imparts* to the body of one / / a yellowish tinge	

Verbs		Structures
Vi₃	/ [who is] *bathing* in it /	N(S)V
Be	but this body of water *is* of such crystalline purity	Coord
Vs	that the body of the bather *appears* of an alabaster whiteness	(Sub)SAdv
Be	[which *is*] still more unnatural	N(S)AdjDel
Vt₁	which / / *produces* a monstrous effect	N(S)Adj
Vt₁Psv Vt₁	/ as the limbs *are distorted* and *magnified* withal /	(Sub)SAdv
Vt₁	*making* fit studies for a Michael Ang. [< That makes fit studies)]	N(S)V

<h3 align="center">A Passage from Mark Twain's Roughing It</h3>
(220 words)

Verbs		Structures
	Sentence 1 So singularly clear was the water, that where it was only twenty or thirty feet deep the bottom was so perfectly distinct that the boat seemed floating in the air.	
Be	So singularly clear *was* the water	Base
Be	that / / the bottom *was* so perfectly distinct	(Sub)SAdv
Be	/ where it *was* only twenty or thirty feet deep /	(Sub)SAdv
Vs	that the boat *seemed* floating in air	(Sub)SAdv
Be	**Sentence 2** Yes, where it *was* even eighty feet deep	(Sub)SAdv
Be	**Sentence 3** Every little pebble was distinct, every speckled trout, every hand's-breadth of sand. Every little pebble *was* distinct, every speckled trout, every hand's-breadth of sand	Base
	Sentence 4 Often, as we lay on our faces, a granite boulder, as large as a village church, would start out of the bottom apparently, and seem climbing up rapidly to the surface, till presently it threatened to touch our faces, and we could not resist the impulse to seize an oar and avert the danger.	

Verbs		Structures
Vi_3 Vs	Often / (1) / a granite boulder / (2) / *would start* out of the bottom apparently and *seem* climbing up rapidly to the surface	Base
Vi_3	/ (1) as we *lay* on our faces /	(Sub)SAdv
Be	/ (2) [which *was*] as large as a village church	N(S)AdjDel
Vt_{to}	till presently it *threatened* to touch our faces	(Sub)SAdv
Vt_1	and we *could* not *resist* the impulse to seize an oar and avert the danger	Coord
Vi_2	Sentence 5 But the boat would float on, and the boulder descend again, and then we could see that when we had been exactly above it, it must still have been twenty or thirty feet below the surface. But the boat *would float* on	Base
Vi_1	and the boulder [*would*] *descend* again	Coord
Vt_3	and then we *could see*	Coord
Be	that / / it must still *have been* twenty or thirty feet below the surface	(Sub)SN
Be	/ when we *had been* exactly above it /	(Sub)SAdv
Be	Sentence 6 Down through the transparency of these great depths, the water was not *merely* transparent, but dazzlingly, brilliantly so. Down through the transparency of these great depths, the water *was* not *merely* transparent, but dazzlingly, brilliantly so.	Base
Vh	Sentence 7 All objects seen through it had a bright, strong vividness, not only of outline, but of every minute detail, which they would not have had when seen simply through the same depth of atmosphere. All objects / / *had* a bright, strong vividness, not only of outline, but of every minute detail	Base
Vt_1Psv	/ [which *were*] / *seen* through it	N(S)V
Vh	which they would not *have had*	N(S)Adj
Vt_1Psv	when [they *were*] *seen* simply through the same depth of atmosphere	(Sub)SAdv
	Sentence 8 So empty and airy did all spaces seem below us, and so strong was the sense of floating high aloft	

Verbs		Structures
	in mid-nothingness, that we called these boat-excursions "balloon-voyages."	
Vs	So empty and airy did all spaces *seem* below us	Base
Be	and so strong *was* the sense of floating high aloft in mid-nothingness	Coord
Vt₃	that we *called* these boat-excursions "balloon voyages."	(Sub) SAdv

Verbs

	Vi₁	Vi₂	Vi₃	Vt₁	Vt₂	Vt₃	Vt_to	Vt_ing	Vb	Vs	Vh	Be	Psv
Thoreau		1	2	10	1	1	1			2	1	11	4
Twain	1	1	2	3		2	1			3	2	10	2

Structures

	Coord	N(S)Adj	N(S)AdjDel	N(S)V	(Sub)SAdv	(Sub)SN
Thoreau	2	3	3	6	6	2
Twain	4	1	1	1	9	1

Verbs. Thoreau uses a total of thirteen VT verbs, compared with Twain's six. If we follow the old saw that "action" verbs are more vigorous than "linking" or other types of verbs, we should expect the passage from *Walden* to be more vigorous and "active" than the passage from *Roughing It.* But such, it seems, is not true. In fact, Twain's prose in the passage under consideration seems to be more active simply because the content describes actions, whereas Thoreau's passage merely describes. As we might expect in passages from descriptive prose, *Be* verbs are prevalent in both passages.

Coord. It is significant and typical that Twain coordinates clauses twice as often as does Thoreau. Coordination tends to give prose the appearance of looseness and spontaneity. Coordination by its very nature does not structure prose as tightly as, say, subordination. Any time a speaker or writer uses a significant amount of coordination, his discourse will appear to be easygoing, not tightly knit.

N(S)Adj. Thoreau uses three complete adjective clauses, whereas Twain uses only one. The effect of the complete adjective clause is amplitude. Compare *The man who is carrying the briefcase is the president of the bank* with *The man carrying the briefcase is the president of the bank.* All told, Thoreau uses six construction deriving from N(S)Adj and N(S)AdjDel; Twain uses two.

N(S)V. It seems to me that one of the most important stylistic features that the analysis reveals is Thoreau's tendency to use verbal constructions. Reference back to the passage from Faulkner quoted earlier shows how typically he relies on the verbal construction to build his sentences and hence his style. The verbal construction presents a handy, abbreviated way of piling construction on construction and hence idea on idea. The verbal construction is also more "artificial" and "literary" than the clause.

(Sub)SAdv. Twain uses more subordinate adverb clauses than does Thoreau, but perhaps the difference is not significant.

We should keep in mind that the analysis presented here is not scientific or even complete; it is paradigmatic. In order to gain an accurate profile of anyone's prose, the analyst must (1) deal with an extensive sample and (2) apply all available criteria. In the paradigms, we have dealt with limited samples and a narrow range of criteria. Nonetheless, the principle demonstrated is valid. Analysis performed with all of the rules of generative grammar on an extensive sample of prose will give an extremely accurate description, even to the point of allowing one to identify prose as surely as fingerprints and voice patterns can be identified. But the quantitative analysis of prose does not bring about value judgments; it merely provides objective data on which discussions of value can be based.

The Value of Style

What, then, is the value of style? This question takes us back to the Aristotelian moral dilemma involving matter versus manner. Is it really moral—to paraphrase Huxley—to paint the fair face of truth with that pestilential cosmetic, rhetoric? The following moves a considerable distance toward a solution to the dilemma:

> The form of any game is of first importance. Game theory, like information theory, has ignored this aspect of game and information movement. Both theories have dealt with the information content of systems, and have observed the "noise" and "deception" factors that divert data. This is like approaching a painting or a musical composition from the point of view of its content. In other words, it is guaranteed to miss the central structural core of the experience. For as it is the *pattern* of a game that gives it relevance to our inner lives, and not who is playing nor the outcome of the game, so it is with information movement. The

selection of our human senses employed makes all the difference say between photo and telegraph. In the arts the particular mix of our senses
in the medium employed is all-important. The ostensible program content
is a lulling distraction needed to enable the structural form to get through
the barriers of conscious attention.[19]

Marshall McLuhan, of course, is telling us again that the medium is the
massage. But his point is all to the good—and actually rather simple. It is,
for instance, futile to criticize television as though it were the movies, just
as it is futile to criticize prose as though it were statistical tabulation. The
element of pure "play" in discourse is the style. "The ostensible program
content is a lulling distraction needed to enable the structural form to get
through the barriers of conscious attention." When we focus on prose as
style, we are focusing on it as art; and when we are focusing on it as art,
we are focusing on style, on the medium. And the medium itself is the
element of mental play, the game, that makes us care about style at all.
Literature can be viewed as documents, as symptoms in the intellectual
history of man; such a stand is not only nonesthetic, it is antiesthetic.
Inevitably the esthetic study of any discourse must turn to pure form, to
style and its extensions beyond the areas where style and form merge, blend,
and redefine themselves at opposite ends of the spectrum.

The appeal of style, finally, is mystic and childlike and hence basic.
Style is wordplay. And art is the most incontrovertible testimony that man
is the playful animal.

McLuhan also says,

All media are active metaphors in their power to translate experience into
new forms. . . . For just as a metaphor transforms and transmits experience, so do the media.[20]

Because the metaphorical effect is, as Hugh Blair said, "made in the mind,"
the metaphor provides an ideal point of departure for a discussion of matter
over manner and hence a springboard for a metarhetoric or a metastylistic.
The discussion of style was weighted preponderantly toward the quantitative, for the quantitative is the most accessible aspect of style, but not the
only one. Though the medium is the message, any medium is only the
outermost of a series of Chinese boxes containing other media, as for instance television contains the drama and the drama contains speech and
action. Style contains message and is at the same time partly message,
and conversely, and paradoxically, is separable from message.

[19] Marshall McLuhan, *Understanding Media: The Extensions of Man* (New York:
McGraw-Hill, Inc., 1965), p. 242.
[20] McLuhan, p. 57.

The Metaphor

The metaphor has a long recognized but seldom analyzed generative capability. I. A. Richards, for instance, quotes Shelley: "Language is vitally metaphorical; this is, it marks the before unapprehended relations of things and perpetuates their apprehension. . . ." This marking of unapprehended relations gives the metaphor the power to fill its own cup of meaning and spill over. André Breton, as quoted by Richards, says, "To compare two objects, as remote from one another in character as possible, or by any other method put them together in a sudden and striking fashion, this remains the highest task to which poetry can aspire." The dialectical process whereby metaphor conjoins "thesis" and "antithesis" to bring "synthesis" is the very process whereby discourse comes into being. For ideas grope for utterance through relations, but random relations also bring ideas into being. The poetic process, for instance, can be a two-way affair: the poet gropes for the proper metaphorical relation to vivify his idea, *or* the relation suggests an idea and hence becomes metaphorical. In this sense, then, the metaphor might generate the poem. An example of this process is "Tintern Abbey," in which the sight of the Abbey sets off a train of thought whereby the Abbey itself becomes metaphorical and a poem.

Herein lies the difference between *symbol* and metaphor. The empty room at dusk, the symbol of my loneliness, becomes a metaphor for my loneliness when I write my poem.

I see no reason to argue with I. A. Richards' basic ideas about the metaphor. He says, of course, that the metaphor consists of *tenor* and *vehicle*. Tenor is the whole meaning in context; vehicle is the device. ". . . the vehicle is not normally a mere embellishment of a tenor which is otherwise unchanged by it but . . . vehicle and tenor in cooperation give a meaning of more varied powers than can be ascribed to either."[21] The device itself involves a comparison, and hence the effective metaphor explodes with the shock of recognition. The effective metaphor is a flashbulb, illuminating one of life's scenes.

Kenneth Burke says,

> Metaphor is a device for seeing something *in terms of* something else. It brings out the thisness of a that, or the thatness of a this. If we employ the word "character" as a general term for whatever can be thought of as distinct (any thing, pattern, situation, structure, nature, person object, act, rôle, process, event, etc.,) then we could say that the metaphor tells us something about one character as considered from the

[21] I. A. Richards, *The Philosophy of Rhetoric* (New York: Oxford University Press, 1936), p. 100.

> point of view of another character. And to consider A from the point of
> view of B is, of course, to use B as a *perspective* upon A.[22]

That is, the metaphor is a medium. When we concentrate on the metaphor,
we concentrate on the medium-istic nature of language. Analogically (and
metaphorically), we can think of a dramatic script that might be presented
(a) on the stage, (b) in the movies, and (c) on TV. Until the script is
translated, metamorphosed, into one of the media, it is strictly literary—
even though the metamorphosis might take place only in the mind of the
reader. (*Visualizing* the play is one of the prime skills in reading drama.)
But each medium will change the nature of the script. Thus, the literalness
of the text will develop into the metaphor of the medium. We can look at
the script through the eyes of the spectator at a play, the eye of the film
camera, or the electronic eye of the television camera.

Just as the camera—electronic or otherwise—has a generative power,
Pygmalionlike transforming materials to its own desires, the metaphor
generates movement that sometimes escapes the control of the speaker or
writer. Kenneth Burke hints at the generative quality of the metaphor when
he says, "Indeed, the metaphor always has about it precisely this revealing
of hitherto unsuspected connectives which we may note in the progressions
of a dream."[23] The metaphor is usually as rationally incongruous as dream
materials:

> He fumbles at your Soul
>
> Doom is the House without the Door
>
> A Plated Life—diversified
> With Gold and Silver Pain
> To prove the presence of the Ore
> In Particles
>
> Revolution is the Pod
> Systems rattle from
> When the Winds of Will are stirred

These, from Emily Dickinson, are as irrational and as illuminating as all
good metaphors and all true dreams.

The Symbol

The symbol is, after all, much like a metaphor. Its vehicle is the
thing: rose, Grim Reaper, spire, cross; its tenor is the whole meaning in

---

[22] From the book, *A Grammar of Motives* by Kenneth Burke, pp. 503–504. © 1950
by Prentice-Hall, Inc. Published by Prentice-Hall, Inc., Englewood Cliffs, New Jersey.
Reprinted with the permission of the publisher.
[23] Kenneth Burke, *Permanence and Change* (Los Altos, Calif.: Hermes Publications,
1954), p. 90.

context. But there is perhaps a fundamental difference between symbol and metaphor: the symbol tends not to be as disjunctive as the metaphor. Very broadly, one might say that the metaphor seeks out similarities in the dissimilar, whereas the symbol emphasizes similarities. Thus, in the following by Edmund Waller we find a controlling symbol:

> Go, lovely rose!
> Tell her that wastes her time and me
> That now she knows,
> When I resemble her to thee,
> How sweet and fair she seems to be.
>
> Tell her that's young
> And shuns to have her graces spied,
> That hadst thou sprung
> In deserts where no men abide,
> Thou must have uncommended died.
>
> Small is the worth
> Of beauty from the light retired;
> Bid her come forth,
> Suffer herself to be desired,
> And not blush so to be admired.
>
> Then die, that she
> The common fate of all things rare
> May read in thee;
> How small a part of time they share
> That are so wondrous sweet and fair!

But in its function the symbol blurs off into a metaphor. If the poet had addressed his beloved as a rose instead of apostrophizing the rose, the utterance would have been metaphorical.

Our interest, however, does not center so much on the nature of the metaphor—a concern that has had countless treatments—or the symbol, but rather on metaphor and symbol as generative devices, as features of discourse that serve to generate discourse.

The symbol often precedes the work. Hawthorne's discovery of the real scarlet "A" generated *The Scarlet Letter*. Under the headline "Playwright Tilted at Windmills," the Los Angeles *Times Calendar* (March 26, 1967) carries a story by Dale Wasserman, the author of the highly successful *Man of La Mancha*. Wasserman tells us that he decided to write a play about Cervantes, a subject more interesting to him than a mere adaptation of *Don Quixote*.

> In style I thought the play would be acerbic, a sort of sober tongue-in-cheek. Witty, I hoped, a smartly cynical comment on man's infinite

capacity for self-deception. To my astonishment the pages that came from the typewriter said no such thing; they marched upon me in an ardent plea for illusion as the most powerful sustaining force in life, the most meaningful function of imagination. In dismay I heard my Cervantes-Quixote saying, "To dream the impossible dream, to fight the unbeatable foe . . . ." And, to a pragmatist proclaiming, "Facts are the enemy of truth." The play was rejecting my intention, imposing quite another of its own.

Once the symbol got going, it assumed a life of its own; it generated its own development. And, in fact, it is a common human experience to seek out the symbolic meaning of this, that, or everything. The symbol generates its own meaning and hence its own discourse.

It is exactly this sort of playful generation that forms the basis of metaphysical poetry. Once Donne has told his reader, "Mark But this flea," the necessary conditions are set up for a systematic exploration of the metaphorical and symbolic meanings that can be discovered in the flea, and in the process the flea becomes the container, the medium, for ideas of marriage, the Trinity, intercourse, innocence, guilt, and so on.

Through the playfulness of style comes that identification which is the most powerful of rhetorical effects.

chapter 6

New Rhetoric:
Form

Generative Grammar and Form

Classical rhetoric—productive and immediately useful though it was—had its own built-in pitfalls, the
dogmas and methods that would spell its demise as
a system of inquiry and an art of discourse. From
Aristotle through Whately and beyond, the condition of rhetoric was stasis, as must have been the situation in a taxonomic art. So much of the rhetorical
material that we have inherited concerns itself with
classification and hence fragmentation: the five "departments" themselves; the parts of the classical
oration; the two hundred or more figures; the topics
—and most important of all, the artificial bifurcation
of the thought process into induction and deduction.
Undoubtedly, the old rhetoric served well; it did for
the field of discourse what classification and taxonomy did for the natural sciences. But as physiology

must go beyond anatomy into process, so rhetoric needed to go beyond its fixation on classification to the more productive inquiry into "generation" and "transformation." A basic fact about rhetoric has been consistently overlooked: the very notion of an "art" of rhetoric implies "a finite number of observations, and it seeks to predict new phenomena by constructing general laws in terms of hypothetical constructs such as (in physics, for example) 'mass' and 'electron.' "[1] The quotation is, of course, from Chomsky's *Syntactic Structures*, and the source of the terms "generation" and "transformation" is obvious.

In fact, generative-transformational grammar is at almost every turn productive for the rhetorician. The ideal of rhetoric—precisely like the ideal of grammar—is to make valid generalizations about discourse and, furthermore, to make these generalizations in such a way that they will be predictive. In one sense, classical rhetoric was "predictive" in its prescriptiveness; that is, one could predict that following the divisions of the classical oration would bring about a conventionally structured classical oration, but the circularity of this proposition is symptomatic of the weakness of taxonomic rhetoric.

In the first place, introspection shows the speaker or writer that on the basic level he does not follow external rules or rubrics to produce discourse; it is unthinkable that any writer should plan sentences in terms of types, except in the most elementary and artificial classroom exercises. That is, the following description of the process of sentence production is ludicrous: *step 1*, formulate idea; *step 2*, choose sentence type; *step 3*, utter or write sentence. In fact, we have no way of knowing what goes on inside the human brain as sentences are formed, and the argument concerning the existence of ideas without language in which to express them turns out to be largely a semantic quibble. In *Philosophy in a New Key*, a book to which we will turn later, Susanne Langer tells the moving story of how Helen Keller finally grasped the concept of the symbol. At the moment when w-a-t-e-r signified " 'the wonderful cool something that was flowing over my hand,' " the girl had broken through the barrier that separates *sign* ("something to act upon, or a means to command action") and *symbol* ("an instrument of thought"). At the point when sign becomes symbol, the possibility of language emerges, to be sure, but to argue that the symbol-less Helen Keller also had no ideas turns on a fruitless quibble about the real meaning of "idea." At best, we can meaningfully discuss the real enunciation of ideas, not their "internal" nature or the psychological processes whereby they gain expression in language. Thus, it is an axiom of grammarians that everyone has an "internal" grammar, but also that we can make meaningful generalizations only about the external, observable grammar.

[1] Noam Chomsky, *Syntactic Structures* (The Hague: Mouton & Cie, 1957), p. 49.

Generalizations about discourse should be productive in a wide sense: in the classroom, they should serve as instructional tools in the way that practice with model sentences does; they should be applicable to the universe of discourse, not merely to the analysis (or outlining) of certain genres. They should give the rhetorician valid insight into the nature of successful—and unsuccessful—discourse, though not into the ways in which the discourse is produced internally. These remarks are not intended to imply that the venerable doctrine of imitation is invalid. And total clarification on this point is imperative. Obviously, we learn to speak at all levels by the process of imitation. No set of formulas, no amount of generalizing about good and bad discourse will supplant the basic exercise of reading or hearing and then consciously or more often unconsciously imitating.

But if the analogy of rhetoric with generative grammar is valid—and we should not push it too far—we should expect that the basic assumptions of generative grammar would in some way be congruent with the basic assumptions of rhetoric. In an exploratory way, then, we ought to find out how extensive the interconnections are—and how profitable these interconnections may be.

First, insofar as generative grammar is a valid description of language functions, its insights should be extendable beyond the sentence. And, in fact, it seems to me that it is precisely at this point that we can begin talking about a "new" rhetoric. As we have seen, in *Syntactic Structures*, Chomsky says,

> The fundamental aim in the linguistic analysis of a language L is to separate the *grammatical* sequences which are the sentences of L from the *ungrammatical sequences* which are not sentences of L and to study the structure of the grammatical sequences. The grammar of L will thus be a device that generates all of the grammatical sequences of L and none of the ungrammatical ones.[2]

Now, the fundamental aim of rhetorical analysis has always been to separate the *suasive sequences* from those that were unsuasive and to study the structure of the suasive sequences. But at this point rhetoric by and large stopped. The rhetorician concentrated on lists of tactics, arrived at by deduction or empirically, and did not speculate on the possibility of a rhetoric that would generate suasive sequences. This failing arose partially from the lack of insight into fundamental principles of discourse structuring, an insight that generative grammar has provided. Stated most baldly, the premise of the new grammar is that on every level of the *sentence*, discourse generates discourse and affords the possibility of systematic transformation. For instance, these two sentences:

[2] Chomsky, p. 13.

> I saw the man
> The man was old

contain the possibility of generating a third: *I saw the old man*—and also of the transformation, *The old man was seen by me*. On a more elementary level, the word "the" in the initial position "contains" the possibility of a following "old" or "tall" or "man," and so forth, but not of "saw," "therefore," and the like. That is, in putting ideas into sentences, we have a wide range of choices, but these choices are controlled by a rather narrow restrictive system called English grammar.

The Generative Quality of Language

We can illustrate this generative quality of language easily enough—and by intuition, every reader has sensed it. Whenever someone talks about incoherence in a paragraph composed of sentences that are in themselves coherent, he is actually talking about the way in which discourse generates more discourse. For instance, the following "paragraph" is incoherent:

> It is a paradox, but the truth nevertheless, that our absence of ideas, the exclusion of ideas from American political life, gives us a superior kind of public morality. The young muggers looked to him like the stuff storm troopers are made of, and he said to himself, "There it goes again!" In the first place, the attack had no idea wrapped around it, it was just plain greed. They were for the victim, whoever he was.

The following paragraph is coherent:

> It is a paradox, but the truth nevertheless, that our absence of ideas, the exclusion of ideas from American political life, gives us a superior kind of public morality. In New York some years ago a German refugee, who was just beginning to breathe freely our sooty but impartial air, was attacked and robbed in broad daylight on First Avenue. The young muggers looked to him like the stuff storm troopers are made of, and he said to himself, "There it goes again!" But there was a vast difference, a difference, as he told the court, that on reflection he was able to appreciate. In the first place, the attack had no idea wrapped around it, it was just plain greed. In the second place, the police had no ideology either. They were for the victim, whoever he was.
> —JACQUES BARZUN, *Democracy and Ideology*

The problem in the first "paragraph" is too obvious for comment. Or is it? Can we ask meaningful questions about the incoherence of the first and the coherence of the second? And might those questions in many ways be of the same order as those probing the "incoherence" of the following "sentence"?

whoever for the they victim were was he

The sentence is a convention, recognized intuitively and more or less adequately describable and definable in terms of grammar, old or new. Is the paragraph a convention describable in analogous terms? And what about longer segments of discourse, such as the essay? If, for instance, a hundred readers agree that essay X is inconclusive, they must base their judgment on some intuitive sense of the convention Essay in much the same way that users of a language have "sentence sense."

The Proposition

Before we go on to the regions that lie ahead in this discussion, it might be well to erect a few directional signs—or, as it were, for the sake of clarity, to tip the hand before it is played. The terminus of the dialectic that is now beginning to emerge looks something like this: invention and arrangement are so nearly the same that they are almost indistinguishable; they are basically the same process. The inventive process controls arrangement, predetermines it. Thus, we ought to reach the synapse where the two venerable departments, invention and arrangement, merge. In this process, style will become a strictly analytical department, useless as a subject of inquiry before the fact. The goal, then, is to bring about a synthesis—not Ramistically to pare departments away—and in the process to develop a theory of rhetoric far more viable than the traditional fragmented and compartmentalized art, an art that often led the rhetorician toward a false notion of how human discourse operates. The discussion at hand will move toward a generative rhetoric, not of the sentence or the paragraph, but of the whole unit of discourse (oration, essay, or whatever).

Consider the following locutions:

The girl opens the door.
The opening of the door by the girl.

The first seems complete; the second seems incomplete and in a way predictive of something to come—or that something must come. The *opening of the door by the girl* is not incomplete because it lacks meaning; in fact, one could argue endlessly and inconclusively about whether the sequence does or does not have a "complete" semantic meaning. But *logically* speaking, the series *The girl opens the door* functions as a proposition, whereas the series *The opening of the door by the girl* does not. Morris Cohen makes the point here clearly:

> What, now, distinguishes a proposition from other significant objects or symbols? It is usual to regard a proposition as an ordered group of words, the order being expressed by inflection or sequence. But a single word *cogito* or *ambulo* is clearly sufficient. The analysis of propositions into *S is P* or *aRb* is often illuminating, but not always fitting. Sometimes it is forced. Mr. Russell makes the distinction between a proposition such as *John walks* and the term *John walking* to consist in that the former asserts something. What is the nature of logical as distinguished from psychological assertion? For the sake of brevity let me say dogmatically that it is *location*—*John's walking* is an unlocated complex. When it is put into a time series it becomes *John walked* or *John is walking*. Some languages like the Chinese often dispense with verbs, but the location is then indicated either by the order of the words or by intonation. When a child says *Moon*, the mother may understand the child from its tone or from its pointing as expressing the proposition, *this is the moon*. The demonstrative is supplied by the gesture.
>
> If such location of an object in some universe is what we mean by existence in general, then propositions assert existence while concepts or terms merely denote or name essences.[3]

The distinction between an assertion and a proposition is crucial. We feel that the assertion contains somehow the urgent generative possibility of a proposition (*The opening of the door by the girl caused a draft*) and that the proposition contains generative possibilities for some kind of elaboration (*and the draft gave me a stiff neck*).[4] Suppose kernels such as

NP	Vt	NP
The boy	sees	the ball

were *systematically*, by the rules of grammar, reducible to something like this:

Gerund Phrase	Prep Phrase (genitive)	Prep Phrase (instrumental)
The seeing	of the ball	by the boy

The grammar that explained the generation of sentences from such kernels would be radically different from that which dealt with *The boy sees the ball*, *The boy runs*, *The boy becomes a man*, and *The boy is good*, which

---

[3] Morris R. Cohen, *A Preface to Logic* (New York: Holt, Rinehart and Winston, Inc., 1965), p. 46. The excerpts in this chapter from *A Preface to Logic* are reprinted with the permission of Holt, Rinehart and Winston, and Routledge & Kegan Paul, Ltd.

[4] For many of the following ideas, I am indebted to Dr. Charles Fillmore of the Ohio State University.

are the types of kernels from which generative grammar now works. But it would also explain the structural basis of the difference between a mere assertion and a proposition. The intriguing possibility here is that basically, in its deepest structure, language is merely assertive, and that only on a succedaneous level of structure does it become propositional—but, furthermore, that *the assertion necessarily generates the proposition.*

Cohen demonstrates clearly that the proposition is formal rather than notional:

> From *Pirots karulize elatically* and A *is a pirot*, we can infer that A *karulizes elatically* without knowing the meaning of the three words or the sense of the three words or the sense of the three sentences. . . . If instead of Pirots we put *"the members of any class of objects"* and instead of *karulize elatically* we put *are members of another class* we have an inference that *a member of the first class is necessarily a member of the second class.*[5]

Apparently, then, the assertion (*The opening of the door* or *the karulizing of the Pirots*) will almost necessarily generate a proposition on the formal level (*The opening of the door caused a draft* or *The karulizing of the Pirots blurged a glud*).

Without reducing the argument *ad absurdum*, we can say also that the sign can generate a symbol—or transform itself into one, as when the sign w-a-t-e-r became a symbol *water* for Helen Keller. In short, there is nothing particularly startling about the assumption that language at all levels contains the generative possibility within a definable system of rules. (Insofar as the rules for constructing a classical oration could generate a classical oration, they were an adequate "grammar.")

Generative grammar, of course, can generate a good many—perhaps most—of the sentences in English.[6] But the moment we go beyond the sentence, we step into an area that so far has been only dimly lit. Generative grammar systematically describes the choices that we *must* make and that we *can* make to produce a sentence. But what about the choices involved in producing a paragraph or an essay?

Topic Sentence

We should like to say that the *topic sentence* of a paragraph has the possibility in a systematic way of generating the paragraph. In a sense, such a view is not inaccurate, but it oversimplifies a complex situation.

[5] Cohen, p. 54.
[6] A word of explanation: generative grammar can generate sentences in that its rules systematically applied will result in English sentences.

First, we must determine rather clearly what is meant by topic sentence. Consider the following paragraph, for example:

> Over a hundred years ago a Scandinavian philosopher, Sören Kierkegaard, made a profound observation about the future. Kierkegaard's remark is of such great, though hidden, importance to our subject that I shall begin by quoting his words. "He who fights the future," remarked the philosopher, "has a dangerous enemy. The future is not, it borrows its strength from the man himself, and when it has tricked him out of this, then it appears outside of him as the enemy he must meet."
>
> —LOREN EISELEY, *The Firmament of Time*[7]

Determining the actual topic sentence of this paragraph is a tricky business. Clearly the first sentence is not the controlling idea, but works as a subordinate, elaborative thought. The second sentence is even more clearly *not* the topic sentence. In fact, when we think in traditional terms, we must conclude that the last sentence in the paragraph is the main, controlling idea: "The future is not, it borrows its strength from the man himself, and when it has tricked him out of this, then it appears outside of him as the enemy he must meet." The first sentence of the next paragraph reinforces the feeling that the last sentence of the paragraph quoted is actually the topic sentence of its paragraph. The paragraph after the one quoted above begins:

> We in the western world have rushed eagerly to embrace the future—and in so doing we have provided that future with a strength it has derived from us and our endeavors.

Or consider another example:

> There is no mystery about why there is such a tendency for popular opinion to be wrong in judging war and peace. Strategic and diplomatic decisions call for a kind of knowledge—not to speak of an experience and a seasoned judgment—which cannot be had by glancing at newspapers, listening to snatches of radio comment, watching politicians perform on television, hearing occasional lectures, and reading a few books. It would not be enough to make a man competent to decide whether to amputate a leg, and it is not enough to qualify him to choose war or peace, to arm or not to arm, to intervene or to withdraw, to fight on or to negotiate.
>
> —WALTER LIPPMANN, *The Public Philosophy*[8]

[7] Excerpts from *The Firmament of Time* by Loren Eiseley. © 1960 by Loren Eiseley. Reprinted by permission of Atheneum Publishers and Victor Gollancz, Ltd.
[8] From *The Public Philosophy* by Walter Lippmann, by permission of Atlantic-Little, Brown and Co. Copyright 1955, by Walter Lippmann.

In this paragraph, the topic sentence is clearly the first. Yet if we look at the paragraph by Eiseley and the one by Lippmann, we feel, I think, that they somehow "work" alike; they are both coherent.

It is hardly revolutionary to mention that sentences get at the same meaning by various routes; if such were not true, synonymy and paraphrase would be impossible. Note the following sequence:

1. The opening of the door by the girl.
2. The girl opens the door.
3. The door is opened by the girl.

We sense, I think, that (1) and (3) are nearer to each other than either (2) and (3) or (1) and (2). But (1) is different from (2) and (3) most notably in that it is "incomplete." If we can use the sentence as an analogy for the paragraph, then, we would assume that somehow "completeness" becomes the main criterion of paragraph versus nonparagraph, but only insofar as the paragraph is a convention. To demonstrate satisfactorily that the paragraph is indeed a convention is not awfully difficult. A. L. Becker reports:

> . . . given a discourse with all paragraph indentations removed, subjects can restore them with a striking degree of agreement. In most cases the subjects paragraph the passages as the authors did, and where they disagree with the author they tend to agree with each other, suggesting that some markers of paragraphs have priority over others in paragraph recognition.[9]

Verifying Becker's conclusion is easy enough. I have found that even relatively unsophisticated "subjects" recognize paragraphs with an amazing degree of consistency.

Now, we should think again of the sequence:

1. The opening of the door by the girl.
2. The girl opens the door.
3. The door is opened by the girl.

It has been proposed that somehow the prepositional phrase is the real irreducible "kernel" of the sentence. If such is indeed true, we can say that (1) expresses the kernel of meaning, and (2) and (3) put that kernel into propositions. That is, meaning is completed by its propositional form, but the proposition is capable of various grammatical arrangements. In this

---

[9] Francis Christensen *et al.*, "Symposium on the Paragraph," *College Composition and Communication*, XVII (May 1966), 69.

sense, we are justified in speaking about "kernels" of paragraphs. The kernel is that "assertion" which gains completion in the "proposition" of the paragraph. Therefore, we ought now to shift our traditional thinking a bit; instead of looking for topic sentences, we ought to look for "kernel" sentences. In the paragraph by Eiseley, the kernel sentence is the last one. In the paragraph by Lippmann, the kernel sentence is the first one. *But the topic sentence and the kernel sentence may or may not be the same sentence.* We shall identify the kernel sentence logically or notionally—in the same way that we can say that *The opening of the door by the girl* is the kernel of *The girl opens the door* and *The door is opened by the girl.* The *topic sentence* is something else again. In fact, we can begin with Francis Christensen's definition:

> . . . the topic sentence of a paragraph is to the supporting sentences what the base clause of a cumulative sentence is to its free modifiers. . . . There are sentences that can be converted into paragraphs merely by changing commas, colons, or semicolons to periods and vice versa. There are sentences that can be converted into paragraphs by converting their added levels back to the sentences from which transformation grammar would derive them. There are paragraphs . . . in which coordinate subtopics are developed some by additions to the subtopic sentence and others by added sentences. Such interchangeability gives strong support to the analogy [between the sentence and the paragraph].[10]

The topic sentence in Christensen's sense is not the notionally most important one in the paragraph; it is the topic sentence only in a generative way; it is "to the supporting sentences what the base clause of a cumulative sentence is to its free modifiers." Therefore, the topic sentence would most frequently, but not always, be the first sentence in a paragraph. Analogically, we can see this same principle work on the sentence level:

> Bedroll, tent, food, and gun—these were what I took.
> I took bedroll, tent, food, and gun.

The last sequence would be the more common; in the first sequence we immediately perceive a figure of grammar. But how does all this work on the paragraph level? Normal paragraph order goes like this:

> In English banks you still see money, and observe the ritual of veneration that goes with it. People are carrying money about. Others sit at tables, counting the stuff, popping it into sacks, weighing it. The visitor feels that he is at the seat of commerce, and anarchy wells up in his spirit.

[10] Christensen *et al.*, "Symposium," p. 61.

But suppose we tamper with the order and also supply a last sentence from a preceding paragraph.

> American banks are flaccid, insipid, effete. But not so English banks. People are carrying money about. Others sit at tables, counting the stuff, popping it into sacks, weighing it. The visitor feels that he is at the seat of commerce, and anarchy wells up in his spirit. In English banks you still see money, and observe the ritual of veneration that goes with it.[11]

In both of these examples the kernel sentence is the same: *In English banks you still see money.* . . . Now in what sense can we say that *People are carrying money about* is the topic sentence in the second example? The old concept of induction is helpful here: by the inductive process one goes from a number of specific instances to a general conclusion—and ideally or theoretically in the scientific method the conclusion will come as a surprise to the investigator.[12] The paragraph seems to move—as does the first example sentence—from a number of specifics to a general conclusion based on them. And there is an element of surprise in the conclusion. However, both the sentence and the paragraph must have some kind of internal coherence; in fact, we sense that they do. This means, then, that in the sentence, one word must "lead" to the next, and in the paragraph, one sentence must "lead" to the next. We can inquire, then, about the ways in which the sentences are meaningfully sequential, about the ways in which they cohere. Read the following arrangements carefully:

> In English banks you still see money, and observe the ritual of veneration that goes with it.
> People are carrying money about.
> Others sit at tables, counting the stuff, popping it into sacks, weighing it.
> The visitor feels that he is at the seat of commerce, and anarchy wells up in his spirit.
>
> People are carrying money about.
> Others sit at tables, counting the stuff, popping it into sacks, weighing it.
> The visitor feels that he is at the seat of commerce, and anarchy wells up in his spirit.
> In English banks you still see money, and observe the ritual of veneration that goes with it.

[11] With apologies to Mr. Malcolm Bradbury for the chopping up of part of his essay "Can We Bring Back the Old-Fashioned Bank Robber?"
[12] Both common sense and modern logic militate against the sharp division of induction and deduction; and we use the term here only in a loose, analogical way.

> In English banks the visitor feels that he is at the seat of commerce, and anarchy wells up in his spirit.
> You still see money, and observe the ritual that goes with it.
>> People are carrying it about.
>> Others sit at tables, counting the stuff, popping it into sacks, weighing it.

All three of these arrangements make coherent paragraphs. But now note the following:

> People are carrying money about.
> The visitor feels that he is at the seat of commerce, and anarchy wells up in his spirit.
> Some people sit at tables counting the stuff, popping it into sacks, weighing it.
> In English banks you still see money, and observe the ritual of veneration that goes with it.

In this arrangement, coherence has evanesced.

The Sentence and the Paragraph

Christensen argues that the sentences in a paragraph have the "grammatical" relations of "coordination and subordination."[13] This means that a series of sentences making up a coherent paragraph will have a "syntax," relating each to the one that precedes it. The following examples illustrate Christensen's sentence analogy and his theory of the paragraph.[14]

A. *Two-Level Sentence*

1   Lincoln's words still linger on the lips—
    2   eloquent and cunning, yes,
    2   vindictive and sarcastic in political debate,
    2   rippling and ribald in jokes,
    2   reverent in the half-formed utterance of prayer.

—ALISTAIR COOKE

A. *Coordinate-Sequence Paragraph*

1   This is the essence of the religious spirit—the sense of power, beauty, greatness, truth infinitely beyond one's own reach, but infinitely to be aspired to.

---

[13] Francis Christensen, "A Generative Rhetoric of the Paragraph," *Notes Toward a New Rhetoric* (New York: Harper & Row, Publishers, 1967), pp. 57–59. The excerpts from Professor Christensen's work are reprinted with the permission of the author.
[14] Christensen, "A Generative Rhetoric," pp. 22–23.

2 It invests men with a pride in a purpose and with humility in accomplishment.

2 It is the source of all true tolerance, for in its light all men see other men as they see themselves, as being capable of being more than they are, and yet falling short, inevitably, of what they can imagine human opportunities to be.

2 It is the supporter of human dignity and pride and the dissolver of vanity.

2 And it is the very creator of the scientific spirit; for without the aspiration to understand and control the miracle of life, no man would have sweated in a laboratory or tortured his brain in the exquisite search after truth.

—DOROTHY THOMPSON, "The Education of the Heart"

B. Multilevel Sentence

1 A small Negro girl develops from the sheet of glare-frosted walk,
2   walking barefooted,
3   her brown legs striking and recoiling from the hot cement,
4   her feet curling in,
5   only the outer edges touching.

B. Subordinate-Sequence Paragraph

1 The process of learning is essential to our lives.
2   All higher animals seek it deliberately.
3   They are inquisitive and they experiment.
4   An experiment is a sort of harmless trial run of some action which we shall have to make in the real world; and this, whether it is made in the laboratory by scientists or by fox-cubs outside their earth.
5   The scientist experiments and the cub plays; both are learning to correct their errors of judgment in a setting in which errors are not fatal.
6   Perhaps this is what gives them both their air of happiness and freedom in these activities.

—J. BRONOWSKI, The Common Sense of Science, (Vintage), p. 111

We can gain many valid insights into the nature of the paragraph, then, especially if we use the sentence analogy as a springboard. In fact, careful examination of an extensive number of paragraphs is a convincing demonstration that we can begin thinking of *structures* beyond the sentence. (The fact that untrained observers can recognize where paragraphs ought to be in unparagraphed discourse is another convincing factor.) But even the extremely helpful work that Christensen has done gives us precious little insight into our reasons for feeling that the first three re-arrangements of the Bradbury paragraph are in themselves paragraphs,

although the fourth is not. For a moment, let us turn to that fourth
arrangement again. If we were to attempt a diagram of the structure of
the paragraph, the result would look like this:

(1)   People are carrying money about.
(2)   The visitor feels that he is at the seat of commerce, and
                             anarchy wells up in his spirit.
(3)   Some people sit at tables, counting the stuff, popping
                             it into sacks, weighing it.
(4)   In English banks you still see money, and observe the ritual of
             veneration that goes with it.

The reason we sense incoherence in this arrangement is fairly obvious; there
is no progressive moment. Sentences (1) and (3) are parallel to each other,
but they are interrupted by (2), a sentence that obviously neither (1) nor
(3) is either coordinate with or subordinate to. Now look at the following
diagrams.

1   We in the western world have rushed eagerly to embrace the future—and
     in so doing have provided that future with a strength it has derived from us
     and our endeavors.
        2   Now, stunned, puzzled and dismayed, we try to withdraw from the
             embrace, not of a necessary tomorrow, but of that future which we
             have invited and of which, at last, we have grown perceptibly afraid.
        2   In a sudden horror we discover that the years now rushing upon us
             have drained our moral resources and have taken shape out of our
             own impotence.
        2   At this moment, if we possess even a modicum of reflective insight,
             we will give heed to Kierkegaard's concluding wisdom: "Through
             the eternal," he enjoins us, "we can conquer the future."

1   The advice is cryptic; the hour late.
1   Moreover, what have we to do with the eternal?
        2   Our age, we know, is littered with the wrecks of war, of outworn
             philosophies, of broken faiths.
        2   We profess little but the new and study only change.

1   Three hundred years have passed since Galileo, with the telescope, opened
     the enormous vista of the night.
        2   In those three centuries the phenomenal world, previously explored
             with the unaided senses, has undergone tremendous alteration in
             our minds.
               3   A misty light so remote as to be scarcely sensed by the un-
                    aided eye has become a galaxy.
               3   Under the microscope the previously unseen has become a
                    cosmos of both beautiful and repugnant life, while the tissues

of the body have been resolved into a cellular hierarchy whose constituents mysteriously produce the human personality.

1   Similarly, the time dimension, by the use of other sensory extensions and the close calculations made possible by our improved knowledge of the elements, has been plumbed as never before, and even its dead, forgotten life has been made to yield remarkable secrets.

2   The great stage, in other words, the world stage where the Elizabethans saw us strutting and mouthing our parts, has the skeletons of dead actors under the floor boards, and the dusty scenery of forgotten dramas lies abandoned in the wings.

3   The idea necessarily comes home to us then with a sudden chill: What if we are not playing on the center stage?

or 3:   4   What if there is no audience beyond the footlights, and the play, in spite of bold villains and posturing heroes, is a shabby repeat performance in an echoing vacuity?

5   Man is a perceptive animal.

6   He hates above all else to appear ridiculous.

6   His explorations of reality in the course of just three hundred years have so enlarged his vision and reduced his ego that his tongue sometimes fumbles. . . .

6   (or 7?) He is beginning to feel alone and to hear nothing but echoes reverberating back.

—LOREN EISELEY, *The Firmament of Time*

These further illustrate the principle of subordination and coordination in paragraphs.

"Formal" Relations

There are certain fairly obvious formal ways in which we see relations among sentences; for instance, pronouns have antecedents, transitional adverbs bridge thought gaps, demonstratives "point" either backward or forward, and so on. Promising work on the analysis of discourse beyond the sentence is being done by tagmemic linguists.[15] Kenneth Pike has stated the basic position:

[15] "In tagmemic theory, the central concept in the process of partitioning patterns is the tagmeme, which can be defined as the class of grammatical forms that function in a particular grammatical relationship." A. L. Becker, "A Tagmemic Approach to Paragraph Analysis," *The Sentence and the Paragraph* (Champaign, Ill.: National Council of Teachers of English, 1966), p. 33.

A bias of mine—not shared by many linguists—is the conviction that *beyond the sentence* lie grammatical structures available to linguistic analysis, describable by technical procedures, and usable by the author for the generation of the literary works through which he reports to us his observations. The studying of these structures has thus far been left largely (but not exclusively) to the literary critic. But even a brief glance in this direction where the linguist has so much to learn has enriched my own experience. . . . The tagmemic approach to linguistic theory . . . claims that certain universal invariants underlie all human experience.[16]

The tagmemic position, then, is twofold: (1) units of discourse larger than the sentence are structurally describable; (2) units of discourse beyond the sentence mirror universal patterns of experience. We shall deal with each of these ideas in order.

The tagmemic theory of paragraphs is still in the process of evolution, but it identifies three "formal signals of the internal tagmemic structure of paragraphs": indention, equivalence classes, and lexical transitions.[17] Indention is to the paragraph what the period is to the sentence; it "sets off a unit which has a certain kind of internal structure allowable by the rules of language." Equivalence classes are best defined by example. For instance, the following paragraph.

If a faction consists of less than a [majority,] relief is supplied by the (republican principle,) which enables the [majority] to defeat *its* sinister views by regular vote. *It* may clog the administration, *it* may convulse the society; but *it* will be unable to execute and mask *its* violence under the (forms of the Constitution.) When a [majority] is included in a *faction*, the (form of popular government), on the other hand, enables *it* to sacrifice to *its* ruling passion or interest both the public good and the rights of other citizens. To secure the public good and private rights against the danger of such a *faction*, and at the same time to preserve the (spirit and form of popular government), is then the great object to which our inquiries are directed.

Three of the equivalence chains in this paragraph, then, are

faction, its, It, it, it, its, faction, it, its, faction

[majority, majority majority]

(republican principle, forms of the constitution, form of popular government, spirit and form of popular government)

The lexical transitions in the paragraph are "on the other hand" and "then." These three principles are not terribly revolutionary, but they

---

[16] Kenneth L. Pike, "Beyond the Sentence," *College Composition and Communication,* XV (October 1964), 129.
[17] Becker, *passim.*

provide a valuable insight into how paragraphs hang together. More than this, they give us a rubric whereby we can define our reasons for saying that the following is not a paragraph:

> The trees are budding. Coal is a form of carbon. He has been singing for three hours now. The world used to be round. It seems enough.[18]

But compare the following sequences:

> The glibby dribblics muriasated kleppently.

> The trees are budding. Nonetheless, coal is a form of carbon. Not only that, he has been singing for three hours now. Then, too, the world used to be round. All of this seems enough.

> Colorless green ideas sleep furiously.
> —NOAM CHOMSKY

In each of these instances, there seems to be a structural meaning, though one would be hard put to it to explain exactly what it says. Apparently, paragraphs, like sentences, have structural as well as lexical meaning:

> Green sleep ideas colorless furiously.
> Colorless green ideas sleep furiously.

A. L. Becker identifies two major paragraph forms, one made up of a topic (T), a restriction (R), and an illustration (I); the other, problem (P) and solution (S). Thus: TRI and PS. The T–R–I sequence is often reordered as I–R–T.[19] A subordinate movement is clearly question (Q) and answer (A). Thus, with the symbols T R I P S Q A, it should be possible to describe the major structure of most paragraphs. The attempt to apply these symbols to paragraphs reveals, as a matter of fact, that they do provide a method of describing the structure of discourse set off by indentions. The following paragraph, by Walter Lippmann,[20] illustrates the principle:

Topic	1	Experience since 1917 indicates that in matters of war and peace the popular answer in the democracies is likely to be No.

---

[18] Richard E. Young and Alton L. Becker, "Toward a Modern Theory of Rhetoric: A Tagmemic Contribution," *Language and Learning*, ed. Janet A. Emig *et al.* (New York: Harcourt, Brace & World, Inc., 1966), p. 202.
[19] Becker, "A Tagmemic Approach to Paragraph Analysis."
[20] From *The Public Philosophy* by Walter Lippmann, by permission of Atlantic-Little, Brown and Co. Copyright 1955, by Walter Lippmann.

Restriction	2	For everything connected with war has become dangerous, painful, disagreeable and exhausting to nearly everyone.
Restriction ("Kernel" sentence)	2	The rule to which there are very few exceptions—the acceptance of the Marshall Plan is one of them—is that at the critical junctures, when the stakes are high, the prevailing mass opinion will impose what amounts to a veto upon changing the course on which the government is at the time proceeding.

Illustration

Question	3	Prepare for war in time of peace?
Answer	4	No. It is bad to raise taxes, to unbalance the budget, to take men away from their schools or jobs, to provoke the enemy.
Question	3	Intervene in a developing conflict?
Answer	4	No. Avoid the risk of war.
Question	3	Withdraw from the area of conflict?
Answer	4	No. The adversary must not be appeased.
Question	3	Reduce your claims on the area?
Answer	4	No. Righteousness cannot be compromised.
Question	3	Negotiate a compromise peace as soon as the opportunity presents itself?
Answer	4	No. The aggressor must be punished.
Question	3	Remain armed to enforce the dictated settlement?
Answer	4	No. The war is over.

The following illustrates a problem-solution paragraph with embedded TRI constructions:

(P) How obsolete is Hearn's judgment? (S₁) (T) On the surface the five gentlemen of Japan do not themselves seem to be throttled by this rigid society of their ancestors. (R) Their world is in fact far looser in its demands upon them than it once was. (I) Industrialization and the influence of the West have progressively softened the texture of the web. Defeat in war badly strained it. A military occupation, committed to producing a democratic Japan, pulled and tore at it. (S₂) (T) But it has not disappeared. (R) It is still the invisible adhesive that seals the nationhood of the Japanese. (I) Shimizu, Sanada, Yamazaki, Kisel and Hirohito were all born within its bonds. Despite their individual work, surroundings and opinions, they have lived most of their lives as cogs geared into a group society. . . .[21]

In summary, the most useful device for analyzing the ways in which coherent discourse beyond the sentence is structured is to begin with the sentence and use it analogically. Like all analogies, this one has a point beyond which it cannot be stretched; however, it is reasonable to assume that the mental processes that bring about a sentence are either extremely similar to or identical with those that bring about larger units of discourse. Because we have no way of determining what goes on inside the human mind, we must take our observations from, and make our analysis of, the sentence as produced and larger units of discourse as produced. There are, however, obvious similarities, both structural and logical, between the sentence and the paragraph. Particularly useful is the generative view of the paragraph.

Paragraphs, according to Christensen, are structured on the principles of coordination and subordination; that is, paragraphs gain coherence because the relations among their sentences are discernibly coordinate or subordinate.

Tagmemics indicates that there are structural features which identify the paragraph and also that paragraphs conform to certain patterns derived from T, R, I, Q, A, P, S in various combinations.

So far, then, we have begun to understand a system whereby paragraphs can be analyzed as structures and whereby we can explain the relations and movements of paragraphs.

The discussion so far has developed the premise that *units of discourse larger than the sentence are structurally describable.* Now to the second premise: *units of discourse beyond the sentence mirror universal patterns of experience.* (Indeed, it is tenable to assume that the sentence itself must mirror the same universal patterns.)

Structural and Lexical Meaning

We have seen that sentences and paragraphs seem to have a structural meaning as well as a lexical meaning. That is, we cannot explain the lexical meaning of some sentences, but we "feel" that they are sentences nonetheless. Such also is true of paragraphs. In other words, there seems to be a sense of form, and, in fact, we have seen that the difference between an assertion and a proposition is largely a matter of form. The best evidence of the function and appeal of pure form is found in music. We can begin with Susanne Langer's premise:

[21] From Frank Gibney, *Five Gentlemen of Japan,* quoted in Becker.

. . . there are certain aspects of the so-called "inner life"—physical or mental—which have formal properties similar to those of music—patterns of motion and rest, of tension and release, of agreement and disagreement, preparation, fulfilment, excitation, sudden change, etc.[22]

Miss Langer argues that music's symbolism is purely formal in that it lacks connotation.[23] And connotation of a symbol "is the conception it conveys. Because the connotation remains with the symbol when the object of its denotation is neither present nor looked for, we are able to *think about* the object without reacting to it overtly at all."[24] Miss Langer's concepts are so important to the argument at hand that I shall quote two passages from her discussion:

. . . music has all the earmarks of a true symbolism, except one: the existence of an *assigned connotation*. It is a form that is capable of connotation, and the meanings to which it is amenable are articulations of emotive, vital, sentient experiences. But its import is never fixed. In music we work essentially with free forms, following inherent psychological laws of "rightness," and take interest in possible articulations suggested entirely by the musical materials.[25]

The real power of music lies in the fact that it can be "true" to the life of the feeling in a way that language cannot; for its significant forms have that *ambivalence* of content which words cannot have. This is, I think, what Hans Mersmann meant, when he wrote: "The possibility of expressing opposites simultaneously gives the most intricate reaches of expressiveness to music as such, and carries it, in this respect, far beyond the limits of the other arts." Music is revealing, where words are obscuring, because it can have not only a content, but a transient play of contents. It can articulate feelings without becoming wedded to them.[26]

What Miss Langer intended to say, I think, is this: music enunciates, not feeling, but the patterns in which feelings (as human experiences) occur. Music, then, is almost pure form, and its appeal is almost purely formal. (The arguments against music's universality being based on sensuous appeal are too involved to introduce here. Suffice it to say that if the appeal of music were purely sensual—like the appeal of creampuffs—it would appeal to the uncultured as well as to the cultured classes.) As music is almost

[22] Susanne K. Langer, *Philosophy in a New Key* (New York: New American Library, 1951), p. 193.
[23] See her chapter "On Significance in Music."
[24] Langer, p. 64.
[25] Langer, p. 203.
[26] Langer, p. 206.

pure form, it can indeed "articulate feelings without becoming wedded to them." We can readily appropriate this concept to explain the basic appeal of other arts. For instance, the bare statement of a poem's theme has little appeal; the poem itself has—and largely for formal reasons, though not, to be sure, for formal reasons exclusively.

Patterns of Experience

Our point here should be fairly obvious: all discourse—not just poetry —gains its coherence because it mirrors what Kenneth Burke calls "patterns of experience." If it does not mirror these patterns, it is incoherent or, at the very least, unsatisfying, in just the same sense that we feel an unresolved chord is unsatisfying. Seemingly, this argument is unassailable, even on biological grounds. The human mechanism is so organized that it can perceive the world only in certain ways; most obviously all perception has a spatial and temporal orientation. But we can borrow terms from the arts to describe other *forms* of experience: climax, resolution, counterpoint, modulation, tension, and so on. Now this inquiry would be futile if it were impossible to find some finite number of patterns in discourse; that is, an infinite series of discrete items always implies precisely lack of meaningful pattern.

We have seen that the paragraph can be described formally, according to patterns, and even when our available means of description fail us with regard to any given paragraph, we know that we are dealing with an entity which *ideally* we ought to be able to describe, insofar at least as a number of observers feel intuitively that the unit they are looking at is a paragraph. (Again the sentence analogy is useful. Everyone has always been able to recognize a sentence, but only in the last few years has anyone been able to approach a defensible definition of it.) As Kenneth Burke says,

> You can't possibly make a statement without its falling into some sort of pattern. Its formality can then be abstracted and named, without reference to any particular subject matter, hence can be looked upon as capable of "reindividuation" in a great variety of subject matters.[27]

Thus, on the sentence level, we can think, say, of polysyndeton as a pure form capable of an infinite number of individuations: *the storm and the stress and the sound and the fury; coffee and tea and milk and water.* On the paragraph level, we can think of the TRI pattern as an abstraction capable of an infinite number of uses. And "the sonnet" is an abstract form

[27] From the book, *A Rhetoric of Motives* by Kenneth Burke, p. 65. © 1950 by Prentice-Hall, Inc. Published by Prentice-Hall, Inc., Englewood Cliffs, New Jersey. Reprinted with the permission of the publisher.

until it becomes "a sonnet." But to speak meaningfully of form as pattern of experience we must go further, must attenuate the discussion to its outer limits.

Logical Patterns

The world may be full of relations that are beyond the power of the human mind to grasp, but insofar as man understands his world, he understands it in terms of relations: he conceives end only in relation to beginning, man only in relation to woman, and so on. And, indeed,

> the kind of world which logic assumes is that of propositions denoting states of affairs which are connected by threads of identity, so that we have unity in diversity. If A implies B, A and B cannot be altogether disparate or unconnected. But if they were completely or numerically identical without any difference we could not distinguish between A and B.[28]

The kind of world that logic assumes is the kind of *world of discourse* that the rhetorician must assume. When we speak of patterns of experience, we are speaking of logical patterns. The metaphors used to describe the artistic experience frequently throw us off the track of this basic truth: this novel is *visceral*, that poem is *sublime*, and such and such a melody is *luscious*. But, as we said before, our reaction to art *is* different from our reaction to gastric difficulties or to a creampuff. We react directly to a stomach ache or to whipped cream. But in art there is an intermediate stage—Addison saw it when he said that one of the pleasures of the imagination is contemplation of the horrible, not directly, but through the medium of art; Longinus saw it when he said that the function of the metaphor was not to persuade, but rather to transport. And the rationale of metaphysical poetry was to show God-ordained relations that had remained undiscovered, so that Donne's flea was not merely a nasty beasty, but at once a flea and a Trinitarian symbol.

Insofar as discourse is coherent, it must express logical relations that exist in the real world, including the real world of the mind. Because man is incapable of apprehending or expressing reality in any terms except those of relations, we must assume that patterns of experience are logical patterns. It cannot be objected that such a view overlooks intuition and the world of the subconscious; the whole Freudian endeavor and accomplishment was discovery of the "logic" of the subconscious.

Thus, patterns of discourse are patterns of experience, and patterns of experience are logical patterns. The most productive thinking along this line has been done by Kenneth Burke. At one point, he says,

[28] Cohen, p. 192.

There are formal patterns which distinguish our experience. They apply in art, since they apply outside of art. The accelerated motion of a falling body, the cycle of a storm, the gradations of a sunrise, the stages of a cholera epidemic, the ripening of crops—in all such instances we find the material of progressive form. Repetitive form applies to all manner of orientation, for we can continue to discuss a subject only by taking up in turns various aspects of it. (Recalling the schoolmen's subdivisions of a topic: *quis, quid, ubi, quibus auxiliis, cur, quo modo, quando*. One talks about a thing by talking about something else.) . . . though forms need not be prior to experience, they are certainly prior to the work of art exemplifying them. Psychology and philosophy may decide whether they are innate or resultant; so far as the work of art is concerned they simply *are*: when one turns to the production or enjoyment of a work of art, a formal equipment is already present, and the effects of art are involved in its utilization.[29]

To say that one needs a formal logic to apprehend these patterns of experience is a gross falsification, like saying that one needs generative grammar to understand sentences. But insofar as logic is an adequate tool for dealing with experience in the real world, it should also be an adequate tool for analyzing and systematically describing form in discourse. (Generative grammar is symbolic logic applied to the sentence.) One of the great limitations of classical rhetoric was its appropriation of Aristotelian logic; the syllogistic mode of reasoning will carry one only so far, and it is applicable to a highly limited spectrum of inquiries. It was with the development of a new logic that a new rhetoric became possible.[30]

Kenneth Burke on Form

In *Counter-Statement*, Kenneth Burke speaks tellingly of the nature of form:

> *Form* in literature is an arousing and fulfillment of desires. A work has form in so far as one part of it leads a reader to anticipate another part, to be gratified by the sequence.[31]

He discusses five kinds of form: (1) *syllogistic progression*, "the form of a perfectly conducted argument, advancing step by step . . . the form of a mystery story, where everything falls together, as in a story of ratiocination by Poe"; (2) *qualitative progression*, the form in which "the presence of

[29] Kenneth Burke, *Counter-Statement* (Los Altos, Calif.: Hermes Publications, 1953), p. 141. Excerpts from *Counter-Statement* are reprinted with the permission of the publisher and Kenneth Burke.
[30] For a discussion of classical logic in rhetoric, see Chapter 2.
[31] Burke, *Counter-Statement*, p. 157.

one quality prepares us for the introduction of another (the grotesque seriousness of the murder scene [in *Macbeth*] preparing us for the grotesque buffoonery of the porter scene)"; (3) *repetitive form*, "the consistent maintaining of a principle under new guises . . . restatement of the same thing in different ways"; (4) *conventional form*, which is self-defining (for example, the sonnet or the classical tragedy); (5) *minor or incidental forms*, such as metaphor, paradox, disclosure, reversal, contraction, expansion, bathos, apostrophe, series, chiasmus.[32]

The idea of form as an arousing and fulfillment of desires is particularly helpful because it leads directly to the question of how these desires are aroused and fulfilled. It seems that this process works on several levels. First, of course, there are purely formal requirements, most notably in music, where the appeal is based almost exclusively on form, or in the assertion, where the phrase seems almost to have an inner life struggling for completion: *The opening of the door by the girl.* Beyond the sentence level, there seems to be a kind of "grammar" of coherent sentences in, say, the paragraph, where the relation almost invariably is one of coordination or subordination. And the paragraph itself seems to have a formal consistency that can be designated by various combinations of the symbols T R I Q A P S. Thus we can summarize:

1. Sentences that relate coherently in units of discourse do so on the basis of coordination and subordination.

2. Coherent paragraphs show relations expressed by T R I Q A P S.

3. Form *qua* form may have the following configurations: syllogistic progression, qualitative progression, conventional form, repetitive form, minor forms.

Insofar as these three axioms give valid descriptions of the way in which discourse functions, they should relate to one another in a logical system, and they should be expressible in terms of logic.

But, second, logic is not merely formal; even the most abstract proposition must have meaning in the lexical sense. Any discussion of the form of discourse must therefore consider not only the interrelations of formal elements but also those of semantic elements.

It is obvious, for instance, that in the discussion of coordination and subordination of sentences within the paragraph we were not speaking of the kind of *formal* coordination and subordination discoverable by analysis within the sentence; rather, we were speaking notionally, of logical coordination and subordination. In my opinion, it is highly doubtful that any symbolic calculus will be able to express the function of a series of sentences in coherent discourse in the way that generative grammar expresses the functions within a single sentence. An example will make this

[32] Burke, *Counter-Statement*, pp. 157–161.

problem clear. Christensen analyzes the structure of the following three sentences (AC, adjective clusters; NC, noun cluster; PP, prepositional phrase; VC, verb cluster; Abs, absolute; RC, relative clause):

  1   He shook his hands,
      2   a quick shake, (NC)
         3   fingers down, (Abs.)
            4   like a pianist. (PP)   —SINCLAIR LEWIS

      2   Calico-coated, (AC)
      2   small bodied, (AC)
      2   with delicate legs and pink faces (PP)
         3   in which their mismatched eyes rolled wild and subdued, (RC)
  1   they huddled,
      2   gaudy motionless and alert, (AC)
      2   wild as deer, (AC)
      2   deadly as rattlesnakes, (AC)
      2   quiet as doves. (AC)   —WILLIAM FAULKNER

  1   The bird's eye, / , remained fixed upon him;
      2   bright and silly as a sequin (AC)
  1   its little bones, /   /, seemed swooning in his hand.
      2   wrapped . . . in a warm padding of feathers. (VC)
                   —STELLA BENSON

All of these relations are analyzable in terms of form, in terms of structural or generative grammar. But what strictly formal criteria does one use to arrive at the diagram of the following paragraph:

  1   Three hundred years have passed since Galileo, with the telescope, opened the enormous vista of the night.
      2   In those three centuries the phenomenal world, previously explored with the unaided senses, has undergone tremendous alteration in our minds.
         3   A misty light so remote as to be scarcely sensed by the unaided eye has become a galaxy.
         3   Under the microscope the previously unseen has become a cosmos of both beautiful and repugnant life, while the tissues of the body have been resolved into a cellular hierarchy whose constituents mysteriously produce the human personality.
                   —LOREN EISELEY

Our determination of subordinate and coordinate relation does not hinge on formal signs, though we can indicate formal reasons for our sense that the paragraph is coherent.

Logic and Form

Problems in logic are particularly revealing of the connection between form and meaning.[33] For instance, the following *sorites*:[34]

All dictatorships are undemocratic.
All undemocratic governments are unstable.
All unstable governments are cruel.
All cruel governments are objects of hate.
All dictatorships are objects of hate.

If this so-called Aristotelian sorites is to be valid, it must follow two formal rules: "1. No more than one premise may be negative; if a premise is negative, it must be the last. 2. No more than one premise may be particular; if a premise is particular, it must be the first." And thus also with the Goclenian sorites:

All sacred things are protected by the state.
All property is sacred.
All trade monopolies are property.
∴. All steel industries are protected by the state.

"1. No more than one premise may be negative; if a premise is negative, it must be first. 2. No more than one premise may be particular; if a premise is particular, it must be last." (For a statement of how the form of the sorites works, look at the alternation of subjects and predicates, and then refer to the definition in footnote 34.) The sorites, then, on a level extended beyond the tripartite syllogism shows both formal and semantic relations in the process of resulting in a logical proposition.[35]

However, any attempt to describe forms of discourse in terms of the old logic must be abortive, for several reasons. In the first place, to state a categorical proposition in traditional logic, one had to reduce it to a sentence of the following type: *All men are mortal* or *Some wars are destruc-*

[33] I do not pretend to be a logician. However, I think it is currently impossible for one to be a rhetorician without understanding the bases of both generative grammar and symbolic logic. For my discussion of logic, I am relying heavily upon an old and conventional, but to my mind highly useful and reliable text. I recommend it to all students of rhetoric: Morris R. Cohen and Ernest Nagel, *An Introduction to Logic* (New York: Harcourt, Brace & World, Inc., 1934). A new and abridged Harbinger edition is now out in paper. It is from this edition that I shall draw my examples, and it is this edition that I particularly recommend to students of rhetoric.

[34] Actually a kind of series of abridged syllogisms—or, more properly, of maxims—arranged in this order: the predicate of the first is the subject of the second, and so on. The conclusion brings about the logical union of the subject of the first maxim with the predicate of the last.

[35] See Cohen and Nagel, pp. 94–95.

tive. That is, one had to state a logical subject (*All men* or *Some wars*) and a logical predicate (*mortal* or *destructive*) and join them by a *copula* (*are*). To make *Germany lost the war* into a categorical proposition, one had to rearrange the statement thus: *Germany is the loser of the last war.* But this kind of sentence represents only one of the kernels or basic types from which English sentences evolve. Generative grammar indicates that there are actually four basic types of sentences:

Noun Phrase	To Be Verb	Predicate	(Adverb)
All men	are	mortal	(in this world)
Noun Phrase	Intransitive Verb		(Adverb)
All men	live		(well)
Noun Phrase	Transitive Verb	Direct Object	(Adverb)
All men	seek	fame	avidly
Noun Phrase	Copulative Verb	Predicate	(Adverb)
All men	grow	smug	(sometimes)

The categorical proposition of classical logic thus forces into one form propositions that are essentially different in grammatical structure and hence in implication; furthermore, the adherence to categorical propositions as a logical tool obviously precludes dealing with some types of statements. (How, for instance, would we turn the last pattern sentence into a categorical proposition without losing essential meaning? *All men are smug sometimes? Smugness is a characteristic of all men at some time?*) Any system of analysis that prescribes or "prestructures" must have limited usefulness; thus, the prestructuring of the rhetorical divisions of the classical oration was more destructive of discourse than it was generative; the old prescriptive grammar brought both pedagogues and scholars to an impasse. The restriction of logic in rhetoric to scholastic logic limited not only logic's usefulness but also the range of rhetoric.

As our text, then, we would adopt this statement:

Languages differ from one another in two ways: different phonetic or ideographic elements are employed in them; and different groups of ideas are expressed by fixed phonetic and graphic elements. But the experiences which a language intends to express and communicate vary in an unlimited manner, while the language employs only a finite number of fundamental linguistic elements, which may be called word stems. *It follows that every language, as we know it, must be based upon a far-reaching classification or categorization of experience. Sense impressions and emotional states are grouped on the basis of broad similarities, although no two of them are identical in every respect. Such groupings indicate, therefore, the presence of a large number of characteristics com-*

mon to each group. Furthermore, various kinds of relations between these several groupings also come to be noted, and require to be expressed in language.[36]

Moving from this text to an analysis of form in discourse, we should search for *general forms* and *relations*. Also, we should expect to be able to list principles of form and relations in a finite but generative series.

Four of the properties of relations identified by logic are *symmetry, transitivity, correlation*, and *connexity*.[37]

Symmetry. A relation is symmetrical when its reverse is true. Thus, *Jeff is as big as Tony* expresses a symmetrical relation because *Tony is as big as Jeff*. But *Italians are preferable to Germans* is asymmetrical because its converse is not true.

Transitivity. The following relation is *intransitive: Jones is the supervisor of Smith, and Smith is the supervisor of Brown*. In this example, Jones is not the supervisor of Brown. But the following relation is transitive: *Jones is richer than Smith, and Smith is richer than Brown* because we can conclude from it that Jones is richer than Brown.

Correlation. The following is a *many-many* correlation: *Jones is the friend of Smith*. Jones may have more friends than just Smith, and Smith may have more friends than just Jones. In the statement *Johann Christian Bach is a son of Johann Sebastian Bach*, we have a *many-one* relation, because J. C. Bach may—and did—have brothers and sisters, but in *J. S. Bach is the father of J. C. Bach*, we have a *one-many* relation. Finally, in *Ten is greater by one than nine*, we have a *one-one* relation.

Connexity. Connexity "depends on whether a relation holds between *every pair* of a collection or not." For instance, in the relations "greater than" or "less than" any two separate numbers will hold the same relation. Put another way: any number is either greater than or less than any other number; hence, either relation holds between any two numbers.

The exploratory question now at hand is whether these relations actually occur in paragraphs (indeed, whether they occur in any segments of discourse, regardless of how extensive). That is, are paragraphs "logical" in any systematic sense? As a beginning, let us see what happens in the rearrangement of a paragraph that we have so far worried almost to death. The original (by Malcolm Bradbury) is

> In English banks you still see money, and observe the ritual of veneration that goes with it. People are carrying money about. Others

---

[36] Cohen and Nagel, p. 117.
[37] Cohen and Nagel, pp. 113–116.

sit at tables, counting the stuff, popping it into sacks, weighing it. The visitor feels that he is at the seat of commerce, and anarchy wells up in his spirit.

But look carefully at this rearrangement:

Since in English banks you still see money, and observe the ritual of veneration that goes with it, the visitor feels that he is at the seat of commerce, and anarchy wells up in his spirit. People are carrying money about. Others sit at tables counting the stuff, popping it into sacks, weighing it.

Now we begin to see why the paragraph is indeed coherent. The first and last sentences conjoined make an enthymeme, which Aristotle defined as the rhetorical syllogism. The paragraph makes sense as a logical proposition followed by illustration—or, in rhetorical terms, followed by amplification. The unity of the paragraph comes from the fact that both the first sentence and the last are necessary to complete the logical form. The two sentences in the middle of the paragraph merely illustrate (amplify). The logical form of the paragraph in question, then, is *enthymemic*.

Now let us look at the logic of another paragraph:

The errors of public opinion in these matters have a common characteristic. The movement of opinion is slower than the movement of events. Because of that, the cycle of subjective sentiments on war and peace is usually out of gear with the cycle of objective developments. Just because they are mass opinions there is an inertia in them. It takes much longer to change many minds than to change a few. It takes time to inform and to persuade and to arouse large scattered varied multitudes of persons. So before the multitude have caught up with the old events there are likely to be new ones coming up over the horizon with which the government should be preparing to deal. But the majority will be more aware of what they have just caught up with near at hand than with what is still distant and in the future. For these reasons the propensity to say No to a change of course sets up a compulsion to make mistakes. The opinion deals with a situation which no longer exists.

—WALTER LIPPMANN[38]

By reconstructing the first three sentences, we begin to see how the logical structure of this paragraph works. Thus:

Because the errors of public opinion in these matters have a common characteristic (namely that the movement of opinion is slower than

[38] Walter Lippmann, *The Public Philosophy*.

the movement of events), the cycle of subjective sentiments on war and peace is usually out of gear with the cycle of objective developments.

We could easily put this into a syllogism, beginning *If the movement of opinion is slower than the movement of events* and so on. But we are still a good way from understanding the logical coherence of the whole paragraph. If we remove from the paragraph all sentences that are not absolutely necessary for it to make sense, we get this:

> The errors of public opinion in these matters have a common characteristic. The movement of opinion is slower than the movement of events. For this reason [these reasons] the propensity to say No to a change of course sets up a compulsion to make mistakes.

The transitivity of this sequence is apparent. Compare it with a sorites:

> All professors are handsome.
> All handsome men are married.
> All married men are well fed.
> ∴. All professors are well fed.

or a syllogism:

> If it rains, I will take my umbrella.
> If I take my umbrella, I am sure to lose it.
> ∴. If it rains, I am sure to lose my umbrella.

Reducing the truncated paragraph to a syllogism or a sorites is difficult, but logical analysis of the truncation is relatively easy. Sentence 1, sentence 2, and the prepositional phrase at the beginning of sentence 3 are identical, thus: *For this reason [the errors of public opinion in these matters have a common characteristic (the movement of opinion is slower than the movement of events)], the propensity to say No to a change of course sets up a compulsion to make mistakes.* The movement of the paragraph in question is clearly what Kenneth Burke calls syllogistic progression, and syllogistic progression clearly involves what the logicians call transitivity or its obverse, intransitivity.

The following paragraph gains coherence because of its propositional asymmetry:

> As events moved, so moved the President. He was not going to act blindly, he assured a group of antislavery churchmen; there was certainly no point in issuing proclamations that "must necessarily be inoperative, like the Pope's bull against the comet." But he did act when ends and

means were fitted, and the Emancipation Proclamation was a masterpiece of practical political sagacity. Lincoln rightly regarded the Proclamation as his chief claim to historical fame, but he was always careful to insist that it was the product of circumstances. He had responded to the changing times. In 1864 he wrote to an admirer: "I claim not to have controlled events, but confess plainly that events have controlled me."

—DAVID DONALD, *Lincoln Reconsidered*

The topic-kernel sentence can be stated as a proposition, thus: *The movements of the president followed the movements of events* or thus: *The movements of events dictated the movements of the president.* In either situation, the converse is *not* true; hence the propositions are asymmetrical. If we view the paragraph as a *discursive development of a proposition,* we can predict that the topic sentence of the paragraph in question will generate a development based on obversatives. And this is exactly what we do find. The second and third sentences of the paragraph illustrate both sides of the obversative relation. Sentences four, five, and six amplify the idea in the third sentence. Another David Donald asymmetrical paragraph:

Refusing to force reality to fit a formula, Lincoln insisted that every problem was unique, that issues could only be decided one at a time, that conflicts need be resolved only when they actually arose. Again and again he told anecdotes to illustrate his view. "The pilots on our Western rivers steer from *point to point* as they call it—setting the course of the boat no farther than they can see," he said, "and that is all I propose to myself. . . ." He was not, he told a questioner, going "to cross 'Big Muddy' until he reached it."

The kernel proposition is *Lincoln insisted on the uniqueness of every problem.* The second sentence amplifies, and the third sentence states the converse.

A symmetrical proposition like this: *Hence the ideal republic is the republic of learning* will result in a paragraph like this:

Hence the ideal republic is the republic of learning. It is the utopia by which all possible actual political republics are measured. The goal toward which we started with the Athenians twenty-five centuries ago is an unlimited republic of learning and a world-wide political republic mutually supporting each other.

—ROBERT M. HUTCHINS, *The Conflict in Education*

Its development is rearrangeable like this:

Hence the ideal republic is the republic of learning. The goal toward which we started with the Athenians twenty-five centuries ago is an unlimited republic of learning and a world-wide political republic mutually supporting each other. It is the utopia by which all actual political republics are measured.

A connexitive paragraph ought to develop this relation: in any set, *a:b :: c:d*. For instance, how might this proposition work out in a paragraph: *As exercise is to the body, so war is to the state?*

> No body can be healthful without exercise, neither natural body nor politic; and certainly, to a kingdom or estate, a just and honourable war is the true exercise. A civil war, indeed, is like the heat of a fever; but a foreign war is like the heat of exercise, and serveth to keep the body in health; for in a slothful peace, both courages will effeminate and manners corrupt. But howsoever it be for happiness, without all question for greatness it maketh to be still for the most part in arms; and the strength of a veteran army (though it be a chargeable business), always on foot, is that which commonly giveth the law, or at least the reputation amongst all neighbor states; as may well be seen in Spain, which hath had, in one part or other, a veteran army, almost continually, now by the space of six-score years.
> —FRANCIS BACON, "Of the True Greatness of Kingdoms and Estates"

A connexitive paragraph (one-one):

> *Self-government is in inverse ratio to numbers.* [Italics mine.] The larger the constituency, the less the value of any particular vote. When he is merely one of millions, the individual elector feels himself to be impotent, a negligible quantity. The candidates he has voted into office are far away, at the top of the pyramid of power. Theoretically they are the servants of the people; but in fact it is the servants who give orders and the people, far off at the base of the pyramid, who must obey. Increasing population and advancing technology have resulted in an increase in the number and complexity of organizations, an increase in the amount of power concentrated in the hands of officials and a corresponding decrease in the amount of control exercised by electors, coupled with a decrease in the public's regard for democratic procedures. Already weakened by the vast impersonal forces at work in the modern world, democratic institutions are now being undermined from within by the politicians and their propagandists.
> —ALDOUS HUXLEY, "The Arts of Selling"

By far the largest number of expository paragraphs, however, will be based on some kind of mere proposition, often categorical:

> In our time it is broadly true that political writing is bad writing.
> —GEORGE ORWELL, "Politics and the English Language"

The distinction between the loss of consideration which a person may rightly incur by defect of prudence or of personal dignity, and the reprobation which is due him for an offence against the rights of others, is not merely a nominal distinction.   —JOHN STUART MILL, *On Liberty*

That government is best which governs least.

Once again, if we view the paragraph as *a discursive development of a proposition*, we can predict that the topic sentence (or kernel sentence) of a paragraph will generate a development based on the relations and requirements of the topic-kernel sentence.

"The Connexion of Ideas"

It is important to remember that only a limited number of paragraphs will conform to the patterns of relations established by logic. Other obvious patterns are prevalent, for instance, chronology and space. Some relations are based not on the logical forms that we have outlined, but on what David Hume called "The Connexion of Ideas":

> 'Tis evident that there is a Principle of Connexion betwixt the different Thoughts or Ideas of the Mind, and that in their Appearance to the Memory or Imagination, they introduce each other with a certain Degree of Method and Regularity. . . . even in our wildest and most wandering Reveries, nay in our very Dreams, we shall find, if we reflect, that the Imagination runs not altogether at Adventures, but that there was still a Connexion upheld among the different Ideas, which succeeded each other.
> —*Philosophical Essays Concerning Human Understanding*

The Connexions that Hume recognizes are "*Resemblance, Contiguity* in Time or Place, and *Cause* or *Effect.*" Resemblance and contiguity demand no intermediary for the establishment of connection, but cause and effect demand the intermediary of experience. That is, the mind immediately perceives relations between things that look alike, act alike, and so on, and between things that are near each other in time or space. But the mind has no way of determining the connection between cause and effect except on the basis of past experience. Until the child has put his hand in the fire (cause), he will not know that the fire will burn him (effect). Whether or not Hume exhausted the possibilities of connection of ideas does not here concern us. His usefulness to us lies in his clear establishment of what we might call *a principle of extralogical coherence*—something, in fact, that we have all sensed. Thinking back to tagmemic theories, we might say that their preoccupation with the forms whereby discourse gains coherence overlooks the obvious, namely, that prediscourse (ideas, chains of mental associations, impressions) also has form brought about through "the Connexion of Ideas," and that this form must appear in the discourse that the prediscourse stimulates.[39] Thus the following brief paragraph:

> Though the Puritans have often been blamed for "blue laws" and censorship, they actually were a great deal freer than they are often given credit for. In his revealing volume *The Not-Quite Puritans* Henry Lawrence refers to no fewer than 66 confessions to fornication in one small town between 1761–65 (that was only those who confessed).
> —HOWARD MOODY, "Toward a New Definition of Obscenity"

In this microparagraph, we shall search in vain for some kind of relation based on formal logic. However, we clearly perceive that the two sentences making up the paragraph possess a close associationistic relation. In fact, Hume would be forced to classify the association as cause–effect by a dialectic something like this: the proposition in the first sentence implies a question of validity, and the question elicits an answer, in this instance, support for the proposition.

For rhetoric, the implications of a doctrine that views form as relational are important. Logic, in all its integrity, needs to be restored to rhetoric.[40] The first sentence in Aristotle's *Rhetoric* has profound implications: "Rhetoric is the counterpart of Dialectic . . . for both have to do with such things as fall, in a way, within the realm of common knowledge, things that do not belong to any one science."

The Symbol as Generating Principle

As a penultimate point—and to bring the present chapter into symmetrical alignment with the chapter on style—we shall turn again to the symbol as a generating principle:

> *The Symbol as Generating Principle.* When the poet has converted his pattern of experience into a Symbolic equivalent, the Symbol becomes a guiding principle in itself. Thus, once our poet suffering self-pity has hit upon the plot of The King and the Peasant, he finds himself with many problems remote from his self-pity. Besides showing his King as a weakling, he must show him as a King—whereupon accounts of court life. Similarly the treatment of the Peasant will entail harvest scenes, dances, descriptions of the Queen and a host of subsidiary characters. As the

[39] *Tristram Shandy* and *Ulysses* are the inevitable examples here.
[40] What happens when rhetoric is stripped of logic is best exemplified by Ramism in the sixteenth century. For a complete discussion of Ramist rhetoric, see Walter J. Ong, *Ramus: Method and the Decay of Dialogue; From the Art of Discourse to the Art of Reason* (Cambridge, Mass.: Harvard University Press, 1958).

Symbol is ramified, Symbols within Symbols will arise, many of these secondary Symbols with no direct bearing upon the pattern of experience behind the key Symbol. These secondary or ramifying Symbols can be said to bear upon the underlying pattern of experience only in so far as they contribute to the workings of the key Symbol.

Again: Symbols will be subtilized in ways not contributory to the pattern. The weak King cannot be too weak, the manly Peasant cannot be too manly—thus we find the poet "defending" to an extent the very character whom he would denigrate, and detracting from the character who is to triumph. Such considerations arise with the adoption of the Symbol, which is the conversion of an experiential pattern into a formula for affecting an audience.

The Symbol, in other words, brings up problems extrinsic to the pattern of experience behind it. The underlying pattern, that is, remains the same whether the poet writes The King and the Peasant, The Man Against the Mob, or A Saint Dying in Neglect. But in each case the Symbol is a generating principle which entails a selection of different subtilizations and ramifications. Thus, the difference between the selectivity of a dream and the selectivity of art is that the dream obeys no principle of selection but the underlying pattern, whereas art, which expands by the ramifying of the Symbol, has the Symbol as a principle of selection.[41]

Now, compare this:

While walking along the streets of one of our provincial towns before the war, I often saw in the window of a small house a pretty young girl sitting quite motionless, not moving even her eyelids, for hours and hours. She resembled an old-fashioned portrait with its dark background encased in a golden frame. This picture, never leaving my mind's eye, became a painful obsession which held me for long. In the monotony of the small town, this image seemed to me the only one worth molding into a literary form. I could think of nothing else, and for years I kept writing only this one story. Moreover, I never succeeded in completing it. (I was unable to make one step forward and away from this particular image-symbol.)[42]

It would be possible to make a whole anthology of statements about the generative power of the symbol, but not a great deal of attention has been paid to the ways in which the symbol controls and gives form to discourse. Symbolism in poetry, to be sure, has been discussed with illumination—and extensively. But the question that concerns a discussion such as the present is the possibility of a calculus of the symbol in discourse.

[41] Burke, Counter-Statement, pp. 198–200.
[42] Eric Kos, "The Writer as Craftsman," Saturday Review, XLIX (August 13, 1966), 12.

The Modes

It is classical rhetoric that provides our final insight into the structure of discourse. Traditionally, rhetoric has spoken of exposition, narration, and description as the modes of discourse. So far, we have concerned ourselves almost exclusively with exposition, for it is by far the most difficult to analyze. "Pure" narration—if there is any such thing—takes its arrangement from a time sequence: first A happened, and then B happened, and then C happened. . . . Description gains coherence from orientation in space:

> The Götaplatsen of Göteberg, a handsome square, centers around one of Milles' finest fountains. As the Kungsportsavenyn slopes gently away from it towards the harbor, it leaves a square of excellent consequence, nearer to the Piazza San Marco than anything to be found in Stockholm, the so-called "Venice of the North." Yet not one of the three buildings which frame the square, neither the City Theatre, nor the Art Museum and gallery nor the Concert Hall adorns the square with a really fine facade. The facades, indeed, embrace great absurdities; but the relation of their walls, the rise of their steps, the quality of the pavements, and perhaps above all the tubs of flowers rising bank on bank combine to support the play of water on the colossal and archaic Poseidon and his humorous entourage to produce a remarkable over-all effect. Would the effect be greater or less had the enveloping buildings been made by greater geniuses, had they more brilliance in their own individual rights? One should not be too quick to say. What can be said with confidence and with no denial of the great quality of 860 Lake Shore Drive in Chicago is that such a Miesian building would be utterly out of place on the Götaplatsen.   —JOHN ELY BURCHARD, "The Urban Aesthetic"

The purely descriptive paragraph is as rare as the purely narrative paragraph.

chapter 7

Pedagogy

The tight little society that constitutes most departments of English stands in serious danger of solipsizing itself. The typical English department, with a perversity almost unimaginable, systematically excludes from its ranks all those who admit to any interest in any aspect of human discourse but the literary—and that narrowly defined. Linguists are suspect, and by and large they have escaped to happier havens outside departments of English (where, it might be added, the linguists can solipsize themselves). Not only are rhetoricians suspect; they are downright unwelcome. Of course, most English departments do tolerate a kind of mugwump rhetorician, the kind who organizes and administers freshman courses in composition (called rhetoric because it pays some attention to grammatical correctness and fifteen methods of developing paragraphs), courses typically based on writing literary analysis and taught by people who do not have the faintest idea of what rhetoric really is. Meantime, rhetoric goes a dismal way in the typical speech department. And as everyone knows, not only will the twain of English and speech never meet, but each is only subconsciously aware of the other's existence. All of these conditions may or may not be symptomatic of a basic malady in American education; nonetheless, the situation is deplorable.

Instead of assuming its responsibility for knowledge about—and advancement of knowledge in—a subject that constitutes perhaps the longest intellectual continuity in the Western tradition, the English department sneers and turns warily and wearily back to *The Faerie Queene*.

Symptomatic of the English department's smalle rhetorique is the scant attention paid to the subject in *The College Teaching of English*.[1] Robert M. Gorrell summarizes the situation:

> Less vigorous and less dramatic than the new enthusiasm for linguistics is a small but probably significant revival of interest in rhetoric. Stimulated partly, perhaps, by the logic of the challenge that freshman English has no subject matter to justify its existence, teachers have been asking themselves what they mean by the title that most commonly designates freshman English, "Composition and Rhetoric." Answers are not the same, but they tend to be serious. There is, for instance, a new interest in the possibilities of classical rhetoric, and teachers are looking with some respect not only at Aristotle but even at figures like Blair or Whately. More promising perhaps are attempts to revise or create a rhetoric compatible with modern linguistics. Both are efforts to replace the rather thin tradition that had developed by the end of the last century, with emphasis on distinguishing the forms of discourse, practicing some set—and not entirely realistic—devices for paragraph development, and going on record in favor of unity, coherence, and emphasis. The "new rhetoricians," who actually are not yet numerous or productive enough to attract this label, are likely to put more emphasis on rhetoric of the sentence—that is, for example, on distinguishing among various kinds of English sentence patterns and evaluating their relative effectiveness. They have also shown a good deal of interest in using rhetorical approaches to literary criticism. At the moment, textbooks, papers at professional meetings, and other evidence of this sort suggest with increasing vigor that something should be done to develop a new rhetoric; there is much to be done.[2]

What Gorrell says is fair enough. And, interestingly, he says just about all that can be said about the current state of rhetoric in departments of English. *The Education of Teachers of English*[3] has no index entry under

---

[1] John C. Gerber, ed. (NCTE Curriculum Series; New York: Appleton-Century-Crofts, 1965).

[2] "Freshman Composition," *The College Teaching of English*, ed. John C. Gerber *et al.* (NCTE Curriculum Series; New York: Appleton-Century-Crofts, 1965), pp. 102–103.

[3] Alfred H. Grommon, ed. (NCTE Curriculum Series; New York: Appleton-Century-Crofts, 1963).

"rhetoric," though the book does in fact deal tangentially with the subject to some extent.

Guth's *English Today and Tomorrow* (1962) has an extensive treatment of rhetoric, but rhetoric interpreted as the teaching of writing—in effect, composition.

Guth's interpretation (or misinterpretation) of what rhetoric actually should do and can do is symptomatic of one of the basic problems in the discipline. No one will pay attention to the premise from which the study of rhetoric develops, namely, that it is the discovery of arguments for any subject whatever. It is analytical in nature. It cuts across many disciplines. And its effectiveness comes about through its two-edged ability to bring about consubstantiality and to explain that ability. Rhetoric always focuses on discourse addressed to *someone somewhere*. Thus it radiates outward (from the ivory tower or elsewhere) into the real world in which real human beings are functioning. Limiting it to the process of writing themes on "My Vacation" or "Character Development in *Lord Jim*" is as futile as limiting the study of grammar to the comma splice. Regarding this two-edged nature of rhetoric, Kenneth Burke is especially helpful. His Pentad, with its rubric Act, Agent, Agency, Scene, Purpose, puts rhetoric exactly where it belongs—in the sphere of human action. Or if rhetoric must be limited, limitation should stop at the point of discourse as a human action within a society. Further narrowing leaves us with—precisely the rhetoric that we have in freshmen English courses. Sad stuff, as any freshman will immediately admit.

A New Breed of Cat

Clearly, if rhetoric is to perform its essential function, a new breed of cat must develop. This new cat must be, above all, the antisolipsist. He needs a broad mind, endless involvement with the human situation, and a wide range of knowledge. We should like to think that he will come from and remain in the English department. And there is some reason for hope. There are stirrings. The Oregon Curriculum, for instance, has this to say:

> We believe that rhetoric is a unified art and that the student should always be conscious of that art in its unity and totality. To be sure, education proceeds sequentially and any program must proceed through a series of shifting emphasis. One kind of problem may appear to be neglected while another kind is being intensively pursued. But the unity of the rhetorical act is constantly emphasized.[4]

[4] *A Curriculum in English, Grades 7–12, Descriptive Essays by the Staff of the Oregon Curriculum Study Center* (Rev. November 1965; Eugene, Ore.: 1965).

The focus of the Nebraska curriculum is narrower than that of the Oregon curriculum; the Nebraska materials confine themselves to style, in an approach developed largely by Professor Francis Christensen. But Christensen's work is, of course, crucial to a new rhetoric.

However hopeful the work now being done may appear, there is, nonetheless, virtually no curriculum in English that includes a segment that might fairly be termed "rhetoric" in our sense of the word. There are courses in composition that more or less systematically talk about organization, style, and invention; there are courses in criticism that *deal with* analysis of discourse; there are courses in literature that analyze discourse. But there is no true rhetoric. The task of this book for the next few pages will be to outline a course in modern rhetoric and to justify it.

As a beginning, we can turn to Jerome S. Bruner:

> How conceive of language as a calculus of thought for ill-formed problems—problems, that is, without unique solutions? I should prefer to look at it from the point of view of the functions that language serves the speaker outwardly, and then to consider which of these functions also serve internally to help us organize our thoughts about things. . . . The shape or style of a mind is, in some measure, the outcome of internalizing the functions inherent in the language we use.[5]

This is a specifically rhetorical view of language, and one that is particularly apt as a starting point for a curriculum in rhetoric.

No evidence necessarily demonstrates that studying rhetoric makes more effective writers and speakers, just as no evidence conclusively demonstrates that the study of grammar makes more effective writers and speakers. As a matter of fact, common sense tells us that one might be able to *describe* a language with great accuracy and nonetheless be relatively inept in the *use* of that language. Analogically, one might be a first-rate rhetorician (for example, student of rhetoric and analyst of discourse) without being a first-rate rhetorician (let us say, effective speaker or writer). We can assume, however, that "how to" courses in speaking and writing will produce more effective speakers and writers. "The Elements of Public Speaking" is more or less effective in its aims; "Freshman Composition" to a greater or lesser degree accomplishes what it sets out to do. (Many would argue that its results are more "lesser" than greater!) But the "how to" portion of rhetoric is a minor part of the whole subject that needs little justification. The "how to" part of rhetoric we can call "Public Speaking" and "Expository Writing," or whatever, according to the predilections of

---

[5] Jerome S. Bruner, *Toward a Theory of Instruction* (Cambridge, Mass.: The Belknap Press of Harvard University Press, 1966), pp. 105–107. The excerpts from *Toward a Theory of Instruction* are reprinted with the permission of the publisher.

the faculties offering these subjects. "Rhetoric" will be a broader kind of course; it will be (a) historical, (b) cultural, (c) theoretical, (d) analytical, (e) practical. Most present-day rhetoric courses are only "practical."

The reasons for this drastically different kind of course are many. Perhaps the most important is that rhetoric is a cultural subject that played an important role in the development of Western thought and culture. To be unaware of the rhetorical tradition is to be largely unaware of "the outcome of internalizing the functions inherent in the language we use," that is, the Western mentality. Rhetoric, like grammar, needs no justification. It has exactly the same reason for being in any curriculum as has history, philosophy, or psychology. Even the most "impractical" discipline has practical fallout, but no one would think of justifying courses in psychology on the basis of their immediately practical application in, say, salesmanship.

Another reason for a course in rhetoric borders on the practical: rhetoric, as we have said, is in part an analytical art; it provides the means for systematically discovering the reasons for the effectiveness of discourse. In this sense, literary criticism is practical, and, in this sense, literary criticism and rhetoric overlap. In the ideal situation, in fact, literary criticism would be rhetorical criticism and vice versa. Any attempt to fragment the study of discourse—poems, novels, plays, TV ads, whatever—must also fragment total understanding. For this reason, Kenneth Burke's rhetoric points toward the ideal situation.

Rhetoric also, as we have pointed out, has its "how to" aspect; that is, courses in public speaking and expository writing are also a segment of rhetoric. One of the main reasons for studying rhetoric as a discipline in itself is to bring some method into the teaching of practicum, to make the course in freshman English less chaotic and also to make it more intellectually justifiable as a valid pursuit in the university, the high school, or even the grade school.

A New Course in Rhetoric

A course in rhetoric would systematically deal with *theory, analysis,* and *practicum.* In grammar, for instance, a theory will attempt to explain how the sentences of a language are generated. Analysis will use this theory to explain the unique characteristics of sentences as produced. And practicum will use the principles of the grammar to help students produce better sentences. Clearly, at some level the theory itself is most important. Practicum, for instance, can take place in the classroom even if the students do not know the theory, for the teacher, who does know the theory, can use its principles to direct the students' efforts; but without the theory, the practicum is impossible. Whether practicum is more efficient if the students understand the theory is a question that need not concern us. The arguments for including grammatical and rhetorical theory in curricula must not be on the level of arguments that include, say, driver training; that is, there are historical, philosophical, and cultural reasons for including the study of both grammar and rhetoric in the curriculum at any and every level.

These statements bring us to the question, "At what point in the spectrum of education should rhetoric be introduced?" We can answer this question with another: "At what point should mathematics be introduced?" Obviously and simply, the earlier the better. Modern learning theory indicates that subject matter of great complexity can be "programmed" for virtually any grade level or any level of intellectual development. To turn once again to Bruner:

> The revolution in our view of the educational process itself is, I think, premised upon several new and startling conceptions. At least they are new in their application and they are certainly startling when put bluntly. One of them has to do with our conception of the child and his intellectual processes. Consider the working hypothesis that *any subject matter can be taught to anybody at any age in some form that is honest.* The question of "when to teach what" must, then, be premised upon some more discerning criterion than "readiness." As I observe the various efforts to construct curricula, I sense that this is indeed the prevailing doctrine. But interestingly enough, it is not a point of view that denies the striking differences between the mind of the child, of the adolescent, and of the adult. Rather, it is a recognition of the fact that, with sufficient effort and imagination, any topic can be rendered into an honest form that is appropriate to the level of comprehension of students at any age.[6]

The first step in creating a curriculum in rhetoric, then, is determining what should be taught, not necessarily how to teach it at any given level.

In fact, the eternal dissatisfaction with present-day bastardized rhetoric courses stems, not primarily from a lack of know-how in methodology, but rather from the lack of a coherent subject matter to which methodology can be applied. Good teachers are good teachers of writing. Great teachers are great teachers of writing. And each has his own method for the "how to" part of rhetoric; but once again we must stress that our concern must go beyond the "how to." Rhetoric is not only—perhaps even not primarily— a "performing art."

The curriculum about to be presented is the subject matter that a satisfactory course in rhetoric should contain. The outline could serve for a course in grade school, high school, or college, depending on the speed

[6] Jerome S. Bruner, "Introduction." *Revolution in Teaching*, A. De Grazia and D. Sohn, Eds. (New York: Bantam, 1964), p. 2.

of presentation and the depth of probing of each unit. Such a rationale is amply justified by modern learning theory.

A curriculum in rhetoric will deal with

Theory: Perhaps enough has been said to justify the inclusion of rhetorical theory. But theory becomes "practical" when it provides both a rationale and a framework for a subject. Our curriculum will use theory both as rationale and as framework.

Analysis: Analysis stands as the intermediary between theory and practice. The venerable (but valid) doctrine of *imitatio* is predicated on emulation *after* analysis. Furthermore, one of rhetoric's most useful aspects is its analytical nature, allowing us to understand the effectiveness of arguments regarding any subject whatever. Just as rhetorical theory would ideally include a theory of mass media, so rhetorical analysis would apply itself to mass media. Just as rhetorical theory would contain a theory of style, so analysis would be applied to style.

Practicum: Rhetoric, as we have said, is also "how to." The curriculum in this book (centered as it is on written discourse) will then suggest a course in composition.

Aristotle

Aristotle's centrality cannot be overstressed. If the rhetorical tradition is worth preservation, *The Art Of Rhetoric* is worth preserving as the first monument in that tradition. I am fully aware that many will wince at the idea of beginning with *the* classical text. But such narrowness is only evidence that the excitement of Aristotle's work needs to be rediscovered. Grade-school children, of course, should not be expected to read the *Rhetoric*, any more than they should be expected to read Euclid. But for high school and college students, Aristotle provides a viable and exciting place to start. In my chapter "Aristotle and Extrapolation" I have attempted something of what can be done with the *Rhetoric*. Undeniably, in it stands the beginning of systematic rhetorical theory. (And I would *not* be averse to abbreviation and summarization.)

Analysis. The *Rhetoric* is concerned with proofs, but the weight of the book focuses on the various kinds of "artistic" proofs in arguments, that is, proofs that must be invented. It is natural, then, to turn the analytical part of the curriculum at this point to discovering various kinds of artistic proofs in discourse. For instance, a class might analyze in detail some kind of recommendation that follows a basically factual report. The recommendations derive from the "facts," but their force depends upon the artistic proofs with which they are presented. A State of the Union Message is a recommendation of precisely this sort.

Practicum. The practicum in any course in rhetoric will be a continuum that is not amenable to fragmentation. But pedagogy in writing can shift its emphasis from unit to unit. Hence, in a suggested situation for practicum, we are speaking of emphasis, not absolutes. The essay—or the poem, play, or short story—is a Gestalt; one cannot judge its rhetorical effectiveness on the basis of one criterion, or even on an isolable set of criteria. But one might, for instance, assign essay topics that will force the student to develop artistic proofs. For instance, "Only Pass and Fail Grades Should Be Assigned in College" is a topic that must be supported by artistic arguments. The point here is not so much the exact assignment as the theory that assignments in practicum should emphasize the theoretical nature of the focus of the unit.

Materials. I have already recommended the Lane Cooper translation of Aristotle's *Rhetoric* (New York: Appleton-Century-Crofts, Inc., 1932, 1960). A workable introduction to classical rhetoric in general is Edward P. J. Corbett, *Classical Rhetoric for the Modern Student* (New York: Oxford University Press, 1965). This is a much more useful book than is Richard E. Hughes and P. Albert Duhamel, *Rhetoric, Principles and Usage* (Englewood Cliffs, N.J.: Prentice-Hall, Inc., 1962).

There are, of course, no texts that present classical rhetoric for the grade-school child. One of the great problems in the long-expected rhetorical revival is the preparation of materials for all levels. Halting steps are now being taken—many of them, unfortunately, destructive of rhetoric as it ought to be conceived. As any publisher's list indicates, a plethora of books attempts to offer better "how to" approaches to writing and speaking. Few of them even tangentially relate to rhetoric as it should be conceived.

Logic

Much of the present volume has concerned the relation of the new logic to rhetoric. Rhetoric and logic have always been sister arts, "counterparts," as Aristotle put it. But the new logic, with its offshoot, generative grammar, has such a direct relation to rhetoric that it is now time to bring the formal study of logic back into the course in rhetoric. Logic concerns, really, what Kenneth Burke calls "patterns of experience." As the present volume has indicated, there is a synapse at which studies of form, style, and invention merge with symbolic logic. The course in rhetoric, then, should exploit this interrelation and enter into "inventio," "dispositio," and style only after the possibilities of new logic have been explored. Our curriculum, then, would take Aristotle as an introduction, a prelude, to set the tone, to state the theme. The course proper would begin with logic— but not merely symbolic logic. The argument here is fairly intricate. Symbolic logic gives hope for showing relations, and relations explain form—

in the phrase, in the sentence, in the paragraph, and beyond. Rhetoric invariably focuses on form. But logic of the symbolic variety does not provide the bread-and-butter rubric necessary for analyzing the chicanery of sophists, nor does it supersede classical logic at all points. Our curriculum will recommend that theory center on abstract logic, that analysis center on logical fallacies, and that practicum center on the enthymeme.

But to take questions in their proper order, we can say that symbolic logic provides the basis for a study of style and organization; a less rigorous kind of logic works perfectly well for analytical and practical purposes. If, however, it is the duty of rhetoric to study style and organization, the theoretical basis for that study is symbolic logic. Thus, a good part of the curriculum in rhetoric will deal with symbolic logic.

Analysis. As Aristotle pointed out, one of the great persuasive devices is the fallacious argument, the fallacy of which the audience does not perceive. It is most instructive to search arguments for their logical fallacies. Ads, presidential speeches, poems—wherever discourse transpires, so do logical fallacies, either intentionally or unintentionally. Another kind of analysis that might well be introduced with the unit on logic is the search for logical "forms" in discourse.

Practicum. Aristotle called the enthymeme "the rhetorical syllogism." The syllogism and enthymeme generally illustrate a *transitive* logical relation, the kind that is easily expressed in a topic sentence such as the following: *Because the society transcends the individual, each man is committed as a social being.* This kind of enthymemic topic sentence implies both organization and development for a piece of discourse. The very relation set up by the enthymeme will control to a large extent the form of a piece of discourse based on it. Taking the enthymeme as its starting place, then, this unit would center on "argumentative" writing, each essay developing from a clear-cut enthymemic statement of the central idea. The virtue of such an exercise is that it is not "artificial" and that it clearly illustrates an elementary principle of form. In fact, the unit will serve as a "way of getting into" the units on grammar and form.

Materials. The student will have been introduced to the enthymeme in Aristotle's *Rhetoric.* It is difficult, however, to judge modern texts in symbolic logic. Many seem to be extremely rough going for the layman, but Morris R. Cohen and Ernest Nagel, *An Introduction to Logic* (New York: Harcourt, Brace & World, Inc., 1962) is, as noted earlier, a workable introduction to both classical logic and symbolic logic. In *An Introduction to Transformational Grammars* (New York: Holt, Rinehart and Winston, Inc., 1964), Emmon Bach includes a chapter, "The Form of Grammars," which deals specifically with logical relations as they pertain to grammar. This book, like several others in the field, however, is only for the intrepid. A real effort needs to be made in the production of theoretically and pedagogically sound texts that conjoin the new logic with the subject matter of rhetoric.

Grammar

Enough has been said in the present volume, perhaps, to indicate the service that generative grammar provides to rhetoric. We can reiterate: the rhetorician must know generative grammar. Thus, in the new curriculum, grammar as well as logic will be subsumed as "departments" of the new rhetoric. Approaching language as it does from the standpoint of symbolic logic, generative grammar provides a synapse between matter and manner—that is, between logical discourse and the style in which the discourse is presented. In fact, symbolic logic, as we have demonstrated, forms a node, from which branch studies of the rationality of discourse, the style of discourse, and the form of discourse. As we have seen, the importance of the new grammar lies, first, in its ability to analyze style precisely and, second, in the kind of suggestions that it provides concerning form in discourse. On the one hand, we can use the word "generative" as a metaphor and trace its implications into such diverse areas as the difference between assertion and proposition and the nature of the metaphor as a "generative" element in discourse. The explorations that took place in the present book were only beginnings, only hints about the undiscovered territory that must lie ahead. Generative grammar may well be regenerative of rhetoric. Thus, the new student in the new course in rhetoric will master generative grammar, and generative grammar will always be presented under rhetorical auspices—where it actually belongs.

Analysis. Criticism is analytical. But it also serves a pedagogical function. That is, when a person understands why discourse functions, he stands some chance of making his own discourse function. When he understands what goes into style, he can develop *a* style. Generative grammar provides a tool for analysis. Students of rhetoric should use it constantly in their probing to determine the effects of discourse brought about through style.

Practicum. The application of generative grammar to practicum, to the "how to" element in any course, is, fortunately, well advanced. By the time this book is published, Professor Francis Christensen's materials will be available, and, as I have elsewhere indicated, they are extremely important. Generative grammar serves as a practical and effective way of teaching style. As Christensen demonstrates, the problem of developing style is one of "sentence building." Already available through NCTE is *The Rhetoric of Short Units of the Composition: A. The Rhetoric of the Sentence* (Nebraska Curriculum Development Center: 1965). These materials, it seems to me, clearly indicate the future in composition courses insofar as the courses focus on developing style.

Form

Again, the present book has discussed theories of form in the light of logic and grammar. A new rhetoric, it seems to me, must maintain this relation, but it must also call upon fairly traditional principles of analysis. These principles are well known: orders of development, orders of arrangement (harking back more or less to classical doctrine), rubrics for getting under way and concluding. Furthermore, a word of caution is necessary: form seldom adheres to logical models; it develops from the process of association of ideas in Hume's sense. Thus, the study of form will be more dialectical than logical. But the idea that there are "patterns of experience" nonetheless guides this dialectic into productive channels.

A theory of form in the new rhetoric will be eclectic and undogmatic; it will also be relational, making tie-ups with logic and grammar.

Analysis. The theory of form becomes analytical when it turns to the analysis of form in discourse. Simply, then, a curriculum in rhetoric will devote some time to the analysis of form in various kinds of discourse.

Practicum. In practicum, form is a matter of emphasis. Pedagogy naturally shifts its focus toward the organization of the student's writing while the class is studying theories of form.

Materials. Most crucial is Kenneth Burke's *Lexicon Rhetoricae*, in *Counter-Statement* (Los Altos, Calif.: Hermes Publications, 1953), first published in 1930. *The Sentence and the Paragraph* (NCTE: 1966) is also extremely valuable. As I have indicated, Langer's *Philosophy in a New Key* and Cohen's *Preface to Logic* were the books that served to stimulate my thinking, but they are only tangentially related to the problem of form in rhetoric, and establishing this relation requires a fairly intricate chain of dialectic. The study of form should also probably draw heavily on modern psychology, but so far no one has made the necessary connection. One must reiterate again and again that there is a tremendous need for texts at all levels.

Invention

The theory of invention will do well to start from Aristotle's *Rhetoric*, but from that center it must radiate in all directions. Perhaps, indeed, invention is not a proper department for rhetoric; it involves the whole man and the whole world of knowledge and feeling. The present book, avowedly at least a fragment of a new rhetoric, conspicuously excludes the venerable department of invention, except by the way. In fact, invention is more profitably pursued in the particular than in general; that is, finding the "topics" in a given piece of discourse is more profitable than the attempt to discover topics in general. Thus, the unit on invention will concentrate on analysis and practicum.

Analysis. The rhetorician takes as his province the discovery of means of persuasion. This means that, like the literary critic, he is concerned with universals and particulars. Theory tells why poetry ought to have such and such elements to be successful; critical analysis discovers the elements of such and such a successful poem. The analytical function of invention is the reason for the countless "readers" that are published year in and year out. The service of rhetoric in this kind of analysis will be to put the materials in a context, to give them a point of view and a purpose.

Practicum. In the practice of writing, the student must sooner or later pay careful attention to the kinds of arguments that he uses in his persuasion. A unit on invention, then, will set the student to listing and evaluating the "topics" in his own essays and in those of his classmates.

Materials. There are diverse sources that discuss methods of development; practically every freshman "rhetoric" does so. One book that for obvious reasons I am partial to is *The Relevance of Rhetoric* by Edward V. Stackpoole and W. Ross Winterowd.

Rhetorical Stance

Rhetorical stance, of course, involves the relation of the rhetorician as writer or speaker to his audience. It involves estimating the audience and then using rhetorical techniques to achieve consubstantiality with listeners or readers. In fact, precious little in rhetorical theory really addresses itself to the problem of rhetorical stance. A paradigm and parody of rhetorical stance is motivational research, which is then translated into an advertisement that will appeal to a given audience for a given reason. And because advertising, too, is rhetoric, an introduction to that most lugubrious of lugubrious subjects might well come into the theory of rhetoric. More appealing is the possibility that the classical doctrine of stance gives for bringing into rhetorical theory a study of the media. Marshall McLuhan is, in a fundamental sense, a rhetorician, and the social and political ramifications of mass rhetoric make it so important that it cannot be overlooked. Thus, we might suggest that the study of rhetorical stance move outward from a position that might be called—as I elsewhere call it—"the intimate audience" to the study of the relation between mass media and audience. This department would, then, involve a study of the media in McLuhan's sense that "the medium is the message."

At a recent symposium, Arthur Knight suggested to a group of English teachers that their departments have the responsibility of teaching the film. There was a general uproar; English departments had clearly defined their role, and that role had nothing to do with the movies. But on second thought: Can we ignore film? And TV? And newspapers? Mr. Knight's question was this: Where better might the film be handled than in the

English department? I personally agree with the premise that the whole function of the English department should be eclectic; the English department should serve as the ecumenical center for a fragmented campus. A revitalization of rhetoric may serve as the Vatican II to get the movement under way.

Analysis. The theory of rhetorical stance will provide an analytical instrument for stance in discourse. The theory of the media will provide an instrument for the analysis of media and the reasons for their effects on people. A unit on rhetorical stance, then, will turn to analyzing movies, TV, newspapers—mass media in general.

Practicum. To paraphrase Mark Twain, one gains a world of experience by picking up a cat by the tail. The best way to learn about the function of media is to use media. I should recommend, then, that students actually practice their rhetoric by making experimental video tapes, films, and slide presentations. I would recommend that they step out of the realm of the strictly verbal into the realm of the verbal-visual, into the realm of what is now being called multimedia.

History

Because rhetoric is a cultural subject, students should have some grasp of its history and development. They should understand, as an absolute minimum, the classical rhetoric of Aristotle and Cicero; Ramism in the Renaissance; and neoclassical rhetoric. The value of such knowledge is not altogether theoretical; there is a good deal of practical fallout from the study of Cicero or Hugh Blair. There is a good deal to be learned from understanding the realignments that Ramus made. Much about force and counterforce in intellectual history is to be learned from the development of the "new" rhetoric in the eighteenth century. My chapter on the neoclassical period indicates how a given period can serve as a paradigm for wide-ranging problems.

Analysis. A given rhetorical climate produces a given kind of discourse. Analysis of Burke's *Speech on Conciliation* as a piece of neoclassical rhetoric illuminates the text itself and the rhetoric that produced it. In a curriculum, the history of rhetoric could well be accompanied by the analysis of pieces of rhetoric from each period.

Practicum. There is no particular reason for relating the students' practice in writing to the study of the history of rhetoric. The point is this: the student should keep writing, week in and week out.

Esthetics

The virtue of a rhetorical approach to literature is that it takes the subject out of the ivory tower and puts it exactly where it belongs, namely,

in the middle of humanity. Our chapter on rhetoric in literature summarizes the problems involved in a rhetorically oriented esthetic. However,
in any such discussion, Kenneth Burke is crucial. His work has given both
esthetics and rhetoric a new direction. Esthetic theory, then, would be
largely the theory of Kenneth Burke.

Analysis. Rhetorical analysis always keep its eye on the *effect on an
audience.* Thus the rhetorical analysis of literature would invariably focus
on the means that literature uses to bring about some reaction in the
audience.

Practicum. It is at this point that imaginative writing properly
enters the curriculum. As Francis Christensen says, the modern composition course has sold its soul for a pot of message. In any course in rhetoric,
the student should have the experience of inventing through the imagination: "Perhaps the main distinction between imagination and invention
lies in the analytical nature of the latter. The inventive process is synthetic
while the imaginative is artificial."[7] Limiting the writing experience to the
synthetic is another pruning that characterizes the narrowness of modern
curricula.

Materials. Virtually everything of Kenneth Burke's is important, as
is Wayne C. Booth's *The Rhetoric of Fiction* (Chicago: The University of
Chicago Press, 1961). Once again, there are no pedagogical texts dealing
with the esthetics of rhetoric or with rhetoric in literature. One of the
needs in the study of rhetoric is a systematic presentation of the contribution that Kenneth Burke has made to the field.

Schematically, the curriculum here tentatively proposed might look like
this:

Theory	Analysis	Practicum
Aristotle, *The Art of Rhetoric*	Artistic and inartistic proofs in arguments	Developing artistic proofs in essays
Grammar	Style	"Sentence building"
Form	Organization	Organization
Invention	Arguments	Development
Rhetorical stance (Media)	Mass persuasion	Work in production
History of rhetoric	Discourse as a product of its age	
Esthetics	Rhetoric in literature	Imaginative writing

[7] Edward V. Stackpoole and W. Ross Winterowd, *The Relevance of Rhetoric* (Boston:
Allyn and Bacon, Inc., 1966), p. 342.

It must be stressed that this curriculum could be implemented on any level. The need, of course, is for materials that will make rhetoric viable at *any* level. This need is perhaps not so great at the university level as at other levels, however. One problem with the current "rhetoric" course is that it is soft in the center. In the first place, it has become a mere service course, teaching putative biologists, engineers, chemists, and so on how to communicate lucidly enough to get through the baccalaureate degree. In the second place, the course itself has no respectable subject matter; the text is usually that dullest of all books, the handbook. When the class becomes lively, the talk is usually about sociology, or literature *qua* literature, or politics—or anything but rhetoric.

The curriculum outlined is an attempt to present rhetoric in a form that is intellectually honest and pedagogically feasible. But it is not the only, and perhaps not even the best, possibility. It does, however, illustrate a way in which the subject matter of rhetoric can be restored to the curriculum. And in this day and age, that is to be devoutly desired.

A Theory of Pedagogy

A theory of pedagogy for rhetoric would be subsumed under a general theory of pedagogy or instruction, a metatheory. When we make the proper alignment, we find that a strange thing happens: the metatheory can be reinterpreted rhetorically, so that we have a rhetoric of pedagogy. The congruence of rhetoric and pedagogy is not after all strange, nor is a treatise on rhetorical pedagogy an exotic hybrid. Almost all rhetorics have been heuristic; thus Quintilian says, "It is my design to lead my reader from the very cradle of speech through all the stages of education which can be of any service to our budding orator till we have reached the very summit of the art." And again:

> My first book will be concerned with the education preliminary to the duties of the teacher of rhetoric. My second will deal with the rudiments of the schools of rhetoric and with problems connected with the essence of rhetoric itself. The next five will be concerned with invention, in which I include Arrangement. The four following will be assigned to Eloquence, under which head I include Memory and Delivery. Finally there will be one book in which our complete orator will be delineated; as far as my feeble powers permit, I shall discuss his character, the rules which should guide him in undertaking, studying and pleading cases, the style of his eloquence, the time at which he should cease to plead cases and the studies to which he should devote himself after such cessation."[8]

---

[8] Quintilian, *The Institutio Oratoria of Quintilian*, trans. H. E. Butler (4 vols.; New York: G. P. Putnam's Sons, 1920), I, 21–22.

Aristotle and Cicero, too, had a heuristic concern. The point, however, is that a new rhetoric needs a new heuristic. In the following pages I shall suggest the direction that a theory of rhetorical instruction might take.

The discussion will be based on that thoroughly remarkable book, *Toward a Theory of Instruction*, by Jerome S. Bruner. And we shall take as our text Bruner's statement that "*the heart of the educational process consists of providing aids and dialogues for translating experience into more powerful systems of notation and ordering*"[9]; that is, the heart of the educational process is rhetorical. In fact, what is to follow might well be termed a rhetorical reinterpretation of Bruner's theory.

Bruner tells us that the etiology of his work involved investigation of the ways—the "strategies"—whereby people attain concepts. What impressed Bruner was the "logic-like or 'rational' quality" of the way in which conceptualization takes place: "One could discern systematic strategies in behavior that had the quality and creases of well practiced rule-governed routines."[10] This discovery is a psychological basis for talking about the "patterns of experience" that are so important to rhetorical theory. Human beings, apparently, do conceptualize according to "forms" that are both recurrent and describable; that is, the mind organizes experience into concepts, and the organization follows given patterns. Because there are patterns of conceptualization, there is also a "logic" of conceptualization, for "pattern" means a series of discernible relations.

Bruner has developed a six-point rubric that describes the process of intellectual growth. This rubric is "rhetorical" in nature, though Bruner does not say so:

1. *Growth is characterized by increasing independence of response from the immediate nature of the stimulus.*

2. *Growth depends upon internalizing events into a "storage system" that corresponds to the environment.*

3. *Intellectual growth involves an increasing capacity to say to oneself and others, by means of words or symbols, what one has done or what one will do.*

4. *Intellectual development depends upon a systematic and contingent interaction between a tutor and a learner. . . .*

5. *Teaching is vastly facilitated by the medium of language, which ends by being not only the medium for exchange but the instrument that the learner can then use himself in bringing order into the environment.*

6. *Intellectual development is marked by increasing capacity to deal with several alternatives simultaneously, to tend to several sequences dur-*

[9] Bruner, *Toward a Theory of Instruction*, p. 21.
[10] Bruner, *Toward a Theory of Instruction*, p. 2.

ing the same period of time, and to allocate time and attention in a manner appropriate to these multiple demands.[11]

These "bench marks" are rhetorical in a number of ways. First, and above all, they point to language as a mediator, between both persons and experience and the person and others. Any such view of language is basically a rhetorical view. Language mediates, for instance, between the response and the immediate nature of the stimulus, it mediates in transferring experience from person to person, and it mediates in the "systematic and contingent interaction" between tutor and learner. The bench marks also point to conceptualization as the ability to deal with contingencies, with the gray areas that constitute probabilities, not certainties (said Aristotle, "And we see that, in Rhetoric, for the most part merely usual and contingent conclusions must be drawn from premises. . ."). It is also the function of rhetoric to mediate between stimulus and response. In matters of public polity, for instance, rhetoric stands between the stimulus (say, an insult to the national pride) and the most direct response (a war).

But Bruner's theory of instruction is even more productive for the rhetorician. He points out that representation occurs through a hierarchy of methods. The first, most basic, and simplest, is through action, the *enactive*. It is virtually impossible to teach anyone to play golf except via the enactive method. Second, is the *iconic*, or, to be blunt, the pictorial. Third is the *symbolic*, that method of representation or conceptualization to which language belongs. This method is

> . . . almost always highly productive or generative in the sense that a language or any symbol system has rules for the formation and transformation of sentences that can turn reality over on its beam ends beyond what is possible through actions or images.[12]

Now, if we accept Bruner's thesis that the language internalized largely controls the kind of conceptualizing that man is capable of, we can conclude that man both metaphorically and literally has a generative intellect, in just the same sense that we can say a grammar or a rhetoric is generative. This conclusion leads to an extremely important hypothesis about pedagogy: any *closed rhetorical system [such as those found in most handbooks] falsifies the very nature of the human mind.* Or, more simply and directly, in the absence of a true generative rhetoric that has the inherent systematic possibilities of generative grammar, the business of teaching rhetorical strategies takes place best via inductive analysis of texts. Let me restate my argument in other terms. Insofar as Bruner is correct in his hypotheses

[11] Bruner, *Toward a Theory of Instruction*, pp. 5–6.
[12] Bruner, *Toward a Theory of Instruction*, p. 11.

about the nature of learning (and hence the nature of the human mind), we can say that the learner will structure a system of rhetoric in just the same way that he structures a system of grammar that gives him the competence to use the language, though he may not be able to describe it. Every speaker has, in fact, an internal generative grammar that he can use intuitively. The external grammar merely provides an accurate description of the processes of the internal, intuitive grammar. The handbook of rhetoric, however, is so limited and limiting that it may well have just the opposite effect from that desired; namely, it may keep the student from gaining strategies that he can add to his internal generative rhetoric.

Thus, a system of pedagogy for rhetoric would lay heavy stress upon the analysis of prose of all kinds. It is in this way, and this way only, that the student will discover strategies that he can internalize and integrate into his own system of rhetoric. More bluntly: the handbook-dominated course is likely to be a failure.

In his chapter, "Teaching a Native Language," Bruner also has suggestions for the rhetorician. Whenever one's capability in language expands, he

> . . . has acquired not only a way of saying something but a powerful instrument for combining experiences, an instrument that can now be used as a tool for organizing thoughts about things to form concepts. It can equally be said that the combinatorial or productive property of language is an invitation to take experience apart and put it together again in new ways.[13]

But not only does language provide this "ordering" device for the data of the world; it also has the strictly rhetorical, "phatic" purpose of "keeping in touch" for the sake of keeping in touch—best illustrated by the "uh-huh" that lets the listener on the other end of a telephone connection know that we are still there and with him. It is best, as a matter of fact, not to separate the two kinds of language functions, for every discourse situation involves a phatic element. Thus pedagogy in discourse must stress not only the pure informational and formational value of language but also its "phatic," socializing nature. In actual practice, this means that *pedagogy should stress discourse as addressed to someone somewhere.* In a course in rhetoric, then, stance would be a pervading concept. In analysis, students must judge the kind of audience that the piece is trying to reach; in writing, the student must, in Bruner's words,

> . . . detach himself from immediate social interaction altogether and conjure up in his own mind a situation appropriate to the written words with which he is dealing.[14]

13 Bruner, *Toward a Theory of Instruction*, p. 105.
14 Bruner, *Toward a Theory of Instruction*, p. 111.

I have dwelt in some detail on Bruner's book, for I think that it illustrates how any discussion of human mental activity, particularly of language activity, becomes inevitably rhetorical. But from *Toward a Theory of Instruction* we can derive certain principles that lead us toward a theory of instruction in rhetoric, that is, toward a *modus operandi* for using the curriculum.

First, it is quite obvious that learning "readiness" is not an absolute concept. The child is ready to learn any subject at an early age, provided instruction is broken down into a series of steps that the youngster can master. Thus, it would seem logical to begin instruction in rhetoric—both as analysis and as "how to"—early in the school years. Specifically, children should be reading analytically and writing in the elementary grades. And these learning activities should take place in the context of a real rhetoric. It seems to me inevitable, for instance, that logic will come back into the curriculum, and I see no reason why it should not enter in, say, the third grade. California recently opted for a grade school language curriculum in generative grammar, a notable step that would have been more meaningful if actual work in the grammar had been preceded by work with symbolic logic. Grade-school children should also have the experience of reading analytically, in precisely the same way that college students learn to analyze prose in the best courses. As we have seen, it is in this way that the child will develop his own "internal" generative rhetoric.

Education, Bruner tells us, is social invention. The great need is to go beyond the imparting of skills: "A curriculum should involve the mastery of skills that in turn lead to the mastery of still more powerful ones, the establishment of self-reward sequences."[15] That is, a "skill" is valuable insofar as it gives the possibility of mastering a skill of a high order, so that the skill itself is only a secondary goal. But in a world characterized by phenomenal change, the great need is for a "skill" that will allow the man to adapt and to cope with that change. He needs a metalanguage or a metaskill. Bruner suggests that mathematics and poetry might be the answer. Poetry, he says, is "the vehicle for searching out unsuspected kinship." I would suggest that rhetoric comes nearest of all disciplines to providing the metalanguage or metaskill whereby man can cope with change. Rhetoric is the tool whereby one may analyze the particularly human aspects of situations. The tools of rhetoric are broadly applicable—Kenneth Burke's Pentad, for instance, a rubric whereby one can cope with discourse as a human activity. Rhetoric is also the art that has no particular subject matter in the sense that medicine or mathematics or biology or history has. Rhetoric synthesizes. It is interesting that a major condemnation of the learned world is its increasing specialization—to advance in education is to learn more and more about less and less. Insofar as the charge is true,

15 Bruner, *Toward a Theory of Instruction*, p. 35.

advanced education, then, systematically incapacitates. Rhetoric's curse and glory is that it forces one to know more and more about more and more. As we have seen, rhetoric today encompasses logic, grammar, ethics, and a host of other subjects, including psychology. The rhetorician must understand a great many areas of knowledge. Furthermore, rhetoric's universal applicability makes it a kind of metalanguage with which to speak about and organize diverse areas of experience and knowledge.

At its best, rhetoric does not defend; it copes. To use one of Bruner's analogies, it does not keep one off the tennis court; rather, it provides a means for being a successful tennis player, in cooperation with another player. So that rhetoric is not only the art of discovering the possible means of persuasion with regard to any subject whatever but also the art of getting on cooperatively with the business of being human.

chapter **8**

Rhetoric
and Poetic

Preliminary

A discussion of the esthetics of rhetoric will be a
fugue, incorporating themes, principally, from Mr.
Wayne Booth, Mr. Northrop Frye, Mr. Kenneth
Burke, and Mr. Aristotle. The following argument
will rely on these and other authorities in the attempt
to transform rhetoric for purposes of poetic. Once the
necessary theoretical basis has been established, the
discussion will turn to the analysis of some poems
and a novel.

But first we must answer the question "Why
transform rhetoric for purposes of poetic?" For instance, Frye tells us that "the lyric is the genre in
which the poet, like the ironic writer, turns his back
on his audience."[1] But rhetoric is the art that *never*

[1] Northrop Frye, *Anatomy of Criticism* (Princeton, N.J.:
Princeton University Press, 1957), p. 271.

173

turns its back on the audience. How can rhetoric, in the sense of audience-oriented discourse, square with the lyric, discourse addressed by the poet to himself? Or is the lyric simply nonrhetorical? What about drama and prose fiction?

No statement could be more antirhetorical then *ars gratia artis*—and the movie studio that adopted this motto must have done so tongue-in-cheek. In fact, motion pictures can serve as a paradigm of the transformation of rhetoric for poetic use. Consider a spectrum of films: the old documentary *March of Time* series, *Dr. Strangelove*, *Never on Sunday*, and a James Bond entertainment. To such a film as *The March of Time*, we can apply rhetorical criticism *mutatis mutandis*, in just the same way that we can apply that kind of criticism to any work of "pure" propaganda appearing under the auspices of "pure" information. *Dr. Strangelove* is a more complex matter. The film is black comedy dealing with the hazards of the hydrogen age and Armageddon via inadvertence; the riotously funny ineptitude of government officials and generals brings about the hydrogen cataclysm. From the viewpoint of poetics, we can judge this film as an imitation of an action in the Aristotelian sense. From the viewpoint of rhetoric, *Dr. Strangelove* becomes a pacifist document, pleading for disarmament and criticizing the conduct of national officials. In effect, then, with an avowedly propagandistic work of art, one can make an attack from the standpoint of *either* rhetoric *or* poetic.

Never on Sunday—a comedy about European innocence versus American "wisdom," that is, Henry James in reverse—is not avowedly propagandistic, but it is a *Tendenzfilm*, a movie with a purpose, a work of art with a message. Its purpose, one might say, is to entertain, but also to make a statement about the natural life. In fact, *Never on Sunday* is typical of most art in that the artistic experience is virtually always both esthetic and philosophical. Poetic holds the means for analyzing and judging a work such as *Never on Sunday*, and one can very well isolate the film from the world of persuasion insofar as art is not persuasive in the sense that, say, a campaign speech is. This observation brings us to *Goldfinger* or *From Russia with Love*, in a way, two purely esthetic films because their end is in no sense persuasion. To the entertainment one can apply the purest esthetic criteria, for the entertainment is a work of art with virtually no rhetorical purpose.

Thus, there is a spectrum running from the totally persuasive on the one end to the purely esthetic on the other. And in effect, the examples used here do not load the dice, for theoretically *Goldfinger* is more of an esthetic endeavor (successful or not) than *Dr. Strangelove* or *Never on Sunday*.

In a way, then, rhetoric and poetic offer two avenues of approach to most works of literature, but not to "pure" literature (or "pure" art, if one does not classify cinema as literature). From the standpoint of one kind of rhetoric, the entertainment—be it James Bond or a lyric—is simply nonfunctional.

Frye helps us out of the dilemma posed by this formulation:

> Rhetoric has from the beginning meant two things: ornamental speech and persuasive speech. These two things seem psychologically opposed to each other, as the desire to ornament is essentially disinterested, and the desire to persuade essentially the reverse. In fact ornamental rhetoric is inseparable from literature itself, or what we have called the hypothetical verbal structure which exists for its own sake. Persuasive rhetoric is applied literature, or the use of literary art to reinforce the power of argument. Ornamental rhetoric acts on its hearers statistically, leading them to admire its own beauty or wit; persuasive rhetoric tries to lead them kinetically toward a course of action. One articulates emotion; the other manipulates it. And whatever we decide about the ultimate literary status of oratory, there seems little doubt that ornamental rhetoric is the *lexis* or verbal texture of poetry. Aristotle remarks, when he comes to *lexis* in the *Poetics,* that that subject belongs more properly to rhetoric. We may, then, adopt the following tentative postulate: that if the direct union of grammar and logic is characteristic of non-literary verbal structures, literature may be described as the rhetorical organization of grammar and logic. Most of the features characteristic of literary form, such as rhyme, alliteration, metre, antithetical balance, the use of exempla, are also rhetorical schemata.[2]

If I understand him correctly, Mr. Frye is saying that there is a rhetoric of transport and a rhetoric of assent, much the same thing that eighteenth-century theorizers concluded after they had "discovered" Longinus. As rhetoric becomes more "ornamental," it more nearly approaches literature; "persuasive" literature approaches rhetoric. However, before we can transform rhetoric to suit our purposes, we must go a bit further, must, in fact, turn to Kenneth Burke to consider *symbolic action.*

Superficially, we can view rhetoric as the art that brings about action, and poetic as the art that concerns actions. It was Aristotle who said in his *Poetics* that "tragedy is an imitation, not of men, but of an action and of life, and life consists in action, and its end is a mode of action, not a quality." Thus, a poetic would judge the success of *imitatio* in the work, but rhetoric would judge, say, how effective the work was in bringing about political reform. We could judge any work of art on both bases. But we must stress that this is at best a superficial view of the difference between rhetoric and poetic.

Aristotle's emphasis of tragedy as an imitation of an action gives us

[2] Frye, p. 245.

the clue that we need. Consider the following formulation: the duel in *Hamlet* is not a duel, but an imitation thereof; *Hamlet* itself is a poetic act, not an imitation thereof. The fencer might criticize the actor's imitation of real swordplay. The drama critic will deal with the illusion created by the actor's imitation of swordplay. The *poetic* act supplies the link with *the* act. Suppose, then, that we consider language from the rhetorical standpoint, not as *ornamental speech* and *persuasive speech* (Frye's formulation), but as *a means of knowledge* and *a mode of action* (Burke's formulation).

> To consider language as a means of *information* or *knowledge* is to consider it epistemology, semantically, in terms of "science." To consider it as a mode of *action* is to consider it in terms of "poetry." For a poem is an act, the symbolic act of the poet who made it—an act of such a nature that, in surviving as a structure or object, it enables us as readers to re-enact it.[3]

Now the transformation of rhetoric into poetic is one step nearer. For we can view all language as action' and apply to its criticism a "dramatistic" viewpoint.

I. A. Richards, says Kenneth Burke, claims that the very nature of literature is its substitution of artistic experience for experience. It is the sign of the refined reader that his actions remain incipient. But, replies Burke, pointedly and simply,

> As an attitude can be the substitute for an act, it can likewise be *the first step towards* an act. Thus, if we arouse in someone an attitude of sympathy towards something, we may be starting him on the road towards overtly sympathetic action with regard to it—hence the rhetoric of advertisers and propagandists who would induce action in behalf of their commodities or their causes by the formation of appropriate attitudes.[4]

The rhetoric of any literature will consist in this very arousing of an attitude of sympathy, but not necessarily toward the work itself. Thus, in the case of one novel, the principal rhetorical purpose might be that of arousing the reader's sympathy for social reform, whereas, on the other hand, the genuinely rhetorical element in a second novel might be the author's intentional or unintentional advocacy on behalf of the book. In either event, both works can be viewed as actions by authors who have consciously or unconsciously chosen means of rhetorical suasion.

[3] From the book, *A Grammar of Motives* by Kenneth Burke, p. 447. © 1950 by Prentice-Hall, Inc. Published by Prentice-Hall, Inc., Englewood Cliffs, New Jersey. Reprinted with the permission of the publisher.
[4] Burke, *A Grammar of Motives*, p. 236.

And there is a more simple and more fundamental point: discourse being of a fabric—in Frye's words, the union of grammar and logic—there is no reason why one should not employ the techniques of either rhetoric or poetic to judge it.

However, the rhetorical realignment of poetics would insist on certain a priori fundamentals: that all discourse is addressed to someone, if only, as with the hypothetical lyric, to the author himself; that discourse being discourse, all of it must function in the moral universe of human society; that efficacy for a purpose is a consideration.

Let us see, then, how the rhetorician might explicate literature.

Rhetorical Criticism

Style

We have no quarrel with the teacher or critic who approaches literature as the history of ideas. In fact, any consideration of literature must deal with ideas—from the *carpe diem* motif of the seventeenth-century lyric to the avowedly political nature of a modern novel. Rationalism, Marxism, Darwinism, existentialism, Freudianism—all these currents in the history of ideas have influenced and produced literature. How might one study Pope without delving into Locke and the rationalists? Pasternak without Marx? Frank Norris without Darwin? Camus without existentialism? Kafka without Freud? In fact, one of the great pleasures of literature is the ideas that it embodies, in an imaginative form, the ideas that literature intuitively, creatively vivifies. Freud himself once said that literature delineates in the round, artistically, what the psychologist delineates in particulars, scientifically. Thus one would be foolish to read *Oedipus Rex* *either* as a pure work of literature *or* as a study in psychology. It is both. And the rhetorician would say that anything that adds meaning and delight to a work of literature is fair game, including the biography of the author.

Finally, however, a course in literature and a course in the history of ideas must be radically different. In the history of ideas, John Locke's *Essay Concerning Human Understanding* is just as valuable as Pope's *Essay on Man*—perhaps more valuable. But in the study of literature, *Essay on Man* is unquestionably more important. One of the many reasons for this is that the student of literature is concerned with style, and style is, unquestionably, one of the reasons that literature has more intrinsic value than has mere history of ideas. (Or, to extend the idea a bit, one reason that art has more intrinsic value than has philosophy.)

The study of style, Aristotle to the contrary, belongs to rhetoric, and the argument for this proposition takes us back to the chapters that discussed Aristotle and Longinus. The *Rhetoric* concerns itself with arguments and with form. Aristotle says that style in rhetoric is primarily a subject that ought to belong to poetic. But it is Longinus who gives us the tip-off, for it was he who pointed out that style can go beyond persuasion to utter transport. It is a fact that some books endure because of their style: *Religio Medici, Sartor Resartus, Euphues, The Stones of Venice, Arabia Deserta.* And it is, of course, a fact that some books endure because of their ideas, in spite of style. But the literary man is concerned with works which have either style or imaginative realization, or both. That is, some books without style survive because of their imaginative realization of an artistic situation. But, by and large, literature consists of works that have style, and that in the most favorable sense of the word. The interesting paradox is that most literature courses—even now, after the years of new critical buffeting— deal almost exclusively with ideas and form, to the exclusion of style. It is interesting to observe that only the rare class in *literature*, only the rare literary critic, spends any considerable amount of time attempting to determine how artistic effects are brought about through style.

The value of style in literature—both stylistics and metastylistics—is most clear in the short lyric poem:

> When as in silks my Julia goes
> Then, then (methinks) how sweetly flows
> That liquefaction of her clothes.
>
> Next, when I cast mine eyes and see
> That brave vibration each way free;
> O how that glittering taketh me!
>
> —ROBERT HERRICK

As Frye points out, the *literal* meaning of the poem is the poem itself, inseparable from the poetic utterance; however, the *paraphrase* meaning of the poem is simple enough: Julia looks beautiful when she is all dressed up in silks, but she looks even better when she is naked. In fact, this little lyric gains everything from style, almost nothing from idea. In teaching the poem, one might (and should) refer to the thematic and formal influence on Herrick of *The Greek Anthology*; one can compare Herrick with his master, Ben Jonson. And so on. But, finally, the small poem stands alone, its own justification its way of saying something.

Form

Form in literature is most easily dealt with in poetry and drama, for prose fiction tends not to be found in patterns that are easily classified in the sense that one can classify "ode" or "sonnet." A distinction between *matrix form* and *developmental form* is useful. For instance, *epic* is a ma-

trix form with certain readily definable characteristics: the work is divided
(in the classical genre) into twenty-four sections; the beginning is *in
medias res*; the Muses are invoked; the purpose of the work is stated at the
beginning:

> Of man's first disobedience, and the fruit
> Of that forbidden tree whose mortal taste
> Brought death into the world, and all our woe,
> With loss of Eden, till one greater Man
> Restore us, and regain the blissful seat,
> Sing, Heavenly Muse. . . .

Once the artist has chosen his matrix form, he is confronted with the
problem of developing his particular subject matter—the journey of Odys-
seus, the founding of Rome, the fall of man. In prose, matrix form is
seldom as clear cut as it is in poetry. This is evidenced by the possibility
of determining to write an epic and then choosing the subject matter, a
process quite different from the decision to write a novel. Or put it another
way: one might be moved to write a poem and find that the sonnet matrix
works for the subject; but one might just as well determine to write a
sonnet and then seek out the subject matter. Wordsworth said,

> Far better to have heard the name
> Of zeal and just ambition, than to live
> Baffled and plagued by a mind that every hour
> Turns recreant to her task; takes heart again,
> Then feels immediately some hollow thought
> Hang like an interdict upon her hopes.
> This is my lot; for either still I find
> Some imperfection in the chosen theme,
> Or see of absolute accomplishment
> Much wanting, so much wanting, in myself,
> That I recoil and droop, and seek repose
> In listlessness from vain perplexity,
> Unprofitably travelling toward the grave,
> Like a false steward who hath much received
> And renders nothing back.
>
> —*The Prelude*, Book I

And Wordsworth, in his desperation to create, was willing to settle for
either a form or a subject, so long as whatever his invention came upon
would rescue him from noncreativeness. It is in this very sense that matrix
form is generative.

Matrix form is much easier to deal with than developmental form.
The form of the classical oration was a useful matrix; the form of each
novel is developmental because it is virtually impossible to describe the

novel satisfactorily. But, to repeat, the work with a clear matrix form will also have a developmental form, and it is on this that our interest centers.

Ideational Content

Because rhetoric is centrifugal, the rhetorical criticism of literature will embrace history of ideas. However, the esthetic concern will be two-fold, both centrifugal and centripetal. That is, the rhetorical critic will ask these questions: How do the ideas in the work go to make up its integrity as a microcosm? How do the ideas in the work influence form? How does form influence the ideas? How does the society that produces the work affect it? How does the work affect the society that produced it?

Identification

When the poet speaks to himself, he addresses someone. When he speaks to someone else, he achieves *identification*. But, as Kenneth Burke points out, no activity is really autonomous. It is possible to speak of "pure" poetry as a theoretical construct, but only as a theoretical construct. For instance, physics must theoretically isolate segments of processes—must make these segments autonomous—in order to explain them via a hypo-thetical construct; but in fact, the physical world is an unbroken and un-breakable continuum of process. Mr. Burke points out—as common sense ought to tell us—that poetic activity, for instance, is carried on by human beings and hence is "impure" in motive, takes place in the continuum of human motives, is isolable only theoretically and momentarily.[5]

Identification comes about whenever the interests of two human beings are joined.[6] Thus, whenever poetry is read, identification (to some degree at least) takes place. And identification is purely rhetorical in that it works toward union rather than disunion. That, after all, *is* the rhetorical motive.

Thus, the controlling idea in the rhetorical criticism of literature is to discover the ways in which a work by an author brings about identification with a reader.[7]

Modus Operandi

Finally, rhetoric must offer a method of proceeding with the analysis of poetry, a sensible and productive "way into" the work itself. There is no

[5] From the book, *A Rhetoric of Motives* by Kenneth Burke, pp. 27–29. © 1950 by Prentice-Hall, Inc. Published by Prentice-Hall, Inc., Englewood Cliffs, New Jersey. Reprinted with the permission of the publisher.
[6] Burke, *A Rhetoric of Motives*, pp. 19–20.
[7] See Kenneth Burke, "Three Adepts of Pure Literature," *Counter-Statement* (Los Altos, Calif.: Hermes Publications, 1953), pp. 1–28.

particular virtue in setting up a hard and fast rubric, however. Rhetoric, like poetic, should be a viable tool that will "open up" the work in the most convenient way for the reader. Interpretation, though, usually proceeds from flashes of insight, the slow unraveling of a difficult passage, the sudden discovery of a telling symbol—that is, by fits and starts and according to the sensibility of the interpreter. There are as many ways into a work of literature as there are readers. The following, an obvious adaptation of Kenneth Burke's Pentad, is one of these ways "in."

The Whole Piece

Initially, the reader must get a sure grasp of what is being said *in general*. What is being said in general is usually what is being said at the surface layer of meaning, and below that surface lie the thermoclines of allegorical, symbolic, implied, and even unintended meaning. To pin down the surface meaning, it is not a bad idea to formulate a one-sentence statement of the "argument" of the work.

> Doing a filthy pleasure is, and short;
> And done, we straight repent us of the sport.
> Let us not, then, rush blindly on unto it
> Like lustful beasts, that only know to do it,
> For lust will languish, and that heat decay.
> But thus, thus, keeping endless holiday,
> Let us together closely lie, and kiss;
> There is no labor, nor no shame in this.
> This hath pleased, doth please, and long will please; never
> Can this decay, but is beginning ever.
>
> —BEN JONSON

The argument of Jonson's poem is

> The intensity of physical love is too brief.
> Anticipation is better than realization.
> Consummation brings about disillusionment.
> It is human to aspire.

And so on. All of the above sentences are relatively accurate *preliminary* statements of the argument of the poem, statements that come about after the first careful reading. Any one of them will provide a useful basis for proceeding with a depth analysis. And, of course, the depth analysis will inevitably expand the first understanding of the poem and probably alter it. It is certain that careful reading and analysis will destroy the one-poem-one-meaning myth. (Each poem means something quite unique and quite personal to each reader. To attempt to strip interpretation of the personal fallacy is to deny the nature of humanity.)

Author

The next step in the process is knowingly, willingly, and eagerly to commit the biographical fallacy. A poem represents the outcome of an action by an *acter*, the poet himself; therefore, it is mere vandalism to view that act as if it were a self-motivated and self-contained phenomenon. Anything that adds to the meaning of the poem is fair game in rhetoric, and the circumstances of the poet add meaning, significance, and interest to the poem. We are interested in a sonnet by Shakespeare because it is a successful work of art, but also *because Shakespeare wrote the poem and it is a poem that Shakespeare wrote*.

The rhetorician is interested in the poem as art, as "message," as a human action of a human acter. Biography adds as much to the poem as the poem does to biography. That is the kind of common sense that scholarly nonsense has too often ignored.

To the Pious Memory of the
Accomplish'd Young Lady,
MRS. ANNE KILLIGREW
Excellent in the Two Sister-Arts
of Poesy and Painting, an Ode

JOHN DRYDEN

I

Thou youngest virgin-daughter of the skies,
Made in the last promotion of the blest;
Whose palms, new pluck'd from paradise,
In spreading branches more sublimely rise,
Rich with immortal green above the rest:
Whether, adopted to some neighboring star,
Thou roll'st above us, in thy wand'ring race,
  Or, in procession fix'd and regular,
  Mov'd with the heavens' majestic pace;
  Or, call'd to more superior bliss,   10
Thou tread'st, with seraphims, the vast abyss;
Whatever happy region is thy place,
Cease thy celestial song a little space;
(Thou wilt have time enough for hymns divine,
  Since heav'n's eternal year is thine.)
Hear then a mortal Muse thy praise rehearse,
  In no ignoble verse!

But such as thy own voice did practice here,
When thy first fruits of poesy were giv'n,
To make thyself a welcome inmate there;　　　　　　　20
　　　While yet a young probationer,
　　　And candidate of heav'n.

II

　　I By traduction came thy mind,
　　　Our wonder is the less to find
A soul so charming from a stock so good;
Thy father was transfus'd into thy blood:
So wert thou born into the tuneful strain,
(An early, rich, and inexhausted vein.)
　　But if thy preëxisting soul
　　Was form'd, at first, with myriads more,　　　　　30
It did thro' all the mighty poets roll,
　　Who Greek or Latin laurels wore,
And was that Sappho last, which once it was before.
　　If so, then cease thy flight, O heav'n-born mind!
　　Thou hast no dross to purge from thy rich ore;
　　Nor can thy soul a fairer mansion find,
Than was the beauteous frame she left behind:
Return, to fill or mend the choir of thy celestial kind.

III

　　May we presume to say, that at thy birth
New joy was sprung in heav'n, as well as here on earth?　　40
　　For sure the milder planets did combine
　　On thy auspicious horoscope to shine,
　　And ev'n the most malicious were in trine.
　　Thy brother-angels at thy birth
　　　Strung each his lyre, and tun'd it high,
　　　That all the people of the sky
　　Might know a poetess was born on earth.
　　　And then, if ever, mortal ears
　　Had heard the music of the spheres!
　　And if no clust'ring swarm of bees　　　　　　　50
　　On thy sweet mouth distill'd their golden dew,
　　　'Twas that such vulgar miracles
　　　Heav'n had not leisure to renew:
　　For all the blest fraternity of love
Solemniz'd there thy birth, and kept thy holiday above.

IV

　　O gracious God! how far have we
Profan'd thy Heav'nly gift of poesy!
Made prostitute and profligate the Muse,
Debas'd to each obscene and impious use,

Whose harmony was first ordain'd above   60
For tongues of angels, and for hymns of love!
O wretched we! why were we hurried down
    This lubric and adult'rate age,
(Nay, added fat pollutions of our own,)
    T' increase the steaming ordures of the stage?
What can we say t' excuse our *second fall?*
Let his thy *vestal*, Heav'n, atone for all:
Her Arethusian stream remains unsoil'd,
Unmix'd with foreign filth, and undefil'd;
Her wit was more than man, her innocence a child!   70

V

Art she had none, yet wanted none;
    For nature did that want supply:
    So rich in treasures of her own,
    She might our boasted stores defy:
Such noble vigor did her verse adorn
That it seem'd borrow'd, where 't was only born.
Her morals too were in her bosom bred,
    By great examples daily fed,
What in the best of books, her father's life, she read.
And to be read herself she need not fear;   80
Each test, and ev'ry light, her Muse will bear,
Tho' Epictetus with his lamp were there.
Ev'n love (for love sometimes her Muse express'd)
Was but a *lambent flame* which play'd about her breast,
Light as the vapors of a morning dream:
So cold herself, whilst she such warmth express'd,
'T was Cupid bathing in Diana's stream.

VI

Born to the spacious empire of the Nine,
One would have thought she should have been content
To manage well that mighty government;   90
But what can young ambitious souls confine?
    To the next realm she stretch'd her sway,
    For *painture* near adjoining lay,
A plenteous province, and alluring prey.
    A *chamber of dependences* was fram'd,
(As conquerors will never want pretense,
    When arm'd, to justify th' offense,)
And the whole fief in right of poetry she claim'd.
The country open lay without defense;
For poets frequent inroads there had made,   100
    And perfectly could represent
    The shape, the face, with ev'ry lineament;

And all the large demains which the *Dumb Sister* sway'd,
   All bow'd beneath her government;
   Receiv'd in triumph wheresoe'er she went.
Her pencil drew whate'er her soul design'd,
And oft the happy draught surpass'd the image in her mind.
   The *sylvan* scenes of herds and flocks,
   And fruitful plains and barren rocks,
   Of shallow brooks that flow'd so clear 110
   The bottom did the top appear;
   Of deeper too and ampler floods,
   Which, as in mirrors, shew'd the woods;
   Of lofty trees, with sacred shades,
   And perspectives of pleasant glades,
   Where nymphs of brightest form appear,
   And shaggy satyrs standing near,
   Which them at once admire and fear:
   The ruins too of some majestic piece,
   Boasting the pow'r of ancient Rome, or Greece, 120
   Whose statues, friezes, columns broken lie,
   And, tho' defac'd, the wonder of the eye:
   What nature, art, bold fiction, e're durst frame,
   Her forming hand gave feature to the name.
   So strange a concourse ne'er was seen before,
But when the peopled ark the whole creation bore.

VII

   The scene then chang'd: with bold erected look
Our martial king the sight with reverence strook;
For, not content t' express his outward part,
Her hand call'd out the image of his heart: 130
His warlike mind, his soul devoid of fear,
His high-designing thoughts were figur'd there,
As when, by magic, ghosts are made appear.
   Our Phoenix queen was portray'd too so bright,
Beauty alone could beauty take so right:
Her dress, her shape, her matchless grace,
Were all observ'd, as well as heav'nly face.
With such a peerless majesty she stands,
As in that day she took the crown from sacred hands;
Before a train of heroines was seen, 140
In beauty foremost, as in rank the queen.
Thus nothing to her *genius* was denied,
   But like a ball of fire the further thrown,
   Still with a greater blaze she shone,
And her bright soul broke out on ev'ry side.
What next she had design'd, Heaven only knows;
To such immod'rate growth her conquest rose
That fate alone its progress could oppose.

VIII

Now all those charms, that blooming grace,
The well-proportion'd shape, and beauteous face,   150
Shall never more be seen by mortal eyes:
In earth the much-lamented virgin lies!
   Not wit, nor piety could fate prevent;
   Nor was the cruel Destiny content
   To finish all the murder at a blow,
   To sweep at once her life and beauty too;
But, like a harden'd felon, took a pride
   To work more mischievously slow,
And plunder'd first, and then destroy'd.
O double sacrilege on things divine,   160
To rob the relic, and deface the shrine!
   But thus Orinda died:
Heav'n, by the same disease, did both translate;
As equal were their souls, so equal was their fate.

IX

Meantime her warlike brother on the seas
His waving streamers to the winds displays,
And vows for his return, with vain devotion, pays.
   Ah, generous youth, that wish forbear,
   The winds too soon will waft thee here!
Slack all thy sails, and fear to come,   170
Alas, thou know'st not, thou art wreck'd at home!
No more shalt thou behold thy sister's face,
Thou hast already had her last embrace.
But look aloft, and if thou kenn'st from far
Among the Pleiads a new kindled star;
If any sparkles than the rest more bright,
'T is she that shines in that propitious light.

X

When in mid-air the golden trump shall sound,
   To raise the nations under ground;
   When in the Valley of Jehosaphat   180
The judging God shall close the book of fate,
   And there the last assizes keep
   For those who wake and those who sleep;
   When rattling bones together fly
   From the four corners of the sky;
When sinews o'er the skeletons are spread,
Those cloth'd with flesh, and life inspires the dead;
The sacred poets first shall hear the sound,
   And foremost from the tomb shall bound,
For they are cover'd with the lightest ground;   190

And straight, with inborn vigor, on the wing,
Like mounting larks, to the new morning sing.
There thou, sweet saint, before the choir shalt go,
As harbinger of heav'n, the way to show,
The way which thou so well hast learn'd below.

Using Dryden as an example of rhetoric in poetry might well be taking unfair advantage, for Dryden was avowedly rhetorical, in some senses a hack exhorting an audience and working in part at least for a living. He was the antithesis of, say, Hart Crane, whose own neuroses drove him to compose, or of Wyatt and Raleigh, whose verses were fashionable exercises (but how glorious!) addressed to an admiring court. Even Shakespeare in his sonnets was working in a gentlemanly tradition. But Dryden was the public poet par excellence. In the 1680s, he defected from the theater and joined the minions of the neoclassical world of journalism.[8] F. N. Lees says,

> Dryden was not a lyric poet, has nothing to offer in the way of illuminating or moving states of mind. His attention is directed outward and it is rather on states of things, on events and the people in them, that he brings his strong and mobile intelligence to bear, his wit, his feeling for language, and his highly trained verse-technique.[9]

And it was in his period as a poetical journalist that he composed the "Ode on Anne Killigrew."

I will not attempt to summarize Dryden's biography, for I could add nothing new. We know that Dryden was an occasional poet par excellence and that "Anne Killigrew" is an occasional poem, written at the urging of Anne's father, who wanted to append the ode to a small volume of his daughter's verse. In 1685, the Catholic monarch James II ascended the throne, and Dryden converted to Catholicism, an act that has caused some controversy regarding the poet's sincerity, but which, by and large, is now viewed (and was viewed by Sir Walter Scott in his biography) as a genuine act of faith. The fact is, however, that Dryden wrote his ode during a time of spiritual crisis and emotional turmoil. (The best argument in favor of Dryden's sincerity in religion is his long justification of Catholicism, *The Hind and the Panther*.)

Compared with other elegiac poems—say, Ransom's "Bells for John Whiteside's Daughter" or Milton's "Methought I saw my late espoused saint"—Dryden's ode sounds insincere; it does not ring with the quality of true grief. We are concerned, then, with the sincerity of the poet, not

---

[8] See Mark Van Doren, *The Poetry of John Dryden* (New York: Harcourt, Brace & World, Inc., 1920), pp. 140–173.
[9] F. N. Lees, "John Dryden," *From Dryden to Johnson*, ed. Boris Ford (Baltimore: Penguin Books, 1965), p. 108.

merely with the apparent insincerity of the poem. Apostrophizing Anne
Killigrew, Dryden says,

> Whatever happy region is thy place,
> Cease thy celestial song a little space;
> (Thou wilt have time enough for hymns divine,
>   Since heav'n's eternal year is thine.)
> Hear then a mortal Muse thy praise rehearse,
>   In no ignoble verse. . . .

The very tone of this is less grief-stricken than

> But, oh! as to embrace me she inclined,
> I waked, she fled, and day brought back my night,

from Milton's great Italian sonnet.

If we do a kind of "factor analysis" of the author as the agent who
made the poem, we shall be able to estimate Dryden's intent (and, by the
way, in the process commit the intentional fallacy and in so doing add
another sin to the process of rhetorical criticism).

The author was an occasional poet—in Van Doren's words, a journalist in verse. Dryden's most successful poetic endeavors are a kind of
"journalism": "MacFlecknoe," "Absalom and Achitophel," "The Hind
and the Panther." The occasional poet—and the poet laureate!—writes
poetry suitable for given occasions; he celebrates the restoration and the
birthdays of monarchs; he writes satires on political intrigues and clandes-
tine lovemaking; he argues the issues of his time in philosophical verse.
When the occasion arises, the poet rises to the occasion with a poem that
is fitting in form and decorum. The occasional poem is ceremonial, with
all of the dispassion of ceremony. One can think analogically here: funeral
masses are general and ceremonial, whereas the funeral oration may be
personal, lyrical, and intensely passionate. This is exactly what E. M. W.
Tillyard means when he says, "Dryden's *Ode* implies a strong agreement
with the contemporary estimation of manners and decorum. It offers a
splendid pompous façade and in so doing protests that a good outward
show is self-valuable."[10]

The biographical point with Dryden as maker of "Anne Killigrew"
is whether or not he was sincere. The answer is that he was not sincere in
grief over the death of Anne Killigrew, but he was most sincere as an
occasional poet writing a ceremonial ode and most sincere as a poet com-
menting on the divine nature of poetry.

We will return to "Anne Killigrew" hereafter.

[10] E. M. W. Tillyard, *Poetry and Its Background Illustrated by Five Poems*, 1470–1870
(London: Chatto & Windus, Ltd., 1961), p. 56.

Circumstances

Poetry is not produced in a vacuum. It is always occasional in some sense of the word. It celebrates something. It is ceremonial in nature in exactly the same way that music is always ceremonial. The circumstantial nature of poetry is best illustrated by the juxtaposition of two poems.

In 1600, Christopher Marlowe's "Passionate Shepherd to His Love" was published:

> Come live with me and be my love,
> And we will all the pleasures prove
> That valleys, groves, hills and fields,
> Woods, or steepy mountain yields.
>
> And will we sit upon the rocks
> Seeing the shepherds feed their flocks,
> By shallow rivers, to whose falls
> Melodious birds sing madrigals.
>
> And I will make thee beds of roses
> And a thousand fragrant posies,
> A cap of flowers, and a kirtle
> Embroidered all with leaves of myrtle.
>
> A gown made of the finest wool,
> Which from our pretty lambs we pull,
> Fair linèd slippers for the cold,
> With buckles of the purest gold.
>
> A belt of straw and ivy buds
> With coral clasps and amber studs:
> And if these pleasures may thee move,
> Come live with me and be my love.
>
> The shepherds' swains shall dance and sing
> For thy delight each May-morning:
> If these delights thy mind may move,
> Then live with me and be my love.

Sir Walter Raleigh replied:

> If all the world and love were young,
> And truth in every shepherd's tongue,
> These pretty pleasures might me move
> To live with thee and be thy love.
>
> Time drives the flocks from field to fold,
> When rivers rage and rocks grow cold,

And Philomel becometh dumb;
The rest complains of cares to come.

The flowers do fade, and wanton fields
To wayward winter reckoning yields.
A honey tongue, a heart of gall,
Is fancy's spring, but sorrow's fall.

Thy gowns, thy shoes, thy beds of roses,
Thy cap, thy kirtle, and thy posies
Soon break, soon wither, soon forgotten:
In folly ripe, in reason rotten.

Thy belt of straw and ivy buds,
Thy coral clasps and amber studs,
All these in me no means can move
To come with thee and be thy love.

But could youth last and love still breed,
Had joys no date nor age no need,
Then these delights my mind might move
To live with thee and be thy love.

Here, then, is a clear-cut instance of circumstance. Other circumstances are not so obvious. But poems are written in time and place. And time and place as motivating factors must be taken into account in any rhetoric of motives.

Medium

Medium has a variety of effects. The influence of periodical publication on Dickens has been widely discussed. The influence of television on the writer is too obvious to need discussion. But medium is not only medium in the modern sense of the singularized plural *media;* it is also matrix form, for we can speak of a sonnet as well as of a poem by Shakespeare, so that medium and form become one at their extremities. We can also speculate about the nature of a multimedia poem, combining the visual, the aural, and the ideational.

When one sets out to write a sonnet, he is writing for the medium as surely as if he were to write a TV or movie script. When the medium controls, that is the time that we focus our interest on it. We become interested in the sonnet *qua* sonnet, not the sonnet *qua* poem; the drama *qua* TV show, not the drama *qua* play. The whole ratio of our values shifts. Thus, for instance, we judge a sonnet against other sonnets, not against a Pindaric ode. This is one of the important things that Marshall McLuhan is saying. The medium can, indeed, be the massage.

Stance

All poems reveal rhetorical stance. Some poems gain a great deal from it.

> To you, my purs, and to noon other wight,
> Complaine I, for ye be my lady dere.
> I am so sory, now that ye be light,
> For certes, but if ye make me hevy cheere,
> Me were as lief be laid upon my beere;
> For which unto youre mercy thus I crye:
> Beeth hevy again, or elles moot I die.
>
> Now voucheth sauf this day er it be night
> That I of you the blisful soun may heere,
> Or see youre colour, lik the sonne bright,
> That of yelownesse hadde nevere peere.
> Ye be my lif, ye be myn hertes steere,
> Queen of comfort and of good compaignye:
> Beeth hevy again, or elles moot I die.
>
> Ye purs, that been to me my lives light
> And Saviour, as in this world down here,
> Out of this tonne helpe me thurgh your might,
> Sith that ye wol nat be my tresorere;
> For I am shave as neigh as any frere.
> But yet I praye unto youre curteisye:
> Beeth hevy again, or elles moot I die.
>
> ### Lenvoy de Chaucer
> O conquerour of Brutus Albioun,
> Which that by line and free eleccioun
> Been verray king, this song to you I sende:
> And ye, that mowen alle oure harmes amende,
> Have minde upon my supplicacioun.

In this delightful poem, Chaucer takes the conventional trappings of the love lyric and uses them to go a-begging to Henry IV. The stance of the author is one of good-humored seriousness; he wants his pension continued (and Henry did continue it). The lovely comic nature of the poem results from the seriousness of the poet juxtaposed against the ridiculousness of the kind of poem that he writes and the purpose of that poem.

Form

As we have seen, matrix form is sometimes synonymous with medium. A sonnet is not only a form, but also a medium. A Platonic dialogue is also a form and a medium. Developmental form is something else again. The most obvious and superficial function of form is its literal use, as in a shaped poem like Herbert's "Easter Wings." Stichomythy is a form that makes for wit in the drama; the smart verbal repartee of many Restoration dramas results from the necessity for quick uptake in verbal duels between two characters. So that in reading, say, *The Way of the World*, we should be on the lookout for stichomythy as a conventional form.

The form "play" brings about more objectivity than the form "novel," for the author cannot explicate within the play. The form "lyric" is likely to be personal, whereas the form "epic" will be public and ceremonial. And so on. Not only does the poet control the form; the form also controls the poet.

There is a logical inevitability to the form of the widely known "To His Coy Mistress," by Andrew Marvell. The stanzas are a stipulation (*if* we had such and such, we would do such and such), a qualification (*but* we do not have such and such), and a conclusion (*therefore* let us do thus and so). In this instance, form becomes extremely important to the effect of the whole.

Style

Briefly, we read some poems and some poets largely for their style. Dryden is one of these, and Pope is another. Both of these poets simply amaze us with their technical mastery, and often we are quite literally less interested in what they say than in how they say it.

Metastyle

Metastyle includes diction, metaphor, symbol, and miscellaneous figures of thought. (Figures of grammar are, of course, stylistic.) In a sense, metastyle is the heart of poetry, for it concerns the language of the poet, his figurative embodiment of concepts, and his symbolic statements. The problem of talking about metastyle in poetry is exactly the same as talking about it in prose, except that the figurative is likely to be more predominant in poetry. For instance, the following:

> She dwelt among the untrodden ways
>   Beside the springs of Dove,
> A Maid whom there were none to praise
>   And very few to love:
>
> A violet by a mossy stone
>   Half hidden from the eye!
> —Fair as a star, when only one
>   Is shining in the sky.

> She lived unknown, and few could know
>   When Lucy ceased to be;
> But she is in her grave, and, oh,
>   The difference to me!

—WORDSWORTH

The second stanza is a metaphorical restatement of the first and is a poem in itself, a sort of haiku.

The importance of the symbol is illustrated by another of Wordsworth's poems:

> My heart leaps up when I behold
>   A rainbow in the sky:
> So was it when my life began;
> So is it now I am a man;
> So be it when I shall grow old,
>   Or let me die!
> The Child is father of the Man;
> And I could wish my days to be
> Bound each to each by natural piety.

Andrew J. George quite rightly says, "This poem is the key-note of all Wordsworth's poetry: it is 'The Prelude' condensed into a lyric."[11] The compression is possible because the rainbow symbolizes so much: temporality, nature, beauty, heavenly affluence, Iris (the messenger of the gods).

Ratios

A given poem will evidence ratios among its elements. Thus, in one work, the predominant force will be metaphor, whereas in another it will be symbol and in another, form.

The whole point is that there are many ways to get into the work. One needs an avenue of entry, but, once that is found, the poem then tends to open up, to reveal itself, layer on layer of meaning. In "My Heart Leaps Up," there is obviously an author-symbol ratio; the lyric gets its import from the reader's knowledge of Wordsworth the man as he expressed himself in the "Intimations Ode" and in "The Prelude" and from the understanding of the rainbow symbol.

The idea of ratios among the elements of a work of art comes from Kenneth Burke. He speaks of ratios in the Pentad (act, scene, agent, agony, purpose), so that, for instance, we can discover a scene-purpose ratio in the witch scene in *Macbeth* or a scene-act ratio in *An Enemy of the People.*[12]

[11] *The Complete Poetical Works of Wordsworth*, ed. Andrew J. George (Boston: Houghton Mifflin Company, 1932), p. 845.
[12] Kenneth Burke, *A Grammar of Motives and A Rhetoric of Motives* ("Meridian Books"; New York: The World Publishing Company, 1962), pp. xvii–20.

"Meaning"

The rhetorical motive is toward *identification*. Rhetoric tries not merely to communicate so many things in almost an equal number of words, but to bring about a kind of consubstantiality between speaker-writer and audience. Rhetorical persuasion goes far beyond the conviction that the facts, the data, or the valid syllogism can bring about. The meaning of a work of literature is much more than the "scientific" meaning, which, as Kenneth Burke said, views language as a means of information.

Meaning is everything in the work—including, of course, formal meaning in the sense that we saw how an apparently meaningless proposition can be semantically almost hollow but formally meaningful: *Pirots karulize elatically; A is a pirot; therefore A karulizes elatically* or *Colorless green ideas sleep furiously*. Meaning also includes the aura that the author casts around a poem that is not anonymous, and it includes the "scene" in which the poem was composed.

To experiment a bit with meaning in a poem, we will turn back to the "Ode on Anne Killigrew" and explore.

The most superficial layer of meaning in the poem is this: "Anne Killigrew" is an elegiac poem on the death of a young poetess. But hardly anyone would be satisfied with such a statement; it ignores too much. A slightly deeper level: Dryden

> . . . used the conventional grief and extravagant adulation to convey certain strongly held opinions and feelings.
> One of these is a heartfelt enthusiasm for the arts, the same enthusiasm that animates Dryden's literary criticism. When he praises Anne Killigrew's accomplishment, he is speaking not for her but for poetry and painting in their entirety; and when at the end he makes the earth lie more lightly on the poets than on other men, he is paying a sincere tribute to the poetic sensibility: a tribute not less sincere for the outrageous assertion that Anne Killigrew will lead the poetic throng to heaven. There is no piety in his references to heavenly music, yet through them he demonstrates how sincerely he prizes the practice of the arts on this earth.[13]

But still any careful reader must feel that there is something more waiting to be apprehended.

Because the poem is not really about its ostensible subject, and because we judge Dryden to be sincere in what he is saying, how far can we go in mining a real import? In choosing the form of the Pindaric, Dryden freed himself of the limitations of the heroic couplet and put his poem into a matrix that could be passionate and allusive and alogical, for the

[13] Tillyard, p. 52.

heroic couplet has built into it the propensity to force a proposition by the time the second end-stop comes. The Pindaric is for Dryden what free verse is for Whitman. The mere form of "Anne Killigrew," then, should tip us off that we will find something more than elegant compliment.

The author's stance is ambivalent, and this ambivalence is a clue to what the poem is getting at. In the ceremonial poem, decorum is everything, particularly, one would think, in the funeral poem. The poem starts by placing the "youngest Virgin-Daughter of the Skies" among the angels. But in the second stanza, we are jarred to find that perhaps Anne is Sappho reincarnate. Sappho was *the* classic poetess, but also the classic *love* poetess, not a Diana, but a Venus. The decorum is cracked. The fourth stanza is an effusion about the corruption of Restoration poesy as compared with that of Anne Killigrew. With these lines,

> O wretched we! why were we hurried down
>   This lubric and adult'rate age,
> (Nay, added fat pollutions of our own,)
>   T' increase the steaming ordures of the stage?

the decorum is shattered. In the last stanza it is annihilated with the grotesque, presumably unintentional comicness of

> The judging God shall close the book of fate,
>   And there the last assizes keep
>   For those who wake and those who sleep;
>   When rattling bones together fly
>   From the four corners of the sky. . . .

Obviously a strange kind of funeral ode, this! And obviously the poet is concerned with the theme of purity versus corruption.

In the infamous Stanza IV,[14] scatological-anal motifs serve to reinforce the idea of Anne's purity. "Steaming ordures" are juxtaposed with "Her Arethusian stream" that "remains unsoil'd, / Unmix'd with foreign filth, and undefil'd. . . ." Now, in the anal context that Dryden so forcefully sets up, only the most innocent reader would fail to attach a double entendre to "Her Arethusian stream," her virginal flow (of poesy). Particularly since Stanza V follows with this:

> Ev'n love (for love sometimes her Muse express'd)
> Was but a *lambent flame* which play'd about her breast,
> Light as the vapors of a morning dream:
> So cold herself, whilst she such warmth express'd,
> 'T was Cupid bathing in Diana's stream.

---

[14] Which Mark Van Doren admires: "The fourth stanza hurls itself with violent alliteration down the steep channel which describes. . . ." Van Doren, p. 199.

At this point, the grotesqueness of Stanza IV becomes meaningful, provided the reader will be honest with himself.

It is the ambivalence and ambiguity of poetry that lends it fascination, so one should not be stopped by what he thinks the "real" meaning *ought to be*. The "real" meaning will be a whole complex of suggestions, overtones, implications, and so on.

It was Tillyard who called "Anne Killigrew" a brilliant façade. The job of the reader is to see what lies behind the façade and at the same time to appreciate the beauty of the façade itself.

Innocence versus experience, virginity versus corruption, purity versus pollution—this is the motif of the poem. In Stanza VI (on painting), we see "pleasant glades,"

> Where nymphs of brightest form appear,
> And shaggy satyrs standing near,
> Which them at once admire and fear. . . .

And in Stanza II, the poet had speculated platonically:

> But if thy preëxisting soul
> Was form'd, at first, with myriads more,
> It did thro' all the mighty poets roll,
> Who Greek or Latin laurels wore. . . .

And, of course, the Platonic ideal is the ultimate in virginity, for its goal is the sluffing off of vile flesh and the return to pure essence.

Authorial stance in the poem, then, is that of the occasional poet writing a poem that is much more than occasional, but in so doing the poet must assume an outward pose of ceremony. The equation between sexual purity and artistic purity must come through implication, not statement; the equation between sexual corruption and anality, that is, also, between lubric poetry and scatology, must be expressed figuratively. In saying what he wants to say, Dryden is using rhetorical subterfuge, hiding behind the trappings of a conventional ceremonial poem.

Rhetoric in a Novel

We will now shift gears and look in detail at the rhetoric of a novel to examine the ways in which an author shapes the viewpoint of his readers. This rhetorical "shaping" may be directed outward, toward the social context in which the novel transpires, or inward, toward the work itself, or both. That is, the author may shape attitudes toward the real world or toward the world of the novel.

As art does not transpire in a vacuum, but rather in a time and a place with given ethical, social, esthetic, and rhetorical preconditions, it is well to examine works in context. Chapter 3 of the present volume looked at the eighteenth century in some detail as a paradigm of rhetorical force and counterforce. A context was established. Thus, to find out how rhetoric functions in the novel, the discussion will turn now to *Amelia*, by Henry Fielding.

The eighteenth century provides a clear example of two theories of human discourse working themselves out. The one (represented by Blair and Campbell) is Aristotelian in nature, a reaction against the "Ciceronianism" that stemmed from the Ramistic rearrangement of rhetorical materials. The other (represented by the elocutionists) is Ciceronian. Of course, it would be futile to speculate that the elocutionists had Cicero directly in mind, as it would be false to say that Ramistic rhetoric was based on the doctrines of Cicero. Nonetheless, Aristotle and Cicero and reinterpretations of Aristotle and Cicero provided the Western world for nearly two millennia with its basic rhetorical materials. Furthermore, Aristotle and Cicero advanced theories of discourse that were in practice at odds with each other and which defined two possibilities for the function of style in rhetorical sausiveness. Cicero's theory approached that of Longinus: style per se has the power to move men. Aristotle emphasized ethical and logical content as the primary suasive devices of rhetoric. Thus, it is both convenient and defensible to speak of rhetorical Aristotelianism and rhetorical Ciceronianism.

"If *Amelia* startled and roused the dull conscience of the British public, it would have achieved its object," says F. Homes Dudden.[15] In his view, at least, *Amelia* is didactic and as such is the forerunner of propagandistic work like *Oliver Twist* and *Bleak House*. Wilbur L. Cross concurs: *Amelia*, although not an expanded pamphlet on crime addressed to lawyers and legislators, nonetheless attempts, through narrative, to show its readers "the moral conditions of London within the immediate jurisdiction of his [Fielding's] court, and warn the unsuspecting against the lures of vice and crime."[16] A. D. McKillop says that, after 1748, Fielding's work "was deeply colored by his immediate concern with the state of public morals."[17] And, of course, we have Fielding's own testimony concerning his avowed purpose in the novel: ". . . the following book is sincerely designed to promote the cause of virtue, and to expose some of the most glaring evils, as well public as private, which at present infest the country. . . ."[18]

How much trust we can put in Fielding's own avowal of his purpose

---

[15] F. Homes Dudden, *Henry Fielding, His Life, Works, and Times* (2 vols.; New York: Oxford University Press, 1952), II, 854.
[16] Wilbur L. Cross, *The History of Henry Fielding* (3 vols.; New Haven, Conn.: Yale University Press, 1918), II, 312.
[17] Alan Dugald McKillop, *The Early Masters of English Fiction* (Lawrence: Kansas University Press, 1956), p. 136.
[18] Henry Fielding, *Amelia* (New York: Doubleday & Company, Inc., 1962), p. 7.

is, of course, a question. A glance at the prefaces and dedications of almost all eighteenth-century novels will reveal the authors expressing their avowed moral purposes. Defoe says he hopes that the reader of *Moll Flanders* "will be more pleased with the moral than the fable, and with the end of the writer than with the life of the person written of." Smollett says that *Roderick Random* will be both "entertaining and universally improving." And so on. More to the point, perhaps, is Fielding's announcement in *The Covent Garden Journal* (No. 8, 1752) that the *Aeneid* was the "noble model" he had used for *Amelia*. Fielding, of course, was preoccupied with the idea of the novel as a prose epic. In *Tom Jones* he points out that the novel, like the epic, can ignore the unity of time; it can seem "to stand still, and sometimes fly." And in *Joseph Andrews* he says that "a comic romance is a comic epic poem in prose." If *Joseph Andrews* was Fielding's comic-epic *Don Quixote*, then *Amelia* was, by his own avowal, a portentously serious *Aeneid*. Within three years after the appearance of *Amelia*, Fielding was to say, indeed, that he preferred "true history" to poetry. He still read Homer and Hesiod with admiration and astonishment, but Herodotus, Thucydides, and Xenophon "with more amusement and satisfaction."[19] Throughout his "Preface" to *The Voyage to Lisbon*, Fielding continually emphasizes the baseness of the lying historian, the superiority of history to poetry, and so forth. In a sense, then, *he* is the lying poet as author of *Amelia*.

It is not by chance that Fielding, like Dante, turned to Virgil as a guide. The *Aeneid* was a poem that, as Gilbert Highet says, expressed "a real spiritual fact: . . . the profound longing for peace, the unvoiced yearning for a world governed by the goodness of God rather than the conflicting desires of men. . . ."[20] Edith Hamilton points out that the sheer consequentiality of the *Aeneid* differentiates it from the *Odyssey* and *Iliad*.[21] In a sense, the *Aeneid* was a *Tendenzroman*, and by his own avowal, Fielding had intended *Amelia* to be *ameliorative* in its effect. The kind of punning—and presumably unintentional or unconscious—logic of the title of the book is curiously indicative of what the author was setting out to do. The *Aeneid*, presumably, furnished "a kind of narrative metaphor" that would allow the author to find a pattern for his work, a way into his subject, "without . . . detracting from the novel's appearance of literal veracity."[22]

Fielding had, in terms of his own experience, moved from the posi-

---

[19] Henry Fielding, "The Voyage to Lisbon," in *The Voyage to Lisbon, Jonathan Wild* (New York: E. P. Dutton & Co., Inc., 1960), pp. 185–186.

[20] Gilbert Highet, *The Classical Tradition* (New York: Oxford University Press, 1957), p. 73.

[21] Edith Hamilton, *The Roman Way to Western Civilization* (New York: New American Library of World Literature, 1957), p. 129.

[22] Ian Watt, *The Rise of the Novel* (Berkeley, Calif.: The University of California Press, 1957), p. 255.

tion of successful writer to that of successful public servant. In his art, he was moving from the comic-epic toward his attitude in *The Voyage to Lisbon*. The first chapter of *Amelia* defines life as an art, in which the "great incidents" are the result of conscious fashioning much like "the several members of a fine statue or a noble poem." And because a "history" such as *Amelia* is a faithful representation of human life, it can best instruct us "in the most useful of all arts, which I call the Art of Life."[23] In *The Voyage to Lisbon*, Fielding had taken an extreme position, and in so doing, he had denied the value of the greater part of his life's labors. Presumably, he would have given a less favorable retrospective judgment on his labors as playwright and novelist than on his work as journalist and magistrate. But *Amelia* was a compromise, a work of art with a serious moral purpose, that is, a rhetorical purpose.

Amelia is obviously a different sort of book from *Tom Jones*, *Joseph Andrews*, and even *Jonathan Wild*; it is more solemn in tone, more serious in intent, even more sententious in execution. It is a book intended by its author to serve a social function. In this sense, it is basically "rhetorical" in purpose. Kenneth Burke would say that the poet works under three component motives: the need to express himself, the need to give that expression artistic form, and the need to persuade.[24] Burke would contend that there is an element of self-expression in activity, an a priori drive toward realization.[25] The poet's drive for revelation is, then, rhetorical as well as self-expressive. That is, depending on the point of view that we choose to take, we can say that the poetic motive is personally cathartic or rhetorically suasive. Or we can rearrange the statement and say that the poetic motive is cathartic in that it is rhetorical. In this sense, Burke is "linguistic" in his view of poetry. Sapir defines language as "a purely human and noninstinctive method of communicating ideas, emotions, and desires by means of a system of voluntarily produced symbols."[26] And Burke says, "We can place in terms of rhetoric all those statements by anthropologists, ethnologists, individual and social psychologists, and the like, that bear upon the *persuasive* aspects of language, the function of language as *addressed*, as direct or roundabout appeal to real or ideal audiences, without or within."[27] So that, categorically, the poetic impulse carried out in language is rhetorical. The artist, agonized with the need to express himself, finds that he also has a desire "to produce effects upon his audience."[28]

---

[23] *Amelia*, p. 16.
[24] See William H. Rueckert, *Kenneth Burke and the Drama of Human Relations* (Minneapolis: University of Minnesota Press, 1963), p. 15.
[25] Kenneth Burke, *Counter-Statement* (Los Altos, Calif.: Hermes Publications, 1953), p. 53.
[26] Edward Sapir, *Language* (New York: Harcourt, Brace & World, Inc., 1949), p. 8.
[27] Burke, *A Rhetoric of Motives*, pp. 43–44.
[28] Burke, *Counter-Statement*, p. 54.

But Burke emphasizes the distinction between the rhetoric of persuasion and the rhetoric of transport. Thus, he says, Longinus recognizes a pure sublimity of effect.

> Where Demosthenes would transport his auditors the better to persuade them, Longinus treats the state of transport as the aim. . . . Indeed, might not the key term, that is usually translated "sublime," come close to what we mean by "moving," not in the rhetorical sense, of moving and audience to a decision, but as when we say of a poem, "How moving!"[29]

This distinction between a rhetoric of persuasion and a rhetoric of transport is crucial to an understanding of the function of the narrator in *Amelia*. Though the fable itself supplies a rhetoric of transport, the narrator uses a rhetoric of persuasion. We can assume that the author-narrator is expressing his own viewpoint whenever he speaks directly to the readers and that whenever he does this, he is using "his own tone of voice" or at least the one he has assumed for the purposes of his art. As in *Tom Jones*, the author-narrator in *Amelia* is very much a character in his own right; he is with us every step of the way. Almost immediately he calls attention to himself as craftsman, as a teller of stories, when he refuses to reveal the discourse between Robinson and Booth in the prison, "which, as it will make a pretty pamphlet of itself, we shall reserve for some future opportunity." Indeed, the author makes a plea for the reader to view him as a faithful historian, even though he must reveal a slight flaw in Dr. Harrison's character.[30] He courteously asks permission to speak the truth and warns the reader to pay attention to the minutiae of the plot.[31]

Most characteristically, however, we see the author in *Amelia* as psychologist, moralist, and explicator.

As psychologist, the author takes the reader aside, as it were, to explain motives of the various characters. Almost compulsively, he attempts to convince the reader of the verisimilitude of *most* of the characters. For instance, on Colonel James:

> His mind was formed of those firm materials of which nature formerly hammered out the Stoic, and upon which sorrows of no man living could make an impression. A man of his temper, who doth not much value danger, will fight for the person he calls his friend, and the man that hath but little value for his money will give it him; but such friendship is never to be absolutely depended on; for, whenever the favorite passion inter-

[29] Burke, *A Rhetoric of Motives*, p. 65.
[30] *Amelia*, p. 446.
[31] *Amelia*, p. 446.

poses with it, it is sure to subside and vanish into air. Whereas the man whose tender disposition really feels the miseries of another will endeavor to relieve them for his own sake; and, in such a mind, friendship will often get the superiority over every other passion.[32]

A survey of the "psychological" passages in the novel reveals that the author never explains the main character. As Dudden points out, Amelia is the only character in Fielding's novels around whom a whole work revolves.[33] He says, and rightly I think, that events and characters gain significance only through their relation to or effect upon Amelia. And Amelia stands unexplicated; she gains life by what she is and what she does, through her controlling motive of love for husband and children, a point from which she never swerves. Though Tom Jones and Joseph Andrews are clearly the central characters in their novels, they do not have as pervasive an influence on the works in which they appear as does the main character in *Amelia*.

In his role as "psychologist," the author, then, is using the rhetoric of persuasion in developing every central character but Amelia. Examples of authorial rhetoric in this respect are numerous.[34] When Fielding the author turns to his audience and becomes a critical commentator on his work, he is applying the kind of rhetoric of "reason" that Aristotle had said should be the basis of persuasion.

Much of the moral tone of the book stems from the author's tendency to supply ethical summation on developments in the plot. Undoubtedly, this moralistic tone contributed in part to the lack of enthusiasm with which *Amelia* was received.[35] Granted, none of the characters in *Amelia* has the verve, humor, or youth of Tom, Joseph, or even Jonathan. The gay young man is, like Colonel James, likely to be thoroughly reprehensible. In fact, not only are Trent and James reprehensible; they are basically corrupt, to the point that the reader loses all sympathy for them though the process takes a while in the case of James.

The author, on behalf of the book, moralizes frequently, always with great seriousness, sometimes lugubriously. For instance, we hear him say,

---

[32] *Amelia*, p. 345.
[33] Dudden, II, 819.
[34] For instance, on Booth's and Miss Matthews' liaison, IV. i, pp. 153–154; on Miss Matthews, IV. ii, pp. 160–161; on Mrs. James, IV. vi, p. 182; on Colonel James, IV. viii, pp. 187–188; on Mrs. Bennett, VII. i, p. 277; on Colonel James, VIII. v, p. 345; on Colonel James again, VIII. viii, pp. 353–354; and on Dr. Harrison, XII. v, pp. 538–539.
[35] The book was a commercial failure. Perhaps the most complete study of the reception of *Amelia* is the detailed account given by Blanchard. He summarizes thus: "As the roll of the 'judicious' is called for the third time, the advocates of *Amelia* are found to be 'few' indeed, far fewer than in the case of *Tom Jones* or even *Joseph Andrews*. The book had gone down to defeat—not entirely, to be sure, because of Amelia's 'vile broken nose,' but because of the distaste of the public for the author's studies in real life." Frederic T. Blanchard, *Fielding the Novelist* (New Haven, Conn.: Yale University Press, 1926), p. 103.

   . . . there is, I believe, something so outrageously suspicious in the nature
of all vice, especially when joined with any great degree of pride, that the
eyes of those whom we imagine privy to our failings are intolerable to us,
and we are apt to aggravate their opinions to disadvantage far beyond
the reality.[36]

Or again:

   Here, reader, give me leave to stop a minute, to lament that so few
are to be found of this benign disposition; that, while wantonness, vanity,
avarice, and ambition are every day rioting and triumphing in the follies
and weakness, the ruin and desolation of mankind, scarce one man in a
thousand is capable of tasting the happiness of others. Nay, give me leave
to wonder that pride, which is constantly struggling, and often imposing
on itself, to gain some little pre-eminence, should so seldom hint to us
the only certain as well as laudable way of setting ourselves above another
man, and that is, by becoming his benefactor.[37]

These bits of moral philosophy, frequently in the form of an apostrophe to the reader, give an urgency to the moral tone of the book, for
while Amelia might present an example of the virtuous woman, the author
exhorts to morality: "Hence, my worthy reader, console thyself, that however few of the other good things of life are thy lot, the best of all things,
which is innocence, is always within thy own power. . . ."[38]

   In at least five places in the novel, the author becomes explicator,
carefully explaining what has happened and why and what will happen.
Again, his presence lends an urgency and seriousness to the novel, for he is
saying, in effect, that the reader must pay attention, must understand in
detail, or the intricacies of a carefully structured book are for nought. For
instance, the author explains that James's anger at Booth sprang from
Miss Matthews' lie about Booth's having traduced James's character.[39]
The whole of XII.i is devoted to explication. And after the completely
irrelevant narration of Trent's history, the author tells us: "After this preface, which we thought necessary to account for a character of which some
of my country and collegiate readers might doubt the existence, I shall
proceed to what more immediately regards Mrs. Booth."[40]

   As a storyteller, the author has certain decided characteristics. One
of these is authorial reticence. At five crucial points in the novel, he states
his inability or unwillingness to describe the scene. For instance:

[36] *Amelia*, p. 161.
[37] *Amelia*, p. 170.
[38] *Amelia*, pp. 334–335.
[39] *Amelia*, p. 230.
[40] *Amelia*, p. 491.

The scene that followed, during some minutes, is beyond my power of description; I must beg the readers' hearts to suggest it to themselves. The children hung on their mother, whom they endeavored in vain to comfort, as Mrs. Atkinson did in vain attempt to pacify them, telling them all would be well, and they would soon see their papa again.

Further, as a moralist, the author tends to convert incidents in the book into paradigms to teach the unwary, as when he titles X.vi "Read, gamester, and observe."

Perhaps more important characteristics of the author as storyteller are his specific rhetoric and style. For it is in a rhetorical medium and by a stylistic vehicle that he tells his story. He has certain mannerisms that appear repeatedly. He is slang-conscious and makes the reader aware of this slang through interpolation of gratuitous phrases that call attention to the usages: "cooled her heels, *as the phrase is*" and "*as the phrase is,* cooled his heels."[41] Again: "The colonel had the curiosity to ask Booth the name of the gentleman who, *in the vulgar language,* had struck, or taken him for a guinea with so much ease and dexterity."[42] In XI.v we find "tipping (as it is called)." Fielding's tendency to call attention to his use of slang makes these instances apparent. As a result, they become a mark of the "unusual" much in the sense that the post-Ramistic Ciceronian would view the unusual as rhetorical device in style. Another such characteristic of the author's "voice" is his tendency to use big or unusual words: *fortitudinous, divellicated, éclaircissement, gallimatias, panegyric, ocular demonstration, chrematistic art,*[43] and *Oneiropolist.*

The author's use of slang and an unusual vocabulary might indicate a style that calls attention to itself. After all, in Book III of the *Rhetoric,* Aristotle had said that one cause of frigidity in style is the use of uncommon words. However, nothing testifies better for the mood that the author establishes and for the way in which he establishes it than does his use of figures in *Amelia.* As a matter of fact, the style of the author in *Amelia* is much more chaste than that of the other three novels. In *Tom Jones,* the Homeric simile had been a typical device of irony, of playfulness, and of hyperbole. Fielding's use of the Homeric simile is characteristically, then, for nonserious purposes, and if *Amelia* is to be primarily or even exclusively a serious book, we should expect to find few Homeric similes or, at the least, to find them used in a different way from that of *Tom Jones.* And that is what we do find. The one Homeric simile in the book appears when Booth informs Amelia that he cannot dine at home:

---

41 *Amelia,* p. 273.
42 *Amelia,* p. 346. Italics mine.
43 Fielding explains in a note: "The art of getting wealth is so called by Aristotle in his Politics." *Amelia,* p. 393.

> As in the delightful month of June, when the sky is all serene, and the whole face of nature looks with a pleasing and smiling aspect, suddenly a dark cloud spreads itself over the hemisphere, the sun vanishes from our sight, and every object is obscured by a dark and horrid gloom; so happened it to Amelia: the joy that had enlightened every feature disappeared in a moment; the luster forsook her shining eyes, and all the little loves that played and wantoned in her cheeks hung their drooping heads, and with a faint trembling voice she repeated her husband's words. . . .[44]

Fielding is very much conscious of the simile, for Dr. Harrison comments on the figure, and the nobleman whom Harrison visits in the country improperly identifies one.

Mid-century rhetoricians apparently held the simile unworthy of notice. Blair and Campbell deal at length with the metaphor, but ignore the simile. Now, if we can accept Herbert Read's thesis that the simile is a clumsier device than the metaphor, that "it belongs to an earlier stage of literary expression"[45]—then we see immediately that it has little place in the good style as defined by Blair and Campbell. Blair says, "As Language makes gradual progress towards refinement, almost every object comes to have a proper name given to it, and Perspicuity and Precision are more studied." Nonetheless, figurative language is language of the passions: the metaphor, of all figures of speech, comes nearest to painting in its immediate impact. "Its peculiar effect is to give light and strength to description; to make intellectual ideas, in some sort, visible to the eye, by giving them colour, and substance, and sensible qualities." But when much art appears, says Blair, "we are always put on our guard against the deceits of eloquence." However, when the speaker's reasoning is sound and his point is strongly made, the figures confirm our belief and warm our minds.

The author's consciousness of simile as device and the dearth of similes in the book, then, is one mark of the novel's being controlled by a stylistic doctrine of perspicuity. But, although only one Homeric simile appears in the book, allegory is a frequent device, and allegory is to metaphor what the Homeric simile is to simile. Blair's definition runs thus:

> An Allegory may be regarded as a continued Metaphor; as it is the representation of some one thing by another that resembles it, and that it is made to stand for it. Thus, in Prior's Henry and Emma, Emma in the following allegorical manner describes her constancy to Henry:
> "Did I but purpose to embark with thee
> On the smooth surface of a summer's sea,
> While gentle zephyrs play with prosperous gales,
> And fortune's favour fills the swelling sails;

---

[44] *Amelia*, pp. 510–511.
[45] Herbert Read, *English Prose Style* (Boston: The Beacon Press, 1955), p. 25.

> But would forsake the ship, and make the shore,
> When the winds whistle, and the tempests roar?"

In *Amelia*, the author uses allegory as conspicuously as the author of *Tom Jones* had used Homeric simile:

> The truth is, that it is almost impossible guilt should miss the discovering of all the snares in its way, as it is constantly prying closely into every corner in order to lay snares for others. Whereas innocence, having no such purpose, walks fearlessly and carelessly through life, and is consequently liable to tread on the gins which cunning hath laid to entrap it. To speak plainly and without allegory or figure, it is not want of sense, but want to suspicion, by which innocence is often betrayed.[46]

But, in fact, the author and his characters distrust the elaborateness of allegory, as the foregoing quotation indicates. Another instance:

> This siege had not continued long before the governor of the garrison became sufficiently apprised of all the works which were carrying on, and, having well reconnoitered the enemy, and discovered who he was, notwithstanding a false name and some disguise of his person, he called a council of war within his own breast. In fact, to drop all allegory, he began to consider whether his wife was not really a more valuable possession than he had lately thought her.[47]

Even Captain Booth cries, "I do not love reasoning in allegories."

To say that the author's rhetoric is devoid of figures would be falsification of the situation, for, of course, the metaphor is basic, and any sentence that employs repetition or parallelism or that is grammatically inverted or that is unusually short is, in traditional terms, employing a figure. However, a "Ramistic" analysis of every locution that appears to be out of the ordinary certainly identifies figures, but it does not move one nearer to an understanding of rhetorical effect.

In fact, the effect of *Amelia*, because of the stance of the author, is argumentative in the rhetorical sense. The argumentative nature of the book becomes clear when we realize that Fielding had the form of the classical oration in mind when he organized *Amelia*. In *De Partitione Oratoria*, Cicero lists five parts of the oration: (1) *exordium*, (2) *narratio*, (3) *confirmatio* (4) *reprehensio* (sometimes aptly called *destructio*), and (5) *peroratio*. The *exordium* gains the favorable attention of the audience, and *narratio* states the speaker's case; *confirmatio* proves the case, after which *reprehensio* refutes the opponent's case. The speech ends with *peroratio*, which is a summing up, including amplification of the speaker's case

[46] *Amelia*, p. 362.
[47] *Amelia*, p. 488.

and recapitulation. We have seen that the author of *Amelia* had in mind an argument against corruption, both moral and political; to a great extent, he was advancing a moral point as the basis of his novel. In fact, Dudden lists five purposes of *Amelia*: reform of the police system, amendment of the laws concerning debtors, prison reform, reform of the legal profession, and improvement of the system of criminal laws.[48] The first chapter of the book contains the exordium ("Chapter I. *Containing the exordium, etc.*"). And virtually all of Books II and III are Booth's narration. Thus, we would assume that Booth's tale and Miss Matthews' account of her misfortunes (I.vii–ix) are a presentation of the "case" of the novel. In fact, Miss Matthews plays a fairly minor role in the book as the plot unravels, and we are immediately aware that Booth's story could have been greatly abridged without affecting the working out of the plot. Dudden recognizes the gaucherie of Fielding's device for introducing the history of Booth and Amelia. He points out that in *Tom Jones* the author gives a fairly brief and straightforward narrative of the histories of Tom, Sophia, and Blifil up to the time that the real action of the book starts. But the long narrative beginning of *Amelia* he calls "a clumsy contrivance."[49] One hesitates to argue with Dudden; the long narrative *is* a clumsy device, and the novel definitely picks up life when the characters are finally set in motion in Book IV.

In his "argument" for social reform and personal morality the author characteristically eschews the pathetic in favor of dialectic. Aristotle had deplored the use of rhetorical "tricks" in speaking; at best, they were regrettable necessities. And in the authorial stance of *Amelia*, we find overtones of the Aristotelian viewpoint. As has been pointed out, the author time and again demurs at the description of scenes of pathos, particularly those that are felicitous. But the author is addressing his "reasoned" argument to "my young readers," those most easily and profitably influenced for good. In *The Rhetoric of Fiction*, Wayne Booth identifies the rhetoric of fiction as elements that are aimed at influencing an audience, not at satisfying the demands of art. Now, the author as moralist is addressing the reader in Booth's sense of the term. But the process of authorial rhetoric, like that of any rhetoric, involves what Kenneth Burke calls "courtship" or the "use of suasive devices for the transcending of social estrangement."[50] Though the author is attempting moral suasion, he nonetheless must exercise "artistic persuasion" in his courting of the reader. And in *Amelia*, on the grounds of accepted rhetorical doctrine, we can logically expect the first chapter to be that in which the principle of courtship is most obviously operative. Fielding, completely aware of the classical tradition and deeply

---

[48] Dudden, II, 843–854.
[49] Dudden, II, p. 810.
[50] Burke, *A Rhetoric of Motives*, p. 208.

immersed therein, would use the exordium for its proper purpose. But the first chapter of *Amelia* is quiet in tone, matter-of-fact and businesslike at first, philosophical and moral ultimately. The first words in the book are "The various accidents which befell a very worthy couple after their uniting in the state of matrimony will be the subject of the following history." As we have noted, however, he immediately begins his little essay on Fortune and on Life as Art. It is the author-narrator who turns the exordium into a moral essay, and Fielding was quite aware of the function of the narrator in a work. At one point, he speaks of the relation between author and reader:

> I shall lay down the general rule; which I believe to be of universal truth between relator and hearer, as it is between author and reader; this is, that the latter never forgive any observation of the former which doth not convey some knowledge that they are sensible they could not possibly have attained of themselves.[51]

Thus, in Fielding's theory at least, the content of the exordium of *Amelia* is not extraneous to the tale, but is integral and necessary. Fielding is trying to reach his readers through the moral of the book. The authorial rhetoric, the element of courtship, works itself out in moral lessons and moral paradigms.

According to the exordium, the thesis of the novel is that life is an art. And the book is largely an illustration of this thesis. Thus, Captain Booth, Amelia's "child," clings tenaciously to a psychology of the passions: "we reason from our heads, but act from our hearts." This, of course, is a philosophy of hopelessness, particularly in the neoclassical frame of reference. But like all good children, Booth sees the error of his ways. He reads Dr. Barrow's sermons and hears Dr. Harrison's comment that hope and fear must subdue the strongest passions; hence, religious passion, the passion for righteousness and salvation, must rule.

Because the childlike Booth did reform, his reward on earth was completely just; he could retire to the country and live out a happy life with Amelia and his family. But what about the unregenerate? Colonel James came to be tyrannized over by an immensely fat Mrs. James. Mrs. Ellison died of drink, and the noble peer had "at last become so rotten that he stunk above-ground." Attorney Murphy was hanged at Tyburn. Thus, the conclusion of the novel exactly supports the moral thesis in the exordium, namely, that life is an art, not chance. And the novel itself illustrates the working out of that proposition.

The pervasiveness of the author in *Amelia*, with his calmness, with his reticence, with his high sense of morality, makes for a somber book, a book

[51] Fielding, *The Voyage to Lisbon*, pp. 148–149.

aimed at convincing the young readers. *Amelia* is argumentative in tone, avoiding the pathetic, arguing for morality and illustrating the consequences of sinfulness and folly, using figures sparingly. It is a perspicuous book.

This very nature of the book makes for an essential flaw in its rhetoric. It is difficult to move very far from Aristotle's definition of rhetoric as the finding of the best means to persuade on any subject whatever. Cicero would extend Aristotle's definition to encompass the rhetoric of style for its own sake, and Longinus would move even one step further, to say that great style goes beyond persuasion in bringing about the transport of assent. It follows, then, that the author of *Amelia* must be viewed as a speaker in behalf of the book, as a rhetorician seeking the available means of persuasion. If he is not that, we deny that the book is aimed at gaining the sympathy of the reader, a clearly untenable position. As a matter of fact, however, the rhetorical flaw in *Amelia* lies precisely in its failure to gain the sympathy of the reader. As a rhetorician, wooing the reader, the author uses one primary device: the moral lesson. His assumption seems to be that the affection of the "young reader" can be won through the presentation of a tale designed to edify. Now, of course, the author as storyteller uses quite another device, that of the tale itself. But the telling of the tale is not authorial rhetoric. The author as moralizer—as speaker arguing the case from the exordium onward—does not engage the reader as does the author *in propria persona* in *Tom Jones*.

And yet the function of the author in *Amelia* is almost a paradigm of mid-century rhetorical theory. First, the author clearly resolves the matter-manner problem in favor of Hugh Blair's theory that

> Logical and Ethical disquisitions move in a higher sphere, and are conversant with objects of a more severe kind; the progress of the understanding in its search after knowledge, and the direction of the will in the proper pursuit of good. They point out to man the improvement of his nature as an intelligent being; and his duties as the subject of moral obligation. Belles Lettres and criticism chiefly consider him as a being endowed with those powers of taste and imagination, which were intended to embellish his mind, and so supply him with rational and useful entertainment.

The failure of the author of *Amelia*, then, is the failure of one trend in eighteenth-century rhetoric—the trend that stressed rationalism and perspicuity.

In a sense, the author functioning as a character in the book provides a frame—or framework—for the fable. Fielding undoubtedly viewed the fable of *Amelia* as sublime. By the time the book appeared, the attitude toward the sublime was fairly well settled in a way that Hugh Blair summarized.[52] The sublime, he said, resides first in the nature of the subject chosen, but requisite to sublimity in poetry are simplicity and conciseness— even to the exclusion of rhymed verse. The sublime reposes in magnitude, and it is heightened by obscurity. Fielding, however, was concerned with the sublime in human nature. It is "that elevation by which the soul of man, raising and extending itself above the order of this creation, and brightened with a certain ray of divinity, looks down on the condition of mortals."[53] This sublimity of human nature is "a perfect work! the Iliad of Nature! ravishing and astonishing," and it "at once fills us with love, wonder, and delight." Although Fielding's definition of the sublime fits Dr. Harrison exactly, Amelia, both physically and morally, is clearly Fielding's greatest achievement in the human sublime. But coincidental with sublimity in human nature might also be the sublimity of physical beauty coupled with a perfect mind, the beauty, for instance, of Amelia, who seemed, as Milton sublimely described Eve,

—Adorn'd
With what all Earth or Heaven could bestow
To make her amiable.

Again,

Grace was in all her steps, Heaven in her eye,
In every gesture, dignity and love.

Or, as Waller sweetly, though less sublimely sings,

Sweetness, truth, and every grace
Which time and use are wont to teach,
The eye may in a moment reach
And read distinctly in her face.[54]

Amelia embodied the sublimity of human nature and mirrored it in her physical form.

There is a strange, almost suspicious, logic to the argument about the sublimity of *Amelia*. The "Dedication to Ralph Allen, Esq." is a part of that logic. "The best man is the properest patron" of a book "sincerely designed to promote the cause of virtue." And Allen would certainly fit Fielding's definition of the truly sublime human being, that mixture of goodness and greatness which gives mankind a glimpse of the divine. Dr.

---

[52] See Chapter 3 above.
[53] Henry Fielding, "Preface to the Miscellanies and Poems," *Fielding's Works*, ed. James P. Browne (11 vols.; London: Bickers and Son, 1872), XI, 94–95.
[54] *Amelia*, p. 237.

Harrison, in his compassion and wisdom, is much like Ralph Allen. But Fielding methodically obviates every objection that the reader might possibly have to this "sublime" character. For instance, why would a man such as Harrison employ a fellow like Attorney Murphy? Murphy had come to Harrison with good recommendations, and no one, including the Doctor, had known of Murphy's "slip . . . perjury and subornation of perjury."

The author argues rationally in behalf of a proposition, but he illustrates the working out of that proposition by a fable that contains elements of the sublime—at least of human nature. It is as though Fielding were illustrating the classic doctrine that literature is meant to edify and pleases only as a means of accomplishing its end. George Campbell said that

> knowledge, the object of the intellect, furnisheth materials for the fancy; the fancy culls, compounds, and, by her mimic art, disposes these materials so as to affect the passions; the passions are the natural spurs to volition, and so need only to be right directed.

In *Amelia*, the author's proposition furnished "materials for the fancy," which compounded a fable designed to affect the passions. If, indeed, Fielding relied upon the sublimity of human nature to bring about his effect, he failed miserably, in his own time, at least.

In placing sublimity in matter rather than manner, Fielding was characteristic of his age. Though the elocutionists had wide popular appeal, serious rhetoricians like Blair and Campbell had definitely stated a position: sublimity is in the subject, and Ciceronianistic manner can vitiate the sublime effect. Of course, Fielding had always turned to Ciceronianism for comic purposes, as a survey of *Tom Jones* and *Joseph Andrews* makes clear. Where, then, in that singularly uncomic novel *Amelia* should we expect to find Ciceronianism? Fielding's earlier use of heightened style is ironic. The apostrophe to love in *Joseph Andrews* is a typical example:

> O love, what monstrous tricks dost thou play with thy votaries of both sexes! How dost thou deceive them, and make them deceive themselves! Their follies are thy delight! Their sighs make thee laugh, and their pangs are thy merriment!
>
> Not the great Rich, who turns men into monkeys, wheelbarrows, and whatever else best humours his fancy, hath so strangely metamorphosed the human shape; nor the great Cibber, who confounds all number, gender, and breaks through every rule of grammar at his will, hath so distorted the English language as thou dost metamorphose and distort the human sense.

The nearest approach to such floridity in *Amelia* is the moral stated figuratively:

Thus did this poor man support his hopes by a dependence on that ticket which he had so dearly purchased of one who pretended to manage the wheels in the great state lottery of preferment. A lottery, indeed, which hath this to recommend it—that many poor wretches feed their imaginations with the prospect of a prize during their whole lives, and never discover they have drawn a blank.

Booth was the object of James's envy.

And why? because this wretch was possessed of the affections of a poor little lamb, which all the vast flocks that were within the power and reach of the colonel could not prevent that glutton's longing for. And sure this image of the lamb is not properly adduced on this occasion; for what was the colonel's desire but to lead this poor lamb, as it were, to the slaughter, in order to purchase a feast of a few days by her final destruction, and to tear her away from the arms of one where she was sure of being fondled and caressed all the days of her life.

Nonetheless, the instances of heightened style in *Amelia* are rare, a fact that is not surprising in view of Fielding's tendency to use Ciceronianism for comic or ironic purposes. Dr. Harrison, the author's alter ego, speaks in much the same tone of voice as the author, eschewing the florid for the grave and sensible, even in his most passionate moments. For instance, in answering Amelia's charge that "all mankind almost are villians in their hearts," the doctor launches into a grave, moving, and beautiful but singularly unfigurative speech:

The nature of man is far from being in itself evil; it abounds with benevolence, charity, and pity, coveting praise and honor, and shunning shame and disgrace. Bad education, bad habits, and bad customs, debauch our nature, and drive it headlong as it were into vice. The governors of the world, and I am afraid of the priesthood, are answerable for the badness of it. Instead of discouraging wickedness to the utmost of their power, both are too apt to connive at it.

Indeed, the characters in the novel tend to mirror their author's predisposition against a Ciceronianistic rhetoric of style.

In fact, Fielding unwittingly carried out Hugh Blair's doctrine that

it is in truth, the sentiment or passion, which lies under the figured expression, that gives it any merit. The Figure is only the dress; the Sentiment is the body and the substance. No Figures will render a cold or an empty composition interesting; whereas, if a sentiment be sublime or pathetic, it can support itself, perfectly well, without any borrowed assistance. Hence several of the most effecting and admired passages of the best authors, are expressed in the simplest language.

This discussion, then, points toward an inevitable conclusion: the author, as a character functioning in the book, applied a rhetoric of persuasion; the fable itself, and the characters who acted it out, supplied a rhetoric of transport through sublimity. And it is in the discrepancy between these two types of rhetoric that one of the failures of *Amelia* lies. Longinus, of course, made the differentiation between persuasion and transport. He pointed out, for instance, that the metaphor properly applied will sweep the reader along with its power, rational considerations aside. In general, the eighteenth century had tended to view sublimity as an inherent property in objects or concepts, but with the intrinsic power to inspire the sublime reaction in the beholder. From Dennis through Blair, the basic theory remained constant, though arguments arose over details. From the sublime of nature through the sublime of magnitude to Fielding's sublime of human nature, no one questioned the ability of that intrinsic quality in some of God's creations to inspire a suprarational response—even frenzy—in the human breast.

But, conversely, the "perspicuous" rhetoricians, beginning in the 1660s and culminating with Blair and Campbell, had in fact or in effect denied the Ciceronian proposition that noble style in itself serves a suprarational suasive function. Fielding's *Amelia* is a curious and disheartening working out of the theory that perspicuity and reason provide the artist with the means for transporting the reader. Because *Amelia* failed to act upon the audience for whom it was intended, it was a rhetorical failure, and that failure illustrates the basic flaw in a whole theory of human discourse.

In short, the persuasive rhetoric of the author left the readers cold; the "sublime" rhetoric of the fable made insufficient appeal to overcome the author's argument. This lack of appeal, of course, does not mean that *Amelia* was an artistic failure. The ultimate esthetic success of the book is not necessarily dependent on its rhetorical success or on its success in a given time and a given place. But any attempt to assess the artistic merits of *Amelia* would carry this discussion far beyond the limits set for it.

A Selected Bibliography

The following bibliography is not intended to be complete. It will serve as a guide to the student and an index to the inclinations of the author. I have made some attempt to indicate the editions and translations that in my opinion are the most satisfactory, but I make no pretense to having read, for instance, all of the versions of Plato's *Phaedrus*. Nor have I attempted to provide a bibliographical roadmap to the publishing history of key books. Kenneth Burke is an example: I have cited only first editions; many of his works are available in later editions.

Rhetorics and related primary sources

Addison, Joseph, ("The Pleasures of the Imagination,") *The Spectator*, Nos. 411–421.

Aristotle, *The "Art" of Rhetoric*, trans. by John Henry Freese. New York: G. P. Putnam's Sons, 1926.

———, *The Rhetoric of Aristotle*, trans. by Lane Cooper. New York: Appleton-Century-Crofts, 1960.

Ascham, Roger, *The Scholemaster* (1570).

Bacon, Francis, *Advancement of Learning* (1605).

Baillie, John, *Essay on the Sublime* (1747), Samuel Holt Monk, ed. Augustan Reprint Society, Publication No. 43; Los Angeles: William Andrews Clark Memorial Library, 1953.

Bain, Alexander, *English Composition and Rhetoric*. New York: American
    Book Company, 1887–1888.
Bascom, John, *Philosophy of Rhetoric*. New York: G. P. Putnam's Sons, 1892.
Bayly, Anselm, *The Alliance of Musick, Poetry and Oratory*. London: John
    Stockdale, 1789.
Blair, Hugh, *Lectures on Rhetoric and Belles Lettres* (1759).
Blundeville, Thomas, *The Arte of Logicke, Plainly taught in the English
    Tongue* . . . (1619).
Burke, Edmund, *A Philosophical Enquiry into the Origin of our Ideas of the
    Sublime and Beautiful* (1757), J. T. Boulton, ed. New York: Columbia
    University Press, 1958.
Burke, Kenneth, *Attitudes toward History*. Two vols.; New York: New Re-
    public, Inc., 1937.
———, *Counter-Statement*. New York: Harcourt, Brace & World, Inc., 1931.
———, *A Grammar of Motives*. Englewood Cliffs, N.J.: Prentice-Hall, Inc.,
    1945.
———, *A Grammar of Motives and a Rhetoric of Motives*. Cleveland: The
    World Publishing Company, 1962.
———, *Permanence and Change: An Anatomy of Purpose*. New York: New
    Republic, Inc., 1935.
———, *The Philosophy of Literary Form, Studies in Symbolic Action*. Baton
    Rouge: Louisiana State University Press, 1941.
———, *A Rhetoric of Motives*. Englewood Cliffs, N.J.: Prentice-Hall, Inc.,
    1950.
———, *The Rhetoric of Religion: Studies in Logology*. Boston: The Beacon
    Press, 1961.
———, *Towards a Better Life, Being a Series of Epistles or Declamations*.
    New York: Harcourt, Brace & World, Inc., 1932.
Campbell, George, *The Philosophy of Rhetoric* (1776).
Cicero, "Brutus," trans. G. L. Hendrickson, in *Brutus, Orator*. Cambridge,
    Mass.: Harvard University Press, 1939.
———, *De Inventione, De Optimo Genere Oratorum, Topica*, trans. H. M.
    Hubbell. Cambridge, Mass.: Harvard University Press, 1949.
———, *De Oratore*, trans. H. Rackham. Two vols.; Cambridge, Mass.: Harvard
    University Press, 1942.
———, *De Partitione Oratoria*, vol. 2 of *De Oratore*.
Cowley, Abraham, "A Proposition for the Advancement of Experimental Phi-
    losophy" (1661).
Cox, Leonard, *The Arte and Crafte of Rhethoryke* (1524).
Demetrius, "On Style," in *Poetics, Aristotle and on Style, Demetrius*, trans.
    T. A. Moxon. New York: E. P. Dutton & Co., Inc. [n.d.].
De Quincey, Thomas, *Essays on Style, Rhetoric and Language*.
Empson, William, *Seven Types of Ambiguity*, 2d rev. ed. Cleveland: The World
    Publishing Company, 1949.
Farnaby, Thomas, *Index Rhetoricus* (1625).
Fénelon, François de la Mothe, *Fénelon's Dialogues on Eloquence*, trans.
    Wilbur Samuel Howell. Princeton, N.J.: Princeton University Press,
    1951.

Fenner, Dudley, *The Artes of Logike and Rethorike, plainly set forth in the English tongue . . .* (1584).

Goldsmith, Oliver, "Of Eloquence (and Popular Preaching)," *The Bee*, November 17, 1759.

Hartley, David, *Various Conjectures on the Perception, Motion, and Generation of Ideas* (1746).

Harvey, Gabriel, "Gabriel Harvey's *Ciceronianus*," trans. Clarence A. Forbes. University of Nebraska Studies in the Humanities, No. 4; Lincoln: 1945.

Hobbes, Thomas, "Aristotle's Rhetoric: A Digest," in *Poetics, Aristotle and On Style, Demetrius*, trans. T. A. Moxon. New York: E. P. Dutton & Co., Inc. [n.d.].

Holmes, John, *The Art of Rhetoric Made Easy* (1739).

Hudson, Hoyt H., "Jewel's Oration against Rhetoric: A Translation," *Quarterly Journal of Speech*, XIV (June 1928), 374–392.

Hughes, John, "Of Style," in *Critical Essays of the Eighteenth Century*, ed. Willard Higley Durham. New York: Russell Sage Foundation, 1961.

Isocrates, "Against the Sophists," in vol. 2 of *Isocrates*, trans. George Norlin. Three vols.; New York: G. P. Putnam's Sons, 1929.

———, "Antidosis," in vol. 2 of *Isocrates*.

Lawson, John, *Lectures Concerning Oratory* (1759).

Leland, Thomas, *A Dissertation on the Principles of Human Eloquence* (1764).

Locke, John, *An Essay Concerning Human Understanding* (1690).

Longinus, "On the Sublime," trans. by W. Rhys Roberts, in *The Great Critics*, James Harry Smith and Edd Winfield Parks, eds. New York: W. W. Norton & Company, Inc., 1939.

Lucian, "A Professor of Public Speaking," in vol. 4 of *Lucian*, trans. A. M. Harmon. Eight vols.; New York: G. P. Putnam's Sons, 1925.

Milton, John, *A Fuller Institution of the Art of Logic, Arranged after the Method of Peter Ramus* (1672).

Newton, John, *An Introduction to the Art of Rhetorick* (1671).

Ogden, C. K., and I. A. Richards, *The Meaning of Meaning*. London: Routledge & Kegan Paul Ltd., 1923.

Pallavicino, Ferrante, *The Whore's Rhetoric* (1683). New York: Ivan Obolensky, Inc., 1961.

Peacham, Henry, *The Garden of Eloquence* (1593). Facsimile ed.; Gainesville, Fla.: Scholars' Facsimiles and Reprints, 1954.

Petronius, *The Satyricon of Petronius*, trans. William Arrowsmith. Ann Arbor: University of Michigan Press [n.d.].

Plato, *Gorgias*, trans. W. R. M. Lamb, in vol. 5 of *Plato*. Eight vols.; New York: G. P. Putnam's Sons, 1925.

———, *Phaedrus*, trans. Harold North Fowler, vol. 1 of *Plato*.

Pope, Alexander, *Essay on Criticism* (1711).

———, *Peri Bathous*.

Quintilian, *The Institutio Oratoria of Quintilian*, trans. H. E. Butler. Four vols.; New York: G. P. Putnam's Sons, 1920.

Ramus, Peter, *The Logike of the Most Excellent Philosopher P. Ramus Martyr . . .* , trans. M. Roll (1581).

Reynolds, Sir Joshua, *Discourse VII* (1778).

Reynolds, Richard (Richard Rainolde), *The Foundacion of Rhetorike* (1563).
New York: Scholars' Facsimiles and Reprints, 1945.

"Rhetorica ad Alexandrum," trans. H. Rackham, in *Aristotle, Problems II,
Books XXII–XXXVIII*. Cambridge, Mass.: Harvard University Press,
1937.

Richards, I. A., *The Philosophy of Rhetoric*. New York: Oxford University
Press, 1936.

———, *Practical Criticism*. New York: Harcourt, Brace & World, Inc., 1929.

Shaftesbury, Anthony Ashley Cooper, *Characteristicks of Men, Manners, Opinions, Times* (1727).

Taverner, Richard, *The second booke of the Garden of wysedome* (1539).

Udall, Nicholas, *Flovres for Latine Spekynge Selected and gathered oute of
Terence, and the same translated in to Englysshe* (1533).

Whately, Richard, *Elements of Rhetoric* (1832).

Wilkins, John, *An Essay Towards a Real Character and a Philosophical Language* (1668).

Wilson, Thomas, *The Rule of Reason* (1551).

The history of rhetoric

Baldwin, Charles Sears, *Ancient Rhetoric and Poetic*. New York: Crowell-
Collier and Macmillan, Inc., 1924.

———, *Medieval Rhetoric and Poetic*. New York: Crowell-Collier and Macmillan, Inc., 1928.

———, *Renaissance Literary Theory and Practice*. New York: Columbia University Press, 1939.

Baldwin, T. H., *William Shakespeare's small Latine & lesse Greeke*. Urbana:
University of Illinois Press, 1944.

Beaumont, Charles Allen, *Swift's Classical Rhetoric*. Athens: University of
Georgia Press, 1961.

Brown, J. Howard, *Elizabethan Schooldays*. New York: Oxford University Press,
1933.

Clark, Donald Lemen, *John Milton at St. Paul's School: A Study of Ancient
Rhetoric in English Renaissance Education*. New York: Columbia University Press, 1948.

———, *Rhetoric in Greco-Roman Education*. New York: Columbia University
Press, 1957.

Cope, Jackson I., *Joseph Glanvill*. Washington University Studies; St. Louis:
1956.

Crane, William G., *Wit and Rhetoric in the Renaissance*. New York: Columbia
University Press, 1937.

Fussell, Paul, *The Rhetorical World of Augustan Humanism: Ethics and Imagery from Swift to Burke*. New York: Oxford University Press, 1966.

Graves, Frank Pierrepont, *Peter Ramus and the Educational Reformation of
the Sixteenth Century*. New York: Crowell-Collier and Macmillan, Inc.,
1912.

Harrison, Benjamin S., "Medieval Rhetoric in the Book of the Duchesse,"
PMLA, XLIX (June 1934), 428–442.

Hornbeak, Katherine Gee, *The Complete Letter-Writer in English, 1568–1800*. Smith College Studies in Modern Languages; Northampton, Mass.: 1934.

Howell, Wilbur Samuel, *Logic and Rhetoric in England, 1500–1700*. Princeton, N.J.: Princeton University Press, 1956.

Howes, Raymond F., ed., *Historical Studies of Rhetoric and Rhetoricians*. Ithaca, N.Y.: Cornell University Press, 1961.

Johnson, F. R., "Two Renaissance Textbooks of Rhetoric: Aphthonius' *Progymnasmata* and Rainolde's A *booke called the Foundacion of Rhetorike*," *Huntington Library Quarterly*, VI (1943), 427–444.

Kennedy, George, *The Art of Persuasion of Greece*. Princeton, N.J.: Princeton University Press, 1963.

———, "The Earliest Rhetorical Handbooks," *American Journal of Philology*, LXXX (April 1959), 169–178.

Kennedy, Milton Boone, *The Oration in Shakespeare*. Chapel Hill: The University of North Carolina Press, 1942.

Kitzhaber, Albert R., *A Bibliography on Rhetoric in American Colleges: 1850–1900*. Denver: Bibliographical Center for Research, Denver Public Library, 1954.

Leonard, Sterling W., *The Doctrine of Correctness in English Usage, 1700–1800*. University of Wisconsin Studies in Language and Literature, No. 25; Madison: 1929.

McKeon, Richard, "Rhetoric in the Middle Ages," *Speculum*, XVII (1942), 3–5.

Miriam Joseph, Sister, *Shakespeare's Use of the Arts of Language*. New York: Columbia University Press, 1947.

Monk, Samuel Holt, *The Sublime: A Study of Critical Theories in XVIII-Century England*. New York: Modern Language Association of America, 1935.

Olson, Elder, "The Argument of Longinus on the Sublime," in *Critics and Criticism*, R. S. Crane, ed. Chicago: University of Chicago Press, 1952.

Ong, Walter J., *Ramus: Method and the Decay of Dialogue; From the Art of Discourse to the Art of Reason*. Cambridge, Mass.: Harvard University Press, 1958.

Roberts, W. Rhys, *Greek Rhetoric and Literary Criticism*. New York: David McKay Company, Inc., 1928.

Taylor, Warren, *Tudor Figures of Rhetoric*. Chicago: University of Chicago Press, 1937.

Tuve, Rosemond, *Elizabethan and Metaphysical Imagery*. Chicago: University of Chicago Press, 1947.

———, "Imagery and Logik: Ramus and Metaphysical Poetics," *Journal of the History of Ideas*, III (February 1942), 365–400.

Wallace, Karl R., *Francis Bacon on Communications and Rhetoric*. Chapel Hill: The University of North Carolina Press, 1943.

Williamson, George, "The Restoration Revolt against Enthusiasm," *Studies in Philology*, XXX (October 1933), 571–603.

———, "The Rhetorical Pattern of Neo-Classical Wit," *Modern Philology*, XXXIII (August 1935), 55–81.

———, *The Senecan Amble*. Chicago: University of Chicago Press, 1951.

————, "Senecan Style in the Seventeenth Century," *Philological Quarterly*, XV (1936), 321–351.

Theory and commentary

Abrams, M. H., *The Mirror and the Lamp*. New York: Oxford University Press, 1953.

Bloomfield, Leonard, *Language*. New York: Holt, Rinehart and Winston, Inc., 1933.

Booth, Wayne C. *The Rhetoric of Fiction*. Chicago: University of Chicago Press, 1961.

Bryant, Donald C., ed., *The Rhetorical Idiom*. Ithaca, N.Y.: Cornell University Press, 1958.

————, "Rhetoric: Its Function and Scope," *Quarterly Journal of Speech*, XXXIX (December 1953), 401–424.

————, "Some Problems of Scope and Method in Rhetorical Scholarship," *Quarterly Journal of Speech*, XXIII (April 1937), 182–189.

Clark, Donald L., "The Place of Rhetoric in Liberal Education," *Quarterly Journal of Speech*, XXXVI (October 1950), 291–295.

Crocker, Lionel, "Rhetoric in the Beginning Course," *Quarterly Journal of Speech*, XXIX (October 1943), 314–317.

Duhamel, P. Albert, "The Function of Rhetoric as Effective Expression," *Journal of the History of Ideas*, X (June 1949), 344–356.

Fogarty, Daniel John, *Roots for a New Rhetoric*. New York: Bureau of Publications, Columbia University, 1959.

Harrington, Elbert W., *Rhetoric and the Scientific Method of Inquiry*. Boulder: University of Colorado Press, 1948.

Henn, T. R., *Longinus and English Criticism*. New York: Cambridge University Press, 1934.

Hochmuth, Marie, "Kenneth Burke and the 'New' Rhetoric," *Quarterly Journal of Speech*, XXXVIII (April 1952), 133–144.

Holland, L. Virginia, *Counterpoint: Kenneth Burke and Aristotle's Theories of Rhetoric*. New York: Philosophical Library, Inc., 1959.

Hunt, Everett L., "Rhetoric and General Education," *Quarterly Journal of Speech*, XXXV (October 1949), 275–283.

Knox, George, *Critical Moments: Kenneth Burke's Categories and Critiques*. Seattle: University of Washington Press, 1957.

Moore, Arthur K., "Rhetoric's Wrung Neck," *Western Humanities Review*, XVII (Winter 1963), 51–62.

Murray, Elwood, "The Semantics of Rhetoric," *Quarterly Journal of Speech*, XXX (February 1949), 31–41.

Natanson, Maurice, "The Limits of Rhetoric," *Quarterly Journal of Speech*, XLI (April 1955), 133–139.

Nichols, Marie Hochmuth, *Rhetoric and Criticism*. Baton Rouge: Louisiana State University Press, 1963.

Ong, Walter J., *The Barbarian Within*. New York: Crowell-Collier and Macmillan, Inc., 1962.

Richards, I. A., *Practical Criticism*. New York: Harcourt, Brace & World, Inc., 1929.

Rueckert, William H., *Kenneth Burke and the Drama of Human Relations*. Minneapolis: University of Minnesota Press, 1963.

Sapir, Edward, *Language*. New York: Harcourt, Brace & World, Inc., 1921.

Sebeok, Thomas A., ed., *Style in Language*. New York: John Wiley & Sons, Inc., 1960.

Simrell, V. E., "Mere Rhetoric," *Quarterly Journal of Speech*, XIV (June 1928), 359–374.

Weaver, Richard M., *The Ethics of Rhetoric*. Chicago: Henry Regnery Company, 1953.

Wimsatt, W. K., Jr., *The Prose Style of Samuel Johnson*. New Haven, Conn.: Yale University Press, 1941.

index